Uncle John's BATHROOM READER® TREASURY

The Bathroom Readers' Institute
&
The Bathroom Readers' Hysterical Society

PORTABLE
PRESS

Ashland, OR, and San Diego, CA

For information, write
The Bathroom Readers' Hysterical Society
Portable Press
5880 Oberlin Drive, San Diego, CA 92121
e-mail: unclejohn@advmkt.com

ISBN: 1-59223-323-6

Project Team:

JoAnn Padgett, Project Manager
Allen Orso, Publisher
Georgine Lidell, Inventory Manager
Michael Brunsfeld (brunsfeldo@comcast.net), Cover Design

THANK YOU HYSTERICAL SCHOLARS!
The Bathroom Readers' Hysterical Society sincerely thanks
everyone who contributed selections to this work.

Printed in the United States of America
First printing: May 2004

04 05 06 07 08   10 9 8 7 6 5 4 3 2 1

CONTENTS

UNCLE JOHN'S BATHROOM READERS— THE ANNUAL EDITIONS

UNCLE JOHN'S PRESENTS SERIES

UNCLE JOHN'S BATHROOM READER PLUNGES INTO SERIES

UNCLE JOHN'S FOR KIDS ONLY SERIES

UNCLE JOHN'S BATHROOM READER PUZZLE BOOKS

INTRODUCTION

Hello New Readers,

Discover the wonders of Uncle John's Bathroom Readers.
Learn why we have five million copies in print. Enough copies for
everyone in Colorado to have a copy, and some could even have
two. Dip into *Uncle John's Bathroom Reader Treasury* and find
selections from:

THE ANNUAL EDITIONS
Uncle John's Ultimate Bathroom Reader
Uncle John's Legendary Lost Bathroom Reader
Uncle John's Great Big Bathroom Reader
Uncle John's Giant 10th Anniversary Bathroom Reader
Uncle John's Absolutely Absorbing Bathroom Reader
Uncle John's All-Purpose Extra-Strength Bathroom Reader
Uncle John's Supremely Satifsying Bathroom Reader
Uncle John's Ahh-Inspiring Bathroom Reader
Uncle John's Unstoppable Bathroom Reader
The Best of Uncle John's Bathroom Reader
Uncle John's Great Big Bathroom Reader, United Kingdom Edition

THE PRESENTS SERIES
Uncle John's Presents Book of the Dumb
Uncle John's Presents Mom's Bathtub Reader

THE PLUNGES INTO SERIES
Uncle John's Bathroom Reader Plunges into History
Uncle John's Bathroom Reader Plunges into The Universe
Uncle John's Bathroom Reader Plunges into Great Lives

THE FOR KIDS ONLY SERIES

Uncle John's For Kids Only
Uncle John's Electrifying Bathroom Reader For Kids Only

THE PUZZLE BOOK SERIES

Uncle John's Bathroom Reader Puzzle Book #1
Uncle John's Bathroom Reader Puzzle Book #2

That's 20 books in all.
So get started and enjoy and if you like them, I'm pretty sure that you will, start creating a library of all our great books.

GO ON GET STARTED!!!!!

Uncle Al
Publisher Portable Press

Uncle John's BATHROOM READER®

PLITZ-PLATZ I WAS TAKING A BATH

As kids, we were all told that trains go "choo-choo" and cars go "beep beep." Check out the sounds they make in other languages.

AAH-CHOO!
Portuguese: Ah-chim!
German: Hat-chee!
Greek: Ap tsou!
Japanese: Hakshon!
Italian: Ekchee!

SPLASH!
Hindi: Dham!
Russian: Plukh!
Danish: Plump!
Spanish: Chof!
Greek: Plitz-platz!

EENY-MEENY-MINY-MO
Arabic: Hadi-badi
Italian: Ambaraba chichicoco
Japanese: Hee-foo-mee-yo
Swedish: Ol-uh dol-uh doff
Polish: Ele mele dudki

CHOO-CHOO!
Chinese: Hong-lung, hong-lung
Danish: Fut fut!
Japanese: Shuppo-shuppo!
Swahili: Chuku-chuku!
Greek: Tsaf-tsouf!

ZZZZZZ...
Arabic: Kh-kh-kh...
Chinese: Hulu...
Italian: Ronf-ronf...
Japanese: Gah-gah...

UPSY-DAISY!
Arabic: Hop-pa!
Italian: Opp-la!
Japanese: Yoisho!
Russian: Nu davai!
Danish: Opse-dasse!

KITCHY-KITCHY-KOO!
Chinese: Gujee!
French: Gheely-gheely!
Greek: Ticki-ticki-ticki!
Swedish: Kille kille kille!

UH-OH!
Chinese: Zao le!
Italian: Ay-may!
Japanese: Ah-ah!
Swahili: Wee!
Swedish: Oy-oy!

BEEP BEEP!
Chinese: Dooo dooo!
Hindi: Pon-pon!
Spanish: Mock mock!
French: Puet puet!
Japanese: Boo boo!

CHUGALUG!
Arabic: Gur-gur-gur!
Hindi: Gat-gat!
Hebrew: Gloog gloog!
Russian: Bool-bool!
Chinese: Goo-doo, goo-doo!

Native Americans spoke more than 133 different languages.

WHEN YOUR HUSBAND GETS HOME...

*Here's a bit of advice taken directly from a 1950s Home Economics
textbook. It was sent in by a reader, along with the comment:
"Times have changed!" No kidding. Believe it or not, this was part of a
course intended to prepare high school girls for married life.*

Have dinner ready: "Plan ahead, even the night before, to
have a delicious meal—on time. This is a way of letting
him know that you have been thinking about him and are
concerned about his needs. Most men are hungry when they come
home and the prospects of a good meal are part of the warm welcome needed."

Prepare yourself: "Take 15 minutes to rest so you will be
refreshed when he arrives. Touch up your makeup, put a ribbon in
your hair and be fresh-looking. He has just been with a lot of
work-weary people. Be a little gay and a little more interesting.
His boring day may need a lift."

Clear away the clutter: "Make one last trip through the main
part of the house just before your husband arrives, gathering up
school books, toys, paper, etc. Then run a dust cloth over the
tables. Your husband will feel he has reached a haven of rest and
order, and it will give you a lift, too."

Prepare the children: "Take a few minutes to wash the children's
hands and faces (if they are small) comb their hair, and if necessary, change their clothes. They are little treasures and he would
like to see them playing the part."

Minimize all noise: "At the time of his arrival, eliminate all noise
of washer, dryer, dishwasher, or vacuum. Try to encourage the children to be quiet. Be happy to see him: Greet him with a warm
smile and be glad to see him."

Some don'ts: Don't greet him with problems or complaints. Don't complain if he's late for dinner. Count this as minor compared with what he might have gone through that day."

Make him comfortable: "Have him lean back in a comfortable chair or suggest he lie down in the bedroom. Have a cool or warm drink ready for him. Arrange his pillow and offer to take off his shoes. Speak in a low, soft, soothing, and pleasant voice. Allow him to relax—unwind."

Listen to him: "You may have a dozen things to tell him, but the moment of his arrival is not the time. Let him talk first."

Making the evening his: "Never complain if he does not take you out to dinner or to other places of entertainment. Instead, try to understand his world of strain and pressure, his need to be home and relax."

* * * *

THE BEST & WORST TIPPERS

According to a poll in Bartender *magazine:*

• Lawyers and doctors are the worst tippers. Normally, doctors are the #1 tightwads. In rougher times, it's lawyers. The reason: "There are more lawyers and less work."

• The biggest tippers are bartenders and "service personnel."

• As smoking gets more restricted, cigar and cigarette smokers—who are now forced to smoke at the bar instead of at restaurant tables—are becoming notably good tippers.

• Other leading tightwads: teachers, computer people, musicians, professional athletes, and pipe smokers.

• Other top tippers: hairstylists, mobsters, tavern owners, regular customers.

• Vodka drinkers are good tippers. People who order drinks topped with umbrellas are bad tippers.

• Democrats tip better than Republicans.

One in 500 humans have one blue eye and one brown eye.

THE WORLD'S MOST FAMOUS CORPSE

More people have seen Lenin's mummy than any other mummy in history. It's a tourist attraction, a cultural artifact, and as you'll see, a political gimmick. How did this weird monument—denounced by Lenin's official historian as an "absurd idea"—come into being? Here's the full story.

> Lenin's tomb in Moscow's Red Square is the best-known landmark in the Soviet Union, as well as the spiritual center of Soviet political ideology. Some 150 million people have visited the mausoleum since it was first built.... There are always long lines, but you should expect to be descending the gloomy stairs into the tomb within 20-30 minutes. Without stopping, you walk around three sides of the glass case in which Lenin lies, stubbly and ashen-faced, wearing a jacket and polka-dot tie.
>
> **—Travel Guide to the Soviet Union**

DEATH OF A LEADER

At 6:50 p.m. on January 21, 1924, Vladimir Ilyich Lenin, first leader of the Soviet Union and father of his country, suffered a stroke and died.

No one was sure how to handle it. Lenin had asked for a simple funeral. He wished to be buried next to his mother and sister in the family burial plot. But when Soviet leaders met to discuss the matter, they came up with another idea—turn the funeral into a "propaganda event" that could help legitimize the Communist regime. They decided to embalm him so he could lie in state for a while.

Then, only three days after his death, the Politburo began discussing the idea of saving the body "a little longer." Lenin's relatives balked at the idea...but Joseph Stalin insisted. As Dmitri Volkogonov writes in *Lenin: A New Biography*, Stalin "came to see [preserving Lenin's body] as the creation of a secular Bolshevik relic with huge propaganda potential." A short time later, the Politburo issued the following orders:

1. The coffin containing V. I. Lenin's corpse is to be kept in a vault which should be made accessible to visitors;

2. The vault is to be formed in the Kremlin wall on Red Square among the communal graves of the fighters of the October Revolution. A commission is being created today for the construction of a mausoleum.

A burial vault was dug along the Kremlin wall, a wooden hut was built over it to keep out the elements, and Lenin's body was placed inside following the funeral.

CORPSE OF ENGINEERS
Meanwhile, the secret police were rounding up the country's top scientists to put them to work figuring out how to embalm Lenin for eternity. A streetcar was towed into Red Square and fitted with beds, hot plates, and washbasins; it served as the terrified scientists' home for the rest of the winter.

But restoring Lenin to his former glory was not so easy. Illness had ravaged him in the final years of his life, leaving him frail-looking and emaciated. And since permanent, *lifelike* embalming had never been attempted before, research on how to accomplish such a task had to begin from scratch. In the meantime, the body continued to deteriorate.

Lenin's cadaver was packed in ice to slow the decay, and by June the scientists finally succeeded in "stabilizing" the body. By then, however, it was a mess. "In those four and a half months," historian Robert Payne writes in *The Life and Death of Lenin*, "remarkable changes had taken place: he was waxen gray, wrinkled, horribly shrunken." Nonetheless, by August 1924, Lenin's body had been cleaned up enough to put on public display.

STAYING IN SHAPE
Work on *improving* Lenin's after-death appearance would continue for more than 25 years. The task was handled by the Research Institute for "Biological Structures" (a Soviet euphemism for cadaver) and its Lenin Mausoleum Laboratory—both of which were so secret that the West did not learn of their existence until after the collapse of the Soviet Union. Part of the routine that was worked out over the years:

Every 7 years, your body grows the equivalent of an entirely new skeleton.

• To prevent Lenin from decomposing, the temperature in the mausoleum is kept at precisely 59° F. The humidity is also kept constant.

• Every Monday and Friday, the mausoleum is closed and a senior official of the institute's "body brigade" (most of whom log 20 years or more on the job before they are allowed to touch the corpse) removes Lenin's clothing and examines the cadaver for any signs of wear and tear. Any dust that has accumulated is carefully brushed away; then a special preservative ointment is applied to the skin. The corpse is then re-dressed and put back on display.

• Every 18 months, the cadaver is bathed in preservatives and injected with chemicals, which displace both water and bacteria in the cells and prevent the tissues from decomposing. Which chemicals are used in the process? Hardly anyone knows—even today, the "recipe" is as closely guarded a secret as the formula for Coca-Cola. Only the eight most senior members of the institute know the precise formula. When the process is completed, the cadaver is given a brand-new, hand-tailored suit.

KEEPING THE FAITH
As of 1996, more than five years after the collapse of the Soviet empire, Lenin's body was still on display in Red Square. Keeping the mausoleum open is no empty gesture—the corpse requires constant attention and a lot of money to keep it in good condition. But for many, it has become the political shrine that Stalin envisioned…and the Russian government fears that giving Lenin a regular burial will create a political backlash. Seventy-two years after he died, Lenin is still—literally—a political presence to be reckoned with.

MUMMIFIED FACTS
• **Wasted effort.** Soviet scientists continued perfecting their embalming techniques until the 1950s…just in time for the death of Joseph Stalin. He, too, was embalmed, then laid to rest alongside Lenin. But *that* turned out to be a waste of time. Eight years later, Nikita Khruschev ordered Stalin's body removed and buried in a more modest grave along the Kremlin wall.

A giraffe's neck has 7 vertebrae; a bird's has 14; a person's has 26.

- **Mummies for sale.** Budget cuts brought on by the collapse of the Soviet Union have forced the Research Institute for Biological Structures to make its services available to the public. The mummification process takes a full year, requires the removal of all organs, and costs around $500,000. "The precise cost depends on the condition of the body," an official explains. "But our work is the best." The $500,000, by the way, only covers the cost of the embalming—you still have to build a mausoleum with temperature and humidity controls, which the institute estimates will cost as much as $5 million...not including the cost of staffing it forever.

- **No-brainer.** In 1924, Lenin's brain was removed and handed over to the Soviet Brain Institute—an organization founded specifically to determine whether the leader's brain was superior to other human brains. Not surprisingly, they reported in 1936 that the brain "possessed such high organization that even during Lenin's illness, it continued to function on a very high level." Alas, it was just propaganda. In 1994, the Brain Institute's director admitted that "in the anatomical structure of Lenin's brain, there is nothing sensational."

CADAVER CONSPIRACY?

Is the body on display in Lenin's Tomb really *his* body? The official word is yes. But throughout the late 1920s, and 1930s, rumors spread that the embalmers had actually failed in their task. According to the story, the body in the mausoleum is a wax dummy.

This rumor is so widely accepted that the Soviet government opened an official "investigation" into the matter and invited a German doctor to participate and report his findings to the world. But the inquiry only heightened suspicions. As Payne reports, the German doctor

> was not permitted to make more than a cursory examination. He reported that he had observed frostbites on the skin, felt the cheeks, and lifted one of Lenin's arms....He inquired about the techniques and was told they were secret but would be fully revealed in three or four years' time when they had been proved effective; and nothing more was ever heard about the secret formula.

Even after the fall of Communism in Russia, no one (except for the government) knows for sure whether the corpse is real.

FAMOUS LAST WORDS

It's never too early to get yours ready.

"Don't let it end like this. Tell them I said something."
—Pancho Villa

"I'd rather be fishing."
—Jimmy Gass, *murderer*

"O.K. I won't."
—Elvis Presley, *responding to his girlfriend's request that he not fall asleep in the bathroom*

"It's very beautiful over there."
—Thomas A. Edison

"Why not? Why not?"
—Timothy Leary

"Make my skin into drumheads for the Bohemian cause."
—John Ziska, *Czech rebel*

"I've never forgiven that smart-alecky reporter who named me 'Butterfingers.'"
—Thomas Moran, *pickpocket*

"I'm tired of fighting. I guess this is going to get me."
—Harry Houdini

"Remember me to my friends, tell them I'm a hell of a mess."
—H. L. Mencken, *essayist*

"Monsieur, I beg your pardon."
—Marie Antoinette, *to her executioner, after stepping on his foot accidentally*

"Dying is a very dull affair. My advice to you is to have nothing whatever to do with it."
—*Author* Somerset Maugham

"But, but, Mister Colonel—"
—Benito Mussolini, *executed 1945*

"This isn't the worst. The worst is that they stole twenty-five years of my life."
—*Director* Erich von Stroheim's *last words to Hollywood*

"I'm not afraid to die, Honey…I know the Lord has his arms wrapped around this big fat sparrow."
—*Blues singer* Ethel Waters

"I am about to, or, I am going to die. Either expression is used."
—Dominique Bouhours, *grammarian*

"Never felt better."
—Douglas Fairbanks, Sr.

DOG DOO! GOOD GOD!

A palindrome is a word or phrase that's spelled the same backward and forward. Word enthusiasts like to say that the first palindrome was uttered in the Garden of Eden when Adam first laid eyes on Eve: "Madam, I'm Adam." (Note that our foremother Eve had a palindromic name, as do people named Otto, Bob, and Anna. As does the sentence "Step on no pets.") Get it?

Your task is to complete the following phrases by filling in the blanks. All the letters you need are there. If the answers don't make a lot of sense to you, remember that in a palindromic world, they're sheer perfection.

1. Dennis _ _ _ _ _ _.

2. Was it a rat _ _ _ _ _?

3. 'Tis in a Desoto _ _ _ _ _ _ _ _ _ _.

4. Red rum, sir, _ _ _ _ _ _ _ _ _.

5. Dammit, _'_ _ _ _ _!

6. Do geese _ _ _ _ _ _ _ _?

7. A slut nixes _ _ _ _ _ _ _ _ _ _ _.

8. Lapses? Order _ _ _ _ _ _ _ _ _ _, _ _ _ _.

9. "Desserts," I _ _ _ _ _ _ _ _ _.

10. If I had a _ _ _-_ _ _...

11. Ed, I saw Harpo Marx _ _ _ _ _ _ _ _ _ _ _ _ _.

12. Yawn. Madonna fan? _ _ _ _ _ _ _ _ _ _.

13. Lisa Bonet ate _ _ _ _ _ _ _ _ _.

14. Do nine men interpret? "_ _ _ _ _ _ _," _ _ _ _ _.

15. Are we not drawn onward, we few, _ _ _ _ _ _ _ _ _ _ _ _ _ _ _ _ _ _?

ANSWER, PAGE 365

* * * * *

PALINDROMIC PEOPLE

Then there are the people who have palindromic names—but only when they're used in sentences like the following. Fill in the first name that begins each of these classic palindromic sentences.

1. _____, am I mayor?
2. _____ and Edna dine.
3. _____ won no wallets
4. _____, I stay away at six A.M.
5. _____, did I moan?
6. _____ is as selfless, as I am, Ron.

ANSWER, PAGE 365

THE KING'S THINGS

Back before we had Michael Jackson to kick around, Elvis Presley served most of our eccentric rock star needs. Here are some of the things Elvis demanded be kept at Graceland at all times. Can you find all 22 of the capitalized words and phrases in the grid?

```
            N O S O
          F E D E A R
          B E S I S A
          C A T N O C
            S C W Y
            N S O G
            U O R N
            B B B I
            R U D D
            E S O D
            G A U U
            R U B P
      T H E U E L A E W A
    S O N E B R E N A P L M
  S I K L I M K M A G H S T J
  F E A I N A R I N I N T I H
  E A T S I H A N A R E P U S
  P S E T F S U T B M E O I T
    C O M E A T L O A F T U
      B L E R D E N J B A
      I E B T A U R R H T
      S R D E T G E C J O
    A C A N B     I Q U E M
  A D U N U         C I S N H
  D O I T O         I C I A F
  H S T I R E     W E Y L T A
  N E S S G O D T O H F Y S O
  R G U R H N T O R A R I I D
  E N S F S N O I N O U W R M
  O A F R E S H F R U I T D S
    R O S R R H U D C T I D
      D E F A A S G O D X
```

BACON
BANANA PUDDING
Six cans of BISCUITS
BROWNIES
CIGARETTES
CONTAC
DRISTAN
FRESH FRUIT

FRESH GROUND BEEF
HAMBURGER BUNS
HOT DOGS
JUICY FRUIT and
    DOUBLEMINT gum
MEATLOAF
MILK
ONIONS

PEANUT BUTTER
Case of PEPSI
POTATOES
SAUERKRAUT
SUCRETS
SUPER ANAHIST

ANSWER, PAGE 367

WIENERS ON WHEELS

*Here's a BRI inside look at the Oscar Mayer Wienermobile,
perhaps the most popular pop-culture icon on four wheels.*

THE EVOLUTION OF THE WIENERMOBILE
In the beginning, there was the "Weiner Wagon," a
horse-drawn cart that the Oscar Mayer Company sent to
Chicago-area butcher shops to promote its products. A German
band rode on the back, oom-pahing for crowds wherever the
wagon stopped.

Modern thinking. In the mid-1920s, Oscar's nephew, Charlie,
joined the company right out of college. He came up with the
idea of hiring a midget to dress up in a chef's uniform and make
appearances with the band. Dubbed "Little Oscar, the world's
smallest chef," the midget sang, plugged Oscar Mayer products,
and gave away prizes at each stop.

Rolling along. In the 1930s, there was a nationwide craze for
vehicles in the shape of products. There were milk bottle-mobiles,
vacuum cleaner-mobiles, cheese-mobiles, and so on. Mayer's
nephew decided to create a special vehicle for Little Oscar. He
paid the General Body Company of Chicago $5,000 to convert an
old car into a 13-foot, open-cockpit hot dog—the first "Wienermobile." It rolled off the assembly line in 1936.

Wieners everywhere. Putting the world's smallest chef behind the
wheel of the World's Largest Wiener, as Oscar Mayer called it,
generated plenty of publicity. In fact, it was such a good promotional gimmick that by the 1940s the company had an entire fleet
of Wienermobiles. Every time they opened a new meat-packing
plant, they commissioned a new Wienermobile to go with it. The
vehicles were on the road continuously from 1936 to 1977, stopping only during World War II gasoline rationing.

Dead dog. By the mid-1970s, it looked like the Wienermobile's
days were running out. Oscar Mayer wanted to move away
from its regional meat plant promotions toward nationwide TV

advertising campaigns…and who knows, maybe it thought the dogs-on-wheels were getting too dorky. So, in 1977, the entire wienie fleet was put up on blocks.

On a roll. The giant wieners might have stayed there forever. But in 1986, the company decided to commemorate the 50th anniversary of the original Wienermobile. As Wienermobile manager Russ Whitacre explains, "We brought the last working one out of storage and put it on the road, driven by two college students for the summer. We got a great deal of response…a lot of nostalgia. Boomers said it was a piece of their lives." When thousands of fans wrote to Oscar Mayer about the vehicles, company officials decided they had something worth preserving, and ordered a brand-new fleet of six to be built. They hit the road in 1988.

LAMBORWIENIE
The pre-1980s Wienermobiles had been pretty spartan as sausages go, but the 1988 models were genuine Wienerbagos, complete with microwave ovens, refrigerators, CB radios, cellular phones, and stereo systems capable of belting out 21 different renditions of the Oscar Mayer Wiener song, including country, rap, and rock 'n' roll versions. Even the car's exhaust system was improved—in addition to ordinary automobile fumes, the Wienermobiles give off a "fondly familiar hot dog scent" during appearances.

The car's V6 engine has a top speed of 110 mph. But the only person known to have driven the car that fast was Al Unser, Jr., who took one of the wienies for a spin at the Indianapolis Motor Speedway. Oscar Mayer hotdoggers (the company's name for Wienerdog drivers) are pretty much stuck driving at the legal speed limit. As Whitacre explains, "Because of the vehicle's visibility, we hear about it if someone drives a Wienermobile in an unsafe manner."

WIENERMOBILE 2000
By 1994, the new Wienermobiles had logged an average of 200,000 miles apiece on American highways and byways, so Oscar Mayer hired California auto designer Harry Bradley—creator of the original Mattel Hot Wheels—to design a Wienermobile for the 21st century. Among his improvements: He extended the wienie theme to the *inside* of the vehicle, giving it a hot dog

dashboard and glove box, a condiment control panel, and relish-colored captain's chairs for the driver and passengers. Estimated total cost of each vehicle: $150,000.

WIENERMOBILE FACTS

• Nine different men played Little Oscar; the last one retired in 1971. Why wasn't he replaced? Oscar Mayer is mum on the subject. Our theory: As times changed, dressing midgets up as chefs could be considered "bad taste."

• What happens to old Wienermobiles? Most are sent to Canada, Mexico, and other countries where Oscar Mayer has affiliates, but at least one is always kept on hand as a "loaner wiener" in case any of the new ones break down.

• Which is harder to get into: Harvard Law School, or the driver's seat of the Wienermobile? Hint: Every year, more than 1,000 recent college graduates apply for the coveted position of "hot-dogger"; only 12 get the nod. Oscar Mayer says "outgoing person-alities and impressive academic credentials" are key qualities for the job.

• Once you're hired on as a hot dogger, you have to put in a week of on-the-dog training at Hot Dog High, the company's Wiener-dog training facility. "The curriculum takes about seven days," hotdogger Brian Spillane explains, "including one day to learn how to drive the 'Dog,' just so no one gets in a pickle when they miss a turn."

• Mastery of hot dog puns is another must. "Go ahead and grill us," Dan Duff, another hotdogger, challenges. "In this job, we're trained to cut the mustard. It's a job to relish…and that's no bologna."

• Wienermobiles log an average of 1,000 miles per week visiting baseball games, children's hospitals, grocery stores, etc. Even so, there have been very few traffic accidents involving the Wiener-mobile—although there was at least one accident involving a Wienermobile fan. As one hotdogger admits: "One guy saw the Weinermobile, and laughed so hard, his false teeth fell out—right into the big air vents on the buns. We never did find them. He really sank his teeth into our buns."

FAMILIAR PHRASES

Here are the origins of some everyday phrases.

HIGHTAIL IT
Meaning: Leave quickly.
Origin: Dates back to the Old West. Cowboys on the Great Plains noticed that wild horses jerked their tails very high just before galloping off. Soon anyone who left quickly was said to have "hightailed it."

RED HERRING
Meaning: Distraction; diversionary tactic.
Origin: Comes from hunting. When herring is smoked, it changes from silvery gray to brownish red and gives off a strong smell. Hunters use red herrings to train dogs to follow a scent...and, by dragging a red herring across the trail, they can also throw a dog *off* a scent.

STUFFED SHIRT
Meaning: Braggart or pompous person.
Origin: In the days before mannequins, clothing shops displayed shirts in their windows by stuffing them with tissue paper or rags. The shirt looked broad-chested, like a strong man, but was really light and flimsy.

RIGHT-HAND MAN
Meaning: Important assistant.
Origin: In 17th-century cavalries, the soldier at the far right of a line of troops had a position of special responsibility or command.

AT THE DROP OF A HAT
Meaning: Quickly; without delay.
Origin: The term dates back to the days when races, prizefights, and other sporting events were literally started with the wave or the drop of a hat.

The average American female will have 3.3 pregnancies in her lifetime.

SPEAK OF THE DEVIL

Here are some random bits of information about the Devil.

THE DEVIL YOU SAY

• The Devil as we think of him—with the horns, pitchfork, etc.—dates back to the 10th and 11th centuries; his popular image was not taken from the Bible. According to the New Testament, the devil takes the form of a lion, a wolf, a dragon, and a serpent. Early Christians sometimes thought of him as a three-headed dog.

So where does the Devil we know come from?
• His beard (goatee), horns, hooves, hairy legs, pointy ears, etc., were borrowed from the goat. Scholars cite two reasons:
1. "The domestic goat was renowned for the size of its phallus," writes historian J.C.J. Metford, and, according to legend, "tempted saints by whispering in their ears lewd details of the sexual pleasures they had relinquished."
2. One of the ways the Church discouraged interest in other religions was by literally "demonizing" gods that competed with theirs. So a lot of the imagery is derived from pagan sources: the goatlike features also come from Pan, the Greek god of shepherds, fertility, and nature.

• His red skin is the color of blood and fire.
• His three-pronged fork, or *triton*, was borrowed from Poseidon, the nasty-tempered Greek god of the sea and of earthquakes, whose main symbol was a three-pronged spear.

DEVOLUTION

• Modern mythology paints the Devil as the kind of all-powerful, evil being who possesses little girls in *The Exorcist* or tries to destroy the world in *The Omen*. But that hasn't always been the case.
• During the Middle Ages in parts of Europe, he was seen as more of a mean-spirited, clumsy, dimwitted lout with a fondness for pranks—like Bluto in the *Popeye* cartoons—that the wise and the holy could easily outsmart. "There was nothing grand about their Satan," historian Charles Mackay writes in his book *Extraordinary*

Popular Delusions and the Madness of Crowds.

> On the contrary, he was a low, mean devil, whom it was easy to circumvent, and fine fun to play tricks with....It was believed that he endeavored to trip people up by laying his long invisible tail in their way, and giving it a sudden whisk when their legs were over it; that he used to get drunk, and swear like a trooper, and be mischievous. ...Some of the saints spat in his face, to his very great annoyance; others chopped off pieces of his tail, which, however, always grew back again.

• Of course, some countries were extremely serious about Satan. Historians estimate that from 1450 to 1750, more than 200,000 alleged witches were executed in Europe and America for "dealing with the Devil."

DEVIL'S FOOD

• How did devil's food cake get its name? One theory: The stuff was so tasty that people assumed that the inventors had to sell their soul to the Devil to get the recipe.

• You've probably eaten pumpernickel bread before...but did you know the word *Pumpernickel* means "Devil's fart" in German? Apparently, when German bakers invented the bread centuries ago, it was awful. The 1756 book *A Grand Tour of Germany* described it as bread "of the very coarsest kind, ill-baked and as black as coal, for they never sift their flour." Locals joked that it was so difficult to digest that even the Devil himself got gas when he ate it.

• In some countries, the Devil is nicknamed "the good man," "the old gentleman," and even "the great fellow." Why? Tradition had it that if you "spoke of the Devil," he would appear. So people didn't.

SATAN ON TRIAL

In 1971, a man named Gerald Mayo filed suit against Satan in the U.S. District Court in Pennsylvania, alleging that "Satan has on numerous occasions caused plaintiff misery and unwarranted threats, against the will of plaintiff, that Satan has placed deliberate obstacles in his path and has caused plaintiff's downfall. Plaintiff alleges that by reason of these acts Satan has deprived him of his constitutional rights."

The case, "Gerald Mayo v. Satan and His Staff." was thrown out of court after Mayo failed to provide the U.S. marshal with instructions on how to serve Satan a subpoena, and could not prove that Satan lived within the jurisdiction of the District Court.

A LITTLE LIST

Can you unscramble the letters below to figure out where danger lurks inside your car, be it RV, SUV, or VW? The lap you save may be your own.

The 3 Most Dangerous Foods to Eat in a Car

1. _ _ _ _ _ _
   E C F E O F

2. _ _ _ _ _
   A S C O T

3. _ _ _ _ _
   I I H L C

ANSWER, PAGE 365

SNAP, CRACKLE, FLOP

For every successful cereal like Frosted Flakes or Wheaties, there are hundreds of bombs like Banana Wackies and Ooboperoos. Here are a few of those legendary cereal flops, along with a few we made up. Can you separate the Wheaties from the chaff and find the fakes?

Mysterios (1959): Each box contained one of four different possible flavors—corn, chocolate, cinnamon, or "fruit." Not any particular fruit...just fruit. Anyway, since most kids were interested in one flavor more than the others, their parents generally just bought cereals that were the flavor their kids wanted.

Kellogg's Kream Crunch (1963): Frosted-oat loops mixed with cubes of freeze-dried vanilla-orange or strawberry ice cream. According to a Kellogg's exec: "The product kind of melted into gooey ice cream in milk. It just wasn't appetizing."

Sugar Smiles (1953): General Mills' first try at sugar cereal. A bizarre mixture of plain Wheaties and sugar-frosted Kix. Slogan: "You can't help smiling the minute you taste it."

Dinos (early 1990s): After the success of Fruity Pebbles, Post tried naming a cereal after the Flintstones' pet dinosaur. "A question that came up constantly," recalls a Post art director, "was 'We've got Cocoa Pebbles and Fruity Pebbles...so what flavor is Dino?'...It sounds like something Fred would be getting off his lawn instead of something you'd want to be eating."

Grape Ape (1976): The Saturday morning cartoon show this cereal was based on didn't last very long, but it lasted longer than the cereal. An adman for Kellogg's said, "It tasted like someone poured milk into grape juice."

Day-O (late 1960s): "The world's first calypso-inspired presweetened cereal," from General Mills.

Post Jelly Donuts (1964): The "donuts" in this cereal weren't very donut-y, but they *were* filled with jelly. Unfortunately, the donuts tended to crack in the box during shipping, and the jelly leaked out, making one big sticky mess.

Ooops (early 1970s): General Mills had so many bombs, they came up with a cereal they actually *said* was based on a mistake. The jingle went: "Ooops, it's a crazy mistake, Ooops, it's a cereal that's great!"

Kellogg's Corn Crackos (1967): The box featured the Waker Upper Bird perched on a bowl of candy-coated twists. An internal company memo said: "It looks like a bird eating worms; who wants worms for breakfast?"

Punch Crunch (1975): A spin-off of Cap'n Crunch. The screaming pink box featured Harry S., an exuberant hippo in a sailor suit, making goo-goo eyes at Cap'n Crunch. Many chain stores perceived the hippo as gay and refused to carry the cereal. Marveled one Quaker salesman: "How that one ever got through, I'll never understand."

ANSWER, PAGE 365

THE BIRTH OF "THE SIMPSONS"

It may be the most popular prime-time cartoon in history. But how did such an outrageous show make it onto the air in the first place? Read on.

OFF THE WALL

In the mid-1980s, producer James L. Brooks was hired to develop a comedy series called *The Tracey Ullman Show* for the fledgling Fox TV network. Ullman was immensely popular in England…but Brooks wasn't sure her humor would play well in the United States. He figured that inserting short cartoon segments between her comedy sketches might help keep the show interesting to American audiences.

Brooks was a fan of counterculture cartoonist Matt Groening (pronounced *Graining*), whose weekly cartoon strip *Life in Hell* runs in *The Village Voice* and more than 200 other "alternative" newspapers. He had a *Life in Hell* poster in his office, and one day he remarked to an assistant, "We should get this guy and have him animate for us."

LOST IN SPACE

So Fox officials approached Groening about animating *Life in Hell* and making its characters—two humans named Akbar and Jeff and three rabbits named Binky, Sheba, and Bongo—part of the show. At first, Groening agreed. Then he ran into a problem: "Fox told me outright, 'We must own the characters and the marketing rights.' The studio was still getting over the fact that a few years ago it gave George Lucas all the licensing rights to *Star Wars*."

Groening was making a pretty good living licensing the *Life in Hell* characters for calendars, mugs, T-shirts, etc., and didn't want to give it up. But rather than walk away from Fox's offer, he came up with another idea. He dashed off a short story based on his real-life family—Homer and Marge Groening (his parents); Lisa and Maggie (his sisters); and an autobiographical character named Bart (an anagram of the word "brat"). He proposed using them instead of the *Life in Hell* characters. Fox agreed to give it a try.

A NEW FAMILY

As Groening developed these characters for TV, they began to lose their resemblance to his real family. (His father, for example, isn't bald, and his mother no longer wears "big hair.") He changed their last name to the all-American sounding "Simpson," and fashioned their lives after old sitcom characters. "I used to spend hours transfixed in front of a TV set watching family situation comedies," he told the *San Francisco Chronicle* in 1990. "It's no accident that the Simpsons live in Springfield—that's the town in *Father Knows Best.*" Later, he added: "What is *The Simpsons* but a hallucination of the sitcom? And that has to be the ultimate American nightmare."

The original sketches were only 15 to 20 seconds long, so Bart was the only well-developed character. "He was like what would have happened if *Leave It to Beaver's* Eddie Haskell got his own show," Groening says. "He was a deviant." Homer—his voice, at least—was a Walter Matthau impersonation, Lisa was supposed to be a "female Bart," and Marge and Maggie weren't much more than backdrops for the other characters.

BUST AND BOOM

The Tracey Ullman Show debuted in 1987. It was a critical success, but ratings were terrible. Despite this, *The Simpsons* attracted a huge cult following, and Fox responded by increasing the length of the sketches from 20 to 90 seconds. Then they introduced a line of Simpsons T-shirts, posters, and other items to cash in on the fad.

But the biggest boost to the Simpsons' popularity came from a candy bar company. The makers of Butterfinger and Baby Ruth licensed the Simpson characters for their candy bar ads—which aired on network TV. So kids who'd never heard of *The Tracey Ullman Show* (or Fox, for that matter) finally got a glimpse of Bart and his family. Their popularity grew.

ON THEIR OWN

In 1988, Fox decided to spin *The Simpsons* off into their own show. It was scheduled to premiere in September 1989. But when the initial 13 episodes came back from Korea, where they were being animated, Groening discovered that the director had added a few unauthorized "jokes" of his own. In one episode, for example, when the Simpsons are watching a TV show called *The Happy Little Elves Meet the Curious Bear Cubs,* the animators inserted a scene in which a bear cub rips off the head of an elf and drinks its blood.

"Not exactly a minor addition," Groening told *The New York Times* in 1990. "When we watched it, we sat in the dark for about two minutes in silence. Then we ran for the door. I thought my career in animation had sunk to the bottom of the sea. Had that gotten on the air, there would be no show today." The director and animators were fired, and the show was postponed until January 1990 while new animators fixed the episodes.

SHOW TIME
The Simpsons as we know it today finally made it onto TV on January 13, 1990. It earned the second-highest ratings in its time slot—pretty impressive when you consider that Fox didn't have as many affiliates around the country as ABC, CBS, or NBC. (*The Tracey Ullman Show* went off the air five months later.) *The Simpsons* went on to become Fox's highest-rated show. In March 1990, it placed 20th in the weekly Nielsen ratings, and in June went all the way to #3. It has, without question, played a key role in establishing Fox as a viable fourth network.

SOUR GRAPES
In 1992, Tracey Ullman filed suit against Fox for $2.25 million, arguing that since *The Simpsons* got their start on her show ("I breast-fed those little devils," she told a reporter), she was entitled to a share of the merchandising profits. In court, however, she ad- mitted that she did not create *The Simpsons,* write any of the shows, or take part in any of the merchandising. She lost the case.

* * *

"The creativity of the way people respond to the show is fantastic. You should see the fan mail. Kids send in their pictures of Bart beating up other cartoon characters."

—*Matt Groening*

Henry Ford was Charles Lindbergh's first passenger in the *Spirit of St. Louis.*

THE MYSTERIOUS OUIJA BOARD

Why did Uncle John write this chapter? Maybe his porcelain Ouija board told him to.

GHOSTWRITER

In the 1890s, spiritualism was a big fad. In the midst of it, someone came up with a new tool for communicating with the dead: a small piece of wood called a "planchette." People would gather around a table or other flat surface, place their hands on the planchette, and watch how it moved. Some had pencils attached that wrote out messages; others pointed at letters, numbers, and words painted on the table and spelled out messages that way. No one could explain why the planchette moved. Skeptics charged that the people who held the planchette were moving it—perhaps unconsciously. But true believers insisted that spirits guided the little thing across the table.

SPELLING IT OUT

William and Isaac Fuld thought the whole thing was a bunch of nonsense, but wanted to cash in on it. They owned a toy company in Maryland, and figured the planchette would make a good game. So they took a board about the size of a cafeteria tray, painted the letters of the alphabet across the middle, and put the numbers 0 through 9 underneath. They also put the words "Yes" and "No" in the left and right corners, and the word "Goodbye" across the bottom. Then they painted the name of the game, "Ouija"—a combination of *oui* and *ja*, the French and German words for "yes"— across the top. Their "Ouija Talking Board" was patented in 1892.

DEAD SERIOUS

It wasn't until World War I that Ouija boards became a big commercial success.

Company legend has it that not long before the war broke out, William Fuld's favorite Ouija board told him to "prepare for big

---

business." So he expanded production...and sure enough, during the war people began using the Ouija to "keep in touch" with loved ones who'd been sent into battle. Sales skyrocketed, and the money poured in.

Since then, Ouija sales have always boomed in times of national crisis, tailed off when conditions improved, then increased again when the next crisis hit. The Ouija board sold well during World War II, the Korean War, and the Vietnam War, and dipped in between. The Fuld Family manufactured Ouija Boards until 1967, when they sold the rights to Parker Brothers.

OUIJA FACTS

• At the time World War I started, the IRS collected a 10% tax on every game sold in the United States and the Fulds didn't want to pay. So they declared the Ouija board to be a "scientific instrument" that didn't qualify for the tax. They fought the case all the way to the Supreme Court...and lost.

• No one can explain how the Ouija planchette moves across the board. "There's nothing special about Ouijas to give it any supernatural powers," one Parker Brothers spokesperson insists. "It's simply a game."

• One reasonable theory: the game works through an "idiomotor action" in much the same way that a dowsing rod finds water. "Unconsciously picturing what you want to have happen can cause your muscles to make it happen," psychology professor Ray Hyman explains. "People think they're not doing anything and that some outside force is making it happen."

* * * *

TRUE STORY

At age 47, the Rolling Stones' bassist, Bill Wyman, began a relationship with 13-year-old Mandy Smith, with her mother's blessing. Six years later, they were married, but the marriage only lasted a year. Not long after, Bill's 30-year-old son Stephen married Mandy's mother, age 46. That made Stephen a stepfather to his former stepmother. If Bill and Mandy had remained married, Stephen would have been his father's father-in-law and his own grandpa.

HOORAY FOR HOLLYWOOD

Hollywood is so closely identified with the "decadent" film industry, that it's hard to imagine that it started out as prim Victorian town...but it did.

HISTORY. In 1886, Kansas prohibitionists Harvey and Daeida Wilcox "bought a 120-acre citrus farm in sleepy Cahuenga Valley, a suburb of Los Angeles, for $150/acre." They built an elaborate Victorian house in the middle of a fig orchard, then began subdividing the property. Liquor wasn't allowed, and only "well-educated, worldly, decent" people were offered the property.

In 1903 the subdivision was big enough to become the city of Hollywood. But that didn't last long. In 1910, the citizens voted to make Hollywood an official district of L.A. The reason: They wanted access to L.A.'s water system. Since then, one historian laments, "Hollywood has been reduced to a mere 'northwest sector of the city of Los Angeles.' "

NAME. While her California house was being built in 1886, Daeida Wilcox went East to visit her family. On the train, she met a woman who described a lovely Illinois summer estate, called Hollywood, that was sprinkled with holly trees.

Wilcox was taken with the idea. She repeatedly tried to grow holly on her citrus farm before deciding that the climate wasn't suitable. Perhaps to console herself, she named their ranch "Hollywood" anyway. In 1887 she registered the name with the Los Angeles recorder.

MAIN INDUSTRY. In the early 1900s, the film industry was centered in both New York City and Fort Lee, New Jersey. But soon movie companies were headed west.

The First West Coast Studio. In 1907, Col. William Selig was producing crude silent movies in Chicago, "whenever the sun was shining—which was not frequently enough to make [his business] a profound success." He happened to read a promotional pamphlet sent East by the Los Angeles Chamber of Commerce that mentioned the city was "bathed in sunshine some 350 days of the year." This impressed Selig, and he sent two men—Francis Boggs and Thomas Parsons—to see if it was true.

To give the area a test, Boggs and Parsons set up a temporary studio in L.A. and began making pictures, recruiting actors off the streets of the city. When they'd completed several pictures, they left to test another location—Colorado—where they compared the climate and photographic possibilities to those on the coast. The West Coast won. Not only was there almost unlimited sunshine, but the varied scenery—mountains, rivers, deserts, and ocean—was unbeatable. Boggs and Parsons shared their discovery with other filmmakers in the east, and in early 1909, Selig went to Los Angeles to build the first L.A. film studio.

The First Hollywood Studio. Ironically, it was the Wilcoxes' puritanism that brought moviemakers to Hollywood. When the couple subdivided their estate, one plot of land wound up in the hands of a tavern owner, who opened a bar there. The outraged Victorians passed a law prohibiting booze, bankrupting the bar. So when the Nestor Moving Picture Company arrived from New Jersey in 1911, it was able to buy the abandoned tavern cheap and convert it into the first Hollywood studio. Within a week, the company had produced Hollywood's first film, *Her Indian Hero,* a Western featuring real Native Americans. Within three months, it was sharing Hollywood with 14 other film companies—despite the "Actors Not Welcome" signs posted all over town.

HOLLYWOOD FACTS

• Early filmmakers who moved West weren't just looking for a place in the sun; they were looking for a place to hide. So many were violating Thomas Edison's motion picture patents that a legal battle known as the Patents War erupted. Southern California was the perfect refuge—as far from the federal government as possible and close enough to the Mexican border for a quick getaway.

• The famous "HOLLYWOOD" sign in the hills above the film capital originally said "HOLLYWOODLAND." It was built in 1923 to promote a real estate development. The last four letters fell down during WW II.

White is the most common color for houses in the United States.

THE LAST LAUGH: EPITAPHS

In the Second Bathroom Reader, *we included some unusual epitaphs sent to us by BRI members. Here's a bunch we've gotten since then.*

Seen in Medway, MA:
In Memory of Peter Daniels, 1688-1746
Beneath this stone, a lump of clay,
Lies Uncle Peter Daniels,
Who too early in the month of May
Took off his winter flannels.

Seen in Ribbesford, England:
Anna Wallace
The children of Israel wanted bread,
And the Lord he sent them manna.
Old clerk Wallace wanted a wife,
And the Devil sent him Anna.

Seen in Westminster Abbey:
John Gay
Life is a joke, and all things show it;
I thought so once and now I know it.

Seen in Death Valley, CA:
May Preston
Here lies the body of fat May Preston
Who's now moved to heaven
To relieve the congestion.

Seen in Falkirk, England:
Jimmy Wyatt
At rest beneath this slab of stone
Lies Stingy Jimmy Wyatt;
He died one morning just at ten
And saved a dinner by it.

Seen in Thanet, England:
Against his will, here lies George Hill
Who from a cliff, fell down quite stiff.
When it happened is not known,
Therefore not mentioned on this stone.

Seen in Shutesbury, MA:
To the Four Husbands of Miss Ivy Saunders
Here lies my husbands, One, Two, Three,
Dumb as men could ever be.
As for my fourth, well, praise be God,
He bides for a little above the sod.
Alex, Ben and Sandy were the first three's names,
And to make things tidy I'll add his—James.

Canada is the second largest country on Earth.

MR. & MS. QUIZ

For all these years, Uncle John has kept his readers up to date on the latest skirmishes in the ongoing Battle of the Sexes. Check the appropriate box to the left of each question when you've figured out which gender is more likely to…

<u>Men</u>   <u>Women</u>

_____   _____   1.   …be naturally blond?

_____   _____   2.   …laugh more?

_____   _____   3.   …sleep more?

_____   _____   4.   …snore?

_____   _____   5.   …be born at night?

_____   _____   6.   …purchase men's clothing in U.S. stores?

_____   _____   7.   …run stoplights?

_____   _____   8.   …switch lanes without signaling?

_____   _____   9.   …be left-handed?

_____   _____   10. …get migraines?

_____   _____   11. …get an ulcer?

_____   _____   12. …get hiccups?

_____   _____   13. …get struck by lightning?

_____   _____   14. …leave their hotel rooms cleaner?

_____   _____   15. …lock themselves out of their hotel rooms?

_____   _____   16. …take longer showers?

_____   _____   17. …blink more?

_____	_____	18.	...stutter as a child?
_____	_____	19.	...buy gifts for Mother's Day?
_____	_____	20.	...fall out of bed while in the hospital?
_____	_____	21.	...talk to their cars?
_____	_____	22.	...hold the TV remote?
_____	_____	23.	...lose the TV remote?
_____	_____	24.	...have a keener sense of smell?

ANSWER, PAGE 366

* * * * *

EYE OF THE BEHOLDER

We knew she bleached her hair, but that's not all; the lovely Marilyn Monroe also enhanced her beauty in four of the following ways. What didn't she have done?

a) She heightened her hairline with electrolysis
b) She had a lump of cartilage removed from the tip of her nose
c) She had a crescent-shaped silicone implant inserted into her jaw to soften its line
d) She had her upper molars removed to emphasize her cheekbones
e) She bleached her teeth

ANSWER, PAGE 368

LEFT-HANDED FACTS

We've considered doing something about left-handedness for several years,
but the question always comes up—are there enough left-handed bathroom readers
to make it worthwhile? After six years, we finally don't care; we
just want to use the information. So here's a section for southpaws.

A re you left-handed? If so, you're not alone—but you're definitely outnumbered; lefties make up only 5% to 15% of the general population. If you're a female southpaw, you're even more unusual—there are roughly 50% more left-handed males than females. For centuries scientists have tried to figure out what makes people left- or right-handed, and they still aren't sure why. (They're not even sure if all lefties are that way for the same reason.) Here are some theories:

WHAT MAKES A LEFTIE?

• Scientists used to think that left- and right-handedness was purely a genetic trait, but now they have doubts. Reason: In 20% of all sets of identical twins, one sibling is left-handed, and the other is right-handed.

• Some scientists think the hand you prefer is determined by whether you're a "right-brained" person or a "left-brained" person. The right half of the brain controls the left side of the body, as well as spatial / musical / aesthetic judgement and perception; the left half controls the right side of the body, plus communication skills. Lefties are generally right-brained.

• Support for this theory: Most children begin demonstrating a preference for one hand over the other at the same time their central nervous system is growing and maturing. This leads some scientists to believe the two processes are linked.

• According to another theory, before birth all babies are right-handed—which means that the left side of their brain is dominant. But during a stressful or difficult birth, oxygen deficiency can cause damage to the left side of the brain, making it weaker and enabling the right side to compete against it for dominance. If the right side wins out, the baby will become left-handed.

"Smut" gets its name from a fungus that lives on corn kernels.

• This theory also explains, researchers claim, why twins, any child born to a smoker, or children born to a mother more than 30 years old are more likely to be left-handed: they are more prone to stressful births. Children of stressful births are also more likely to stammer and suffer dyslexia, traits that are more common in lefties.

LEFT-HANDED HISTORY
No matter what makes southpaws what they are, they've been discriminated against for thousands of years—in nearly every culture on Earth. Some examples:

• The artwork found in ancient Egyptian tombs portrays most Egyptians as right-handed. But their enemies are portrayed as left-handers, a sign they saw left-handedness as an undesirable trait.

• Ancient Greeks never crossed their left leg over their right, and believed a person's sex was determined by their position in the womb—with the female, or "lesser sex," sitting on the left side of the womb.

• The Romans placed special significance on right-handedness as well. Custom dictated that they enter friends' homes "with the right foot forward"…and turn their heads to the right to sneeze. Their language showed the same bias: the Latin word for left was *sinister* (which also meant "evil" or "ominous"), the word for right was *dexter* (which came to mean "skillful," or "adroit"). Even the word ambidextrous literally means "right-handed with both hands."

• The Ango-Saxon root for left is *lyft*, which means "weak," "broken," or "worthless." *Riht* means "straight," "just," or "erect."

BIBLICAL BIAS
• The Bible is biased in favor of right-handed people. Both the Old and New Testament refer to "the right hand of God." One Old Testament town, Nineveh, is so wicked that its citizens "cannot discern between their right hand and their left hand."

• The saints also followed the right-hand rule; according to early Christian legend, they were so pious even as infants that they refused to nurse from their mother's left breast.

• The distinction is made even in religious art: Jesus and God are nearly always drawn giving blessings with their right hand, and the Devil is usually portrayed doing evil with his left hand.

Close encounters: 10% of Americans swear they've "been in the presence of a ghost."

PHRASE ORIGINS

Here are the origins of some more famous phrases.

THE HANDWRITING IS ON THE WALL
Meaning: The outcome (usually negative) is obvious.
Background: The expression comes from a Babylonian legend in which the evil King Belshazzar drank from a sacred vessel looted from the Temple in Jerusalem. According to one version of the legend, "A mysterious hand appeared after this act of sacrilege and to the astonishment of the king wrote four strange words on the wall of the banquet room. Only the Hebrew prophet, Daniel, could interpret the mysterious message. He boldly told the ruler that they spelled disaster for him and for his nation. Soon afterward, Belshazzar was defeated and slain, just as Daniel said." The scene was a popular subject for tapestries and paintings during the Middle Ages.

OLD STOMPING GROUND
Meaning: Places where you spent a lot of time in your youth or in years past.
Background: The prairie chicken, which is found in Indiana and Illinois, is famous for the courtship dance it performs when looking for a mate. Large groups of males gather together in the morning to strut about, stamp their feet, and make booming noises with their throats. The original settlers used to get up early just to watch them; and the well-worn patches of earth became known as *stomping grounds.*

JIMINY CRICKET
Meaning: The name of the cricket character in the Walt Disney film *Pinocchio*; also a mild expletive.
Background: The name Jiminy Cricket predates *Pinocchio*...and has nothing to do with crickets. It is believed to have originated in the American colonies as "a roundabout way of invoking Jesus Christ." (Since the Puritans strictly forbade taking the Lord's name in vain, an entire new set of kinder, gentler swear words—darn, dang, heck, etc.—were invented to replace them.

More shoplifters are arrested on Wednesdays in January than at any other time of the year.

THE BITTER END

Meaning: The very end—often an unpleasant one.

Background: Has nothing to do with bitterness. It's a sailing term that refers to end of a mooring line or anchor line that is attached to the *bitts*, sturdy wooden or metal posts that are mounted to the ship's deck.

HAVE A SCREW LOOSE

Meaning: Something is wrong with a person or mechanism.

Background: The phrase comes from the cotton industry and dates back as far as the 1780s, when the industrial revolution made mass production of textiles possible for the first time. Huge mills sprang up to take advantage of the new technology (and the cheap labor), but it was difficult to keep all the machines running properly; any machine that broke down or produced defective cloth was said to have "a screw loose" somewhere.

MAKE THINGS HUM

Meaning: Make things run properly, smoothly, quickly, and efficiently.

Background: Another cotton term: the guy who fixed the loose screws on the broken—and thus *silent*—machines was known as the person who *made them hum* again.

IF THE SHOE FITS, WEAR IT

Meaning: "If something applies to you, accept it."

Background: The term is a direct descendant of the early 18th-century term "if the cap fits, put it on," which referred specifically to *fool's caps.*

PLEASED AS PUNCH

Meaning: Delighted.

Background: Believe it or not, the expression has nothing to do with party beverages—it has to do with the rascally puppet character Punch (of Punch and Judy fame), who derived enormous sadistic pleasure from his many evil deeds. The phrase was so popular that even Charles Dickens used it in his 1854 book, *Hard Times.*

There's enough salt in the world's oceans to cover the entire U.S. with a layer 1 1/2 miles deep.

MUMMY'S THE WORD

Mummies are as much a part of American pop culture as they are a part of Ancient Egyptian culture. But how much do you know about them?

RAG TIME

As long as there have been people in Egypt, there have been mummies—not necessarily *man-made* mummies, but mummies nonetheless. The extreme conditions of the desert environment guaranteed that any corpse exposed to the elements for more than a day or two dried out completely, a process that halted decomposition in its tracks.

The ancient Egyptian culture that arose on the banks of the Nile River believed very strongly in preserving human bodies, which they believed were as necessary a part of the afterlife as they were a part of daily life. The formula was simple: no body, no afterlife—you couldn't have one without the other. The only problem: As Egyptian civilization advanced and burial tombs became increasingly elaborate, bodies also became more insulated from the very elements—high temperatures and dry air—that made natural preservation possible in the first place.

The result was that a new science emerged: artificial mummification. From 3100 B.C. to 649 A.D., the ancient Egyptians deliberately mummified the bodies of their dead, using methods that became more sophisticated and successful over time.

MUMMY SECRETS

Scientists have yet to unlock all of the secrets of Egyptian mummification, but they have a pretty good idea of how the process worked:

• When a king or other high official died, the embalmers slit open the body and removed nearly all the organs, which they preserved separately in special ceremonial jars. A few of the important organs, like the heart and kidneys, were left in place. (The Egyptians apparently thought the brain was useless and in most cases they shredded it with small hooks inserted through the nostrils, pulled it out the nose using tiny spoons, and then threw it away.)

Some Egyptian mummies wore dentures.

- Next, the embalmers packed the body in oil of cedar (similar to turpentine) and natron, a special mineral with a high salt content. The chemicals slowly dried the body out, a process that took from 40 to 70 days.
- The body was now completely dried out and "preserved," but the process invariably left it shrunken and wrinkled like a prune, so the next step was to stuff the mouth, nose, chest cavities, etc., with sawdust, pottery, cloth, and other items to fill it out and make it look more human. In many cases the eyes were removed and artificial ones put in their place.
- Then the embalmers doused the body with a waterproofing substance similar to tar, which protected the dried body from moisture. In fact, the word mummy comes from the Persian word *mumiai*, which means "pitch" or "asphalt," and was originally used to describe the preservatives themselves, not the corpse that had been preserved.
- Finally, the body was carefully wrapped in narrow strips of linen and a funerary mask resembling the deceased was placed on the head. Afterwards it was placed in a large coffin that was also carved and painted to look like the deceased, and the coffin was placed in a tomb outfitted with the everyday items that the deceased would need in the afterlife.

THE MUMMY GLUT

Pharaohs weren't the only ancient Egyptians who were mummified—nearly anyone in Egyptian society who could afford it had it done. The result: By the end of the Late Period of Ancient Egypt in the seventh century A.D., the country contained an estimated 500 million mummies, far more than anyone knew what to do with. They were too numerous to count, too disconnected from modern Egyptian life to have any sacred spiritual value, and in most cases were thought to be too insignificant to be worthy of study. Egyptians from the 1100s onward thought of them as more of a natural resource than as the bodies of distant relatives, and treated them as such.

Well into the 19th century, mummies were used as a major fuel source for locomotives of the Egyptian railroad, which bought them by the ton (or by the graveyard). They were cheaper than wood and burned very well.

For more than 400 years, mummies were one of Egypt's largest export industries, and the supply was so plentiful that by 1600 you could buy a pound of mummy powder in Scotland for about 8 shillings. As early as 1100 A.D., Arabs and Christians ground them up for use as medicine, which was often rubbed into wounds, mixed into food, or stirred into tea.

By the 1600s, the medicinal use of mummies began to decline, as many doctors began to question the practice. "Not only does this wretched drug do no good to the sick," the French surgeon Ambrose Paré wrote in his medical journal, "…but it causes them great pain in their stomach, gives them evil smelling breath, and brings on serious vomiting which is more likely to stir up the blood and worsen hemorrhaging than to stop it." He recommended using mummies as fish bait.

By the 1800s, mummies were imported only as curiosities, where it was fashionable to unwrap them during dinner parties.

Mummies were also one of the first sources of recycled paper: During one 19th-century rag shortage (in the days when paper was made from *cloth* fibers, not wood fibers), one Canadian paper manufacturer literally imported Egyptian mummies as a source of raw materials: he unwrapped the cloth and made it into sturdy brown paper, which he sold to butchers and grocers for use as a food wrap. The scheme died out after only a few months, when employees in charge of unwrapping them began coming down with cholera.

Note: What happened when the supply of mummies became scarce? A grisly "instant mummy" industry sprang up in which fresh corpses of criminals and beggars were hastily embalmed and sold as real mummies.)

MUMMY FACTS

• Scientists in South America have discovered mummies from the ancient civilization of Chinchorros that are more than 7,800 years old—nearly twice as old as the oldest Egyptian mummy. And, just as in Egypt, the mummies are plentiful there. "Every time we dug in the garden or dug to add a section to our house, we found bodies," one elderly South American woman told *Discover* magazine. "But I got used to it. We'd throw their bones out on a hill, and the dogs would take them away."

Among many other things, Thomas Jefferson is the inventor of the calendar clock.

- The average Egyptian mummy contains more than 20 layers of cloth that, laid end-to-end, would be more than four football fields long.
- In 1977, an Egyptian scientist discovered that the mummy of Pharaoh Ramses II, more than 3,000 years old, was infested with beetles. So they sent it to France for treatment, complete with an Egyptian passport describing his occupation as "King, deceased."
- What's the quickest way to tell if an Egyptian mummy still has its brains? Shake the skull—if it rattles, the brain is still in there.
- The Egyptians were also fond of mummifying animals. To date, scientists have discovered the preserved remains of bulls, cats, baboons, birds, crocodiles, fish, scorpions, insects...even wild dogs. One tomb contained the remains of more than one *million* mummified birds.
- Some mummies have been discovered in coffins containing chicken bones. Some scientists believe the bones have special religious meaning, but (no kidding) other experts theorize that the bones are actually leftover garbage from the embalmer's lunch.

* * * *

CELEBRITY MUMMY

Jeremy Bentham and his "Auto Icon." Bentham was a famous 19th-century English philosopher. When he died in 1832, he left instructions with a surgeon friend that his body be beheaded, mummified, dressed in his everyday clothes, and propped up in a chair, and that a wax head be placed on his neck to give the corpse a more realistic appearance. He further instructed that his real head also be mummified and placed at his feet, and that the whole arrangement be put on public display. The corpse and its head(s) can still be seen at University College in London, where they sit in a glass case specially built for that purpose.

A column of air one inch square and 600 miles high weighs about 15 lbs.

GROUNDS FOR DIVORCE

Think you're in a bad relationship? Take a look at these folks.

In Loving, New Mexico, a woman divorced her husband because he made her salute him and address him as "Major" whenever he walked by.

One Tarittville, Connecticut, man filed for divorce after his wife left him a note on the refrigerator. It read, "I won't be home when you return from work. Have gone to the bridge club. There'll be a recipe for your dinner at 7 o'clock on Channel 2."

In Lynch Heights, Delaware, a woman filed for divorce because her husband "regularly put itching powder in her underwear when she wasn't looking."

In Honolulu, Hawaii, a man filed for divorce from his wife, because she "served pea soup for breakfast and dinner…and packed his lunch with pea sandwiches."

In Hazard, Kentucky, a man divorced his wife because she "beat him whenever he removed onions from his hamburger without first asking for permission."

In Frackville, Pennsylvania, a woman filed for divorce because her husband insisted on "shooting tin cans off of her head with a slingshot."

One Winthrop, Maine, man divorced his wife because she "wore earplugs whenever his mother came to visit."

A Smelterville, Idaho, man won divorce from his wife on similar grounds. "His wife dressed up as a ghost and tried to scare his elderly mother out of the house."

In Canon City, Colorado, a woman divorced her husband because he made her "duck under the dashboard whenever they drove past his girlfriend's house."

No escape: In Bennettsville, South Carolina, a deaf man filed for divorce from his wife because "she was always nagging him in sign language."

The Last Straw: In Hardwick, Georgia, a woman actually divorced her husband because he "stayed home too much and was much too affectionate."

Ayatollah Ruhollah Khomeini had a weakness for cologne.

WESTERN NICKNAMES

Wild Bill...Black Bart...Billy the Kid...Butch and Sundance. Western heroes had colorful nicknames—but they weren't all as complimentary as they sound. Here's some info on a few of the names.

James Butler "Wild Bill" Hickok. Had a long nose and a protruding lip, and was originally nicknamed "Duck Bill."

William "Bat" Masterson. The famous sheriff of Ford County, Kansas, hit more lawbreakers over the head with his cane than he shot with his gun, and thus earned the nickname "Bat."

Robert LeRoy "Butch Cassidy" Parker. As a teenager, Parker idolized a criminal named Mike Cassidy, and eventually began using his friend's last name as an alias. He picked up the name "Butch" while working in a Rock Springs, Wyoming, butcher shop.

Harry "The Sundance Kid" Longabaugh. As a teenager during the 1880s, Longabaugh spent $1\frac{1}{2}$ years in the Sundance Jail in Wyoming, serving out a sentence for horse stealing.

William "Billy the Kid" Bonney. Looked like a kid.

Henry "Billy the Kid" McCarty. Looked like a goat.

John "Doc" Holliday. A professional dentist by trade, he became a gunslinger and professional gambler after a bout with tuberculosis forced him to move West in search of a drier climate. Even at the height of his criminal career, he practiced dentistry part-time. Holliday's girlfriend was a prostitute named "Big Nose" Kate Elder.

Charles E. "Black Bart" Boles. Came up with the name himself after he became a stagecoach robber by accident. Originally a schoolteacher in northern California's gold country, Boles had a friend who was a Wells Fargo stagecoach driver and decided to play a trick on him. One day in 1875, he covered his face with a scarf, found a stick about the size of a pistol, and jumped out in front of the coach hoping to scare his friend. To his surprise, the driver threw down the strongbox and rode off before Boles could tell him it was only a joke. Opening the strongbox, Boles discovered a fortune in gold coins and bullion. Realizing there was more money in stickups than there was in education, Boles quit his teaching job and began holding up stagecoaches full time. He robbed 28 stagecoaches between 1875 and 1883.

After each robbery, he penned a short poem and left it behind in the empty strongbox where he knew investigators would find it. He always signed it "Black Fart, Po-8." One read: "Blame me not for what I've done, I don't deserve your curses/and if for some cause I must be hung/Let it be for my verses." Boles was eventually caught and sentenced to four years in San Quentin prison, but returned to stagecoach robbing within a few weeks of his release. This time Wells Fargo detectives cut a deal with Boles behind the scene: According to legend, they offered Boles a lifelong pension of $200 a month in exchange for his agreement to give up crime. Whether or not the story is true, the robberies stopped immediately.

...and now, folks, we'd like you to meet the dumbest train robber in the West.

Al Jennings, a successful Oklahoma lawyer in the early 1890s, and his brother Frank, also a lawyer, gave up their chosen profession and began second career: sticking up trains—or at least trying to.

In 1897 they tried to rob a mail car on a Santa Fe train, but the conductor chased them away. Two weeks later the brothers tried to stop another train by blocking the track with railroad ties, but the train steamed right through the barrier. In another robbery attempt, they tried to dynamite open two safes, but succeeded only in blowing up the boxcar the safes were on.

The law eventually caught up with them. Frank got five years in prison and Al was sentenced to life in prison, but President Theodore Roosevelt granted him a "full citizenship" pardon in 1907.

Jennings returned to his law practice and eventually ran for county attorney under the slogan, "When I was a train robber I was a good train robber, and if you choose me, I will be a good prosecuting attorney." He lost. In 1914 he ran for governor of Oklahoma (this time his slogan was "It takes the same sort of nerve to be an honest governor as to rob a train or bank") and lost that too.

MONEY FACTS

A few odds and ends about almost everyone's favorite subject.

THE FDR DIME

Here's how FDR wound up on our 10¢ coin:

• Franklin D. Roosevelt, who was crippled by polio in 1921, escaped from his disability by swimming whenever he could. One of his favorite swimming holes was Warm Springs, Georgia, a natural spring. In 1926 the future president donated enough money to start a polio foundation at the site, so that other polio sufferers could enjoy the waters too.

• Despite the large donation, the foundation was always running out of money.

• Singer Eddie Cantor (a popular radio personality) knew about Roosevelt's concern for the foundation, and in 1937 he proposed to the president that he ask every American to send a dime to the White House to be used for polio research. Cantor suggested a name for the promotion: The March of Dimes.

• Roosevelt took his suggestion and made the appeal. The public response was enormous: on some days the White House was flooded with as many 150,000 letters containing dimes.

• The president became so closely associated with the March of Dimes that after his death in 1945, Congress voted to create the Roosevelt dime in his honor. The first ones were released to the public on January 30, 1946, Roosevelt's birthday—and the traditional start of the March of Dimes annual fund-raising campaign.

• The vaccine for polio was announced on April 12, 1955, on the 10-year anniversary of Roosevelt's death.

CATTLE CALL

• In about 2000 B.C., man began trading bronze ingots shaped like cows (which had about the same value as a real cow). The value of these "coins" was measured by weighing them—which meant that any time a transaction was made, someone had to get out a scale to measure the value of the money.

• Around 800 B.C., the Lydians of Anatolia—who traded bean-shaped ingots made of a gold-silver alloy called *electrum*—began

---

A productive life: A queen ant can lay 30,000 eggs a month for up to 10 years.

stamping the ingot's value onto its face. This eliminated the need for a scale and made transactions much easier.

• But switching to countable coins from weighed ones increased the chances of fraud—precious metals could be chipped or shaved off the edges of the coins. One of the techniques designed to prevent this is still evident on modern U.S. coins, even though they no longer contain precious metals. What is it? Feel the edges of a dime or a quarter. Those grooves were originally a way to tell if any metal had been shaved off.

ARE YOUR BILLS REAL?

Here are some anticounterfeit features of U.S. paper currency you probably didn't know about:

• The currency paper is fluorescent under ultraviolet light.

• The ink is slightly magnetic—not enough for household magnets to detect, but enough for special machines to notice.

• The paper has thousands of tiny microscopic holes "drilled" into it. Reason: when the money is examined under a microscope, tiny points of light shine through.

COIN FACTS

• The Director of the Mint gets to decide who appears on our coins, but the decisions have to be approved by the Treasury Secretary—and changes on any coin can't be made more than once every 25 years.

• Prior to the assassination of President Lincoln, it was a long-standing tradition *not* to have portraits on U.S. coins. Symbols of liberty were used instead. The only reason Lincoln's face got the nod: he was considered a human embodiment of liberty.

• If you design a portrait that gets used on a coin, you get to have your initials stamped in the coin alongside it. That's normally an innocuous addition to the coin, but there have been exceptions: When the Roosevelt dime was released in 1946, some concerned anticommunists thought the initials "JS" (for designer John Sinnock) stood for Joseph Stalin. And when the John F. Kennedy memorial half-dollar was issued in 1964, some conspiracy theorists thought the letters "GR" (for Gilroy Roberts) were a tiny rendition of the communist hammer and sickle.

CAFFEINE FACTS

What's America's favorite drug? You guessed it—caffeine. We use more caffeine than all other drugs—legal or illegal—combined. Want to know what the stuff is doing to you? Here's a quick overview.

BACKGROUND
If you start the day with a strong cup of coffee or tea, you're not alone. Americans ingest the caffeine equivalent of 530 million cups of coffee *every day.* Caffeine is the world's most popular mood-altering drug. It's also one of the oldest: according to archaeologists, man has been brewing beverages from caffeine-based plants since the Stone Age.

HOW IT PICKS YOU UP
Caffeine doesn't keep you awake by supplying extra energy; rather, it fools your body into thinking it isn't tired.
• When your brain is tired and wants to slow down, it releases a chemical called *adenosine.*
• Adenosine travels to special cells called *receptors,* where it goes to work counteracting the chemicals that stimulate your brain.
• Caffeine mimics adenosine; so it can "plug up" your receptors and prevent adenosine from getting through. Result: Your brain never gets the signal to slow down, and keeps building up stimulants.

JAVA JUNKIES
• After a while, your brain figures out what's going on, and increases the number of receptor cells so it has enough for both caffeine *and* adenosine.
• When that happens, caffeine can't keep you awake anymore... unless you *increase* the amount you drink so it can "plug up" the new receptor cells as well.
• This whole process only takes about a week. In that time, you essentially become a caffeine addict. Your brain is literally restructuring itself to run on caffeine; take the caffeine away and your brain has too many receptor cells to operate properly.

Experts say: Humans and elephants are the only animals that can stand on their heads.

• If you quit ingesting caffeine "cold turkey," your brain begins to reduce the number of receptors right away. But the process takes about two weeks, and during that time your body sends out mild "distress signals" in the form of headaches, lethargy, fatigue, muscle pain, nausea, and sometimes even stiffness and flu-like symptoms. As a result, most doctors recommend cutting out caffeine gradually.

CAFFEINE'S EFFECTS
• **Good:** Caffeine has been scientifically proven to temporarily increase alertness, comprehension, memory, reflexes, and even the rate of learning. It also helps increase clarity of thought.
• **Bad:** Too much caffeine can cause hand tremors, loss of coordination or appetite, insomnia, and in extreme cases, trembling, nausea, heart palpitations, and diarrhea.
• Widely varying the amount of caffeine you ingest can put a strain on your liver, pancreas, heart, and nervous system. And if you're prone to ulcers, caffeine can make your situation worse.
• If you manage to consume the equivalent of 70-100 cups of coffee in one sitting, you'll experience convulsions, and may even die.

CAFFEINE FACTS
• The average American drinks 210 milligrams of caffeine a day. That's equal to 2–3 cups of coffee, depending on how strong it is.
• How you make your coffee has a lot to do with how much caffeine you get. Instant coffee contains 65 milligrams of caffeine per serving; coffee brewed in a percolator has 80 milligrams; and coffee made using the "drip method" has 155 milligrams.
• Top four sources of caffeine in the American diet: coffee, soft drinks, tea, and chocolate, in that order. The average American gets 75% of their caffeine from coffee. Other sources include over-the-counter pain killers, appetite suppressants, cold remedies, and some prescription drugs.
• What happens to the caffeine that's removed from decaf coffee? Most of it is sold to soda companies and put into soft drinks. (Cola contains some caffeine naturally, but they like to add even more.)
• Do you drink more caffeine than your kids do? If you correct for body weight, probably not. Pound for pound, kids often get as much caffeine from chocolate and soft drinks as their parents get from coffee, tea, and other sources.

THE HISTORY OF ASPIRIN

Today we take aspirin so much for granted that it's hard to believe that when it was first discovered, it was considered one of the most miraculous drugs ever invented. It turns out that the history of aspirin also makes a good story.

PAIN KILLER

In the late 1890s, Felix Hoffman, a chemist with Germany's Friedrich Bayer (pronounced "By-er") & Company, started looking for a new treatment to help relieve his father's painful rheumatism.

Drugs to treat the pain and inflammation of rheumatism had been around for 2,000 years. In 200 B.C., Hippocrates, the father of medicine, observed that chewing on the bark of the white willow tree soothed aches and pains. In 1823, chemists had finally succeeded in isolating the bark's active ingredient. It was salicylic acid.

TOUGH STUFF

The problem was, salicylic acid wasn't safe. In its pure form, it was so powerful that it did damage at the same time it was doing good. Unless you mixed it with water, it would burn your mouth and throat. And even *with* water, it was so hard on the stomach lining that people who took it became violently ill, complaining that their stomachs felt like they were "crawling with ants."

Salicylic acid had given Hoffman's father multiple ulcers. He had literally burned holes in his stomach trying to relieve his rheumatism pain, and was desperate for something milder. So Hoffman read through all the scientific literature he could find. He discovered that every scientist who had tried to neutralize the acidic properties of salicylic acid had failed...except one. In 1853, a French chemist named Charles Frederic Gerhart had improved the acid by adding sodium and acetyl chloride—creating a new compound called acetylsalicylic acid. However, the substance was so unstable and difficult to make that Gerhart had abandoned it.

No Pain, No Gain

Hoffman decided to make his own batch of Gerhart's acetylsalicylic acid. Working on it in his spare time, he managed to produce a purer, more stable form than anyone had ever been able to make. He tested the powder on himself successfully. Then he gave some to his father. It eased the elder Hoffman's pain, with virtually no side effects.

The Bayer Facts

Hoffman reported his findings to his superiors at Bayer. His immediate supervisor was Heinrich Dreser, the inventor of heroin. (At the time, it was thought to be a non-addictive substitute for morphine. Heroin was a brand name, selected to describe the drug's *heroic* painkilling properties.) Dreser studied Hoffman's acid, found that it worked, and in 1899 Bayer began selling their patented acetylsalicylic acid powder to physicians under the brand name *aspirin*. The name was derived from the Latin term for the "queen of the meadow" plant, *Spiraea ulmaria*, which was an important source of salicylic acid. A year later, they introduced aspirin pills.

IN THE BEGINNING

Within ten years of its introduction, aspirin became the most commonly prescribed patent medicine in the world for two reasons: (1) it actually worked, and (2) unlike heroin, morphine, and other powerful drugs of the time, it had few side effects. There was nothing on the market like it, and when it proved effective at reducing fever during the influenza epidemics at the start of the twentieth century, its reputation as a miracle drug spread around the world.

"This was a period of time when a person only had a life expectancy of 44 years because there were no medications available," says Bayer spokesman Dr. Steven Weisman. "Aspirin very quickly became the most important drug available." It seemed to be able to solve any problem, large or small—gargling aspirin dissolved in water eased sore throats, and rubbing aspirin against a baby's gums even helped sooth teething pain.

UPS AND DOWNS

Aspirin was initially a prescription-only medication, but it became available over the counter in 1915. Sales exploded, and demand for the new drug grew at a faster rate than ever. Since Bayer owned the patent on aspirin—and there were no other drugs like it—the company didn't have to worry about competition; it had the worldwide market to itself.

But the forces of history would soon get in the way.

HEADACHE MATERIAL

In 1916, Bayer used its aspirin profits to build a massive new factory in upstate New York. They immediately started manufacturing the drug for the American market and sold $6 million worth in the first year.

Then they ran into problems. World War I made Germany America's enemy, and in 1918 the U.S. Government seized Bayer's American assets under the Trading With the Enemy Act. They auctioned the factory off to the Sterling Products Company of West Virginia. (The two Bayers would not reunite again until 1995, when the German Bayer bought Sterling's over-the-counter drug business for $1 billion.) Sterling continued marketing aspirin under the Bayer brand name, which by now had been Americanized to "Bay-er."

The original American patent for aspirin expired in 1917, and the "Aspirin" trademark was lost in 1921. Anyone who wanted to make and sell aspirin was now legally free to do so. By the 1930s there were more than a thousand brands of pure aspirin on the market; there were also hundreds of products (Anacin, for example) that combined aspirin with caffeine or other drugs. A bottle of aspirin in the medicine cabinet was as common in American households as salt and pepper were on the kitchen table.

Ready for more? "Aspirin: the Miracle Drug" is on page 58.

Historical note: In 1763, an English clergyman named Edward Stone administered tea, water, and beer laced with powdered willow bark to more than fifty people suffering from fever. They all got better, proving that willow bark reduced fever, too.

The odors that most commonly turn women off are barbecued meat, cherries, and men's cologne.

BRAND NAMES

We all know these names—many are a part of our everyday lives. But where did they come from?

SEALY MATTRESS. In 1881, an inventor from Sealy, Texas, developed a cotton-filled mattress. Word spread around the Southwest, and people began asking for the "mattress from Sealy." Eventually it became known simply as the "Sealy mattress."

SAMSONITE LUGGAGE. Named after Samson, the biblical strong man, to symbolize "strength and durability."

DORITOS. Rough translation from Spanish: "little bit of gold."

SANYO. Means "three oceans" in Japanese. Toshio Iue, who founded the company in 1947, planned to sell worldwide—across the Atlantic, Pacific, and Indian Oceans.

HUSH PUPPIES. At a dinner in 1957, Jim Muir, sales manager for Wolverine World Wide, Inc., was served tiny fried balls of corn dough known in the South as "hush puppies." When he wondered about the name, his host explained that local farmers used the food to quiet barking dogs. Muir decided it was a perfect name for a new pigskin shoe his company was developing. The reason: the shoe "could soothe a customer's aching feet, a.k.a. their 'barking dogs.'"

AMANA. In 1854, a German religious sect moved to Iowa and founded the Amana Colonies. Nearly a century later (1932) George Foerstner, a member of the group, started a business making freezers. It was run by the Amana community under their own brand name until 1943, when they sold it back to Foerstner. He kept the name.

MINOLTA. A loose acronym for **M**achinery and **IN**struments **O**ptica**L** by Kazuo **TA**shima (founder of the Japanese-German Camera Company). The first Minolta-brand camera was introduced in 1932.

THE JIG IS UP

Everything has a history—even jigsaw puzzles. They started as a toy for rich kids...became a hobby for wealthy adults...and then, when mass production made it possible, became a pastime for the rest of us.

THE FIRST JIGSAW PUZZLE

Jigsaw puzzles were one of Western Europe's first educational toys. In 1762, a London mapmaker/printer named John Spilsbury glued a few of his maps onto thin wood panels. Then, using a small hand-saw, he cut them up along the borders of each country. He called them "dissected maps," and sold them to well-to-do parents "for the edification of the young." It was the beginning of an industry.

Spilsbury's timing was excellent—the first children's books had been published only a year earlier, and there was a blossoming interest in new ways to educate the young. By 1800 twenty different London publishers were cranking puzzles out. Most featured historical subjects and moral lessons—and Bible stories. Religious puzzles were an especially popular diversion on Sundays, when ordinary "secular" play was not permitted.

REAL JIGSAW PUZZLES

Until the late 19th century, jigsaw puzzles were made one at a time, gluing expensive prints to fine mahogany or cedar. Each piece was cut out with a hand saw, and each puzzle had no more than 50 pieces. Only the border pieces interlocked; anything more complicated would have cost too much money—and there was a limit to what even wealthy parents were willing to pay. Early jigsaw puzzles cost the equivalent of a week's wages for a common laborer.

Then, in 1876, the power scroll saw, also known as the *jigsaw*, was exhibited at the Philadelphia Centennial Exposition. It was inexpensive (some foot-powered treadle saws sold for as little as $3), and was capable of making incredibly intricate cuts. It immediately revolutionized furniture design. By the 1890s it had an impact on puzzles, too: craftsmen began making completely interlocking puzzles with smaller pieces...which could challenge adults as well as children.

PUZZLE-MANIA

The new puzzles were a hit in high-society circles. Their popularity grew until, in 1908, a jigsaw puzzle craze swept America. No
one was left out; if you couldn't afford to buy puzzles, there were
puzzle lending libraries, and even puzzle *rental* companies. Sales
were so strong that Parker Brothers gave up manufacturing games
for a year to focus exclusively on puzzles. (It was during the 1908
craze that the company pioneered the idea of cutting the pieces
into shapes that people could recognize—stars, ducks, dogs, flowers, snowflakes, etc.).

THE GOLDEN AGE OF PUZZLES

When the craze died down, jigsaw puzzles had become a part of
American life. By the 1920s, they were so cheap that just about
anyone could afford them...manufacturers were using softer
woods, which were easier to saw, and fancy engraving had been
replaced by black and white lithographs that kids could paint with
stencils and watercolors. By 1930, wood and jigsaws had given way
to cardboard and die-cutting, so it was possible to buy a beautiful
puzzle for as little as 10¢.

As America got deeper into the Great Depression, these inexpensive puzzles became increasingly attractive family entertainment. The result: people went on another puzzle-buying binge. For
about six months in the early 1930s, the U.S. could not get
enough puzzles. At the peak of the fad, Americans were purchasing 6 million puzzles *a week*. Things got so frantic that newsstands
began offering a service called "puzzle-a-week," with new puzzles
hitting the shelves every Wednesday. In less than a year, manufacturers sold more than $100 million worth of jigsaw puzzles (in
1930s money!).

STAND-UP GUY

Puzzles remained more or less unchanged after the 1930s. The artwork improved and special "luxury" puzzle makers sprang up to
handcraft custom puzzles for movie stars and captains of industry,
but they were really just more of the same thing. By the 1980s,
puzzles had become a stale staple of the toy industry.

Then in 1989, a Canadian broadcasting executive named Paul
Gallant decided to start a toy company. But he wasn't sure what

kind of toys he wanted to make. "I started thinking about puzzles, and how they hadn't changed much since the 1700s," he told the *New York Times* in 1997, "and wondered why no one had ever made a three-dimensional puzzle." He experimented with ordinary cardboard puzzle pieces, but they fell over when he tried to stand them up. So he made some out of the same kind of polyethylene foam that is used to insulate airliner cockpits. The pieces were sturdy enough to build miniature walls.

Gallant made a 3-D puzzle resembling a Victorian mansion and took it to the F.A.O. Schwartz toy store in Manhattan, where he showed it to the store's toy and game buyer. "I took the puzzle and I threw it in the air," Gallant says. It didn't break. "I said, 'No glue, no pins, no nothing, it just stays like this interlocking.' And I pushed the wall off and I separated the pieces and showed him this was really a puzzle. And he said, 'Wow, where did you get that?'" F.A.O. Schwartz bought 74 puzzles that afternoon in 1991; Gallant's company now sells more than $100 million worth of 3-D puzzles—shaped like skyscrapers, castles, the Eiffel Tower, the Titanic, and even *Star Wars* spaceships—every year, making it another of the biggest puzzle fads in history.

PUZZLING INNOVATIONS
Has it been a while since you've bought a puzzle? Here are some new products you might find on your next trip to the toy store:

• **Mono-colored Puzzles.** No pretty pictures, just puzzle pieces, hundreds of them, all painted the same color so that there are no clues as to where they belong in the puzzle.

• **Multiple-border Puzzles.** Pieces with straight edges that appear to be border pieces, but actually are inner pieces.

• **Impossibles.** 750-piece borderless puzzles with too many pieces. No taking the easy way out by connecting outer edges first, because edge pieces look like inner pieces. To make it even more puzzling: five extra pieces that don't fit anywhere in the puzzle.

• **Triazzles.** All of the pieces are triangle shaped with similar designs, but with only one correct solution.

• **The World's Most Difficult Jigsaw Puzzles.** Double-sided puzzles with 529 pieces. The same artwork is on both sides, rotated 90 degrees with respect to each other.

First female boxing match in the U.S.: March 16, 1876. The winner got a silver butter dish.

FILL IN THE LIMERICKS

You probably know a few limericks of your own (naughty, naughty) and you may recognize the following as some of Uncle John's favorites. But just how well do you remember them? See if you can fill in the blanks (one for each missing letter) to complete each little ditty.

1. A cat in despondency sighed,
   And resolved to commit __ __ __ __ __ __ __;
   She passed under the wheels
   Of eight __ __ __ __ __ __ __ __ __ __ __
   And after the ninth one she __ __ __ __ __.

2. There was a young fellow of Leeds,
   Who swallowed six packets of __ __ __ __ __ __.
   In a month, silly ass,
   He was covered with __ __ __ __ __ __.
   And he couldn't sit down for the __ __ __ __ __ __.

3. There was a young lady of Ryde,
   Who ate some green apples and __ __ __ __ __;
   The apples __ __ __ __ __ __ __ __ __
   Inside the lamented,
   And made cider inside her __ __ __ __ __ __.

4. There was a young athlete named Tribbling,
   Whose hobby was basketball
   __ __ __ __ __ __ __ __ __ __;
   But he dribbled one day
   On a busy __ __ __ __ __ __ __ __.
   Now his sister is missing a __ __ __ __ __ __ __ __.

5. There was a hillbilly named Shaw
   Who envied his maw and his __ __ __.
   To share in their life
   He adopted his __ __ __ __ __
   And became his own
   __ __ __ __ __ __-__ __-__ __ __.

6. A rocket explorer named Wright
   Once traveled much faster than __ __ __ __.
   He set out one day
   In a relative __ __ __,
   And returned on the previous __ __ __ __.

7. There was a young lady from Lynn
   Who was sunk in original __ __ __.
   When they said, "Do be good,"
   She replied, "If I __ __ __ __ __...."
   But I'd do wrong right over __ __ __ __"

8. There was an old fellow named Cager
   Who, as the result of a __ __ __ __ __,
   Offered to fart
   The whole oboe __ __ __ __
   Of Mozart's "Quartet in F __ __ __ __ __."

9. An epicure, dining in Crewe,
   Once found a large mouse in his __ __ __ __.
   Said the waiter: "Don't shout,
   Or wave it __ __ __ __ __,
   Or the rest will be wanting one, __ __ __."

10. There was a young belle of old __ __ __ __ __ __ __
    Whose garments were always in patchez.
    When comment arose
    On the state of her __ __ __ __ __ __ __ __,
    She drawled, "When Ah itchez,
    Ah __ __ __ __ __ __ __ __ __ __!"

ANSWER, PAGE 368

FOUNDING FATHERS

You already know their names. Here's who they belonged to.

Jerome Smuckers. Started out selling apple butter in Orrville, Ohio, in 1897; in 1923 he branched out to jams and jellies.

Abraham and Mahala Stouffer. Cleveland, Ohio, restaurateurs. Their Stouffer's restaurants were so popular that they began freezing entrees for customers to eat at home. By 1957, they were selling frozen foods in supermarkets; and by the late 1960s they were supplying frozen dinners for the Apollo space program.

John Deere. In 1837, Deere invented the first practical steel plow, which unlike iron plows, cut through black, sticky prairie soil without bogging down in the thick muck. Today John Deere is the largest agricultural machinery manufacturer in the world.

Jack Mack. Mack and his brother Augustus were wagon builders in Brooklyn at the turn of the century. In 1900, they built the first bus in the U.S. It was used to carry tourists around Brooklyn's Prospect Park. The bus was so reliable—it logged more than 1 million miles over 25 years—that Jack and Augustus were swamped with orders. They and three other brothers formed the Mack Brothers Company a short time later. Jack designed the company's first truck in 1905.

The Smith Brothers. The first commercial typewriters were available in 1873, but it wasn't until 1895 that someone invented a typewriter that allowed you to see the words as you were typing. When Union Typewriter Co. balked at making the new machine in 1903, Lyman, Wilbert, Monroe, and Hurlbut Smith left the company and founded the L.C. Smith Brothers Typewriting Co. In 1925 they merged with the Corona Typewriting to become Smith-Corona.

Herman Fisher and Irving Price. Together with Helen Schelle, they founded the Fisher-Price toy company in 1930 to make toys out of Ponderosa Pine. Their first big hit: Snoopy Sniffer, a "loose-jointed, floppy-eared pull toy who woofed when you pulled his wagging spring tail," in 1938. The company made its first plastic toys in 1949.

A chameleon's tongue is twice the length of its body.

YOU'RE MY INSPIRATION

It's always fascinating to find out who, or what, inspired familiar characters. Here are some we've come across.

DON CORLEONE, the Mafia leader in *The Godfather*, Mario Puzo's bestselling novel.
Inspired by: Puzo's mother. "Like the don," he explains, "she could be extremely warm and extremely ruthless....[For example], my father was committed to an insane asylum. When he could have returned home, my mother made the decision not to let him out—he would have been a burden on the family. That's a Mafia decision."

MOBY DICK, the Great White Whale, title character of Herman Melville's classic novel.
Inspired by: Mocha Dick, a real white sperm whale that was the terror of the seas in the first half of the 19th century. (He was named for Mocha Island, near Chile.) Mocha Dick was said to have wrecked or destroyed nearly thirty whaling boats and killed thirty men, beginning in 1819. Historians say Melville first read of him in an 1839 issue of *Knickerbocker* magazine.

WINNIE THE POOH, Christopher Robin's stuffed bear.
Inspired by: A Canadian black bear. In 1914, Harry Colebourne, a Canadian soldier, was traveling east on a troop train headed for England and World War I. When the train stopped in White River, Ontario, Harry bought a black bear cub from a hunter. He called it Winnie, after his hometown of Winnipeg, and took it to England as a mascot.

Colebourne was eventually stationed in France, and while he was gone, he loaned Winnie to the London Zoo. By the time he returned, the bear had become so popular that he decided to leave it there.

A few years later, a four-year-old named Christopher Milne brought his favorite stuffed bear, Edward, to the zoo. Christopher

In the time it takes to hatch one egg, the male Emperor penguin loses 1/3 of its body weight.

saw Winnie and became so excited that he decided to rename Edward. "Pooh" was his nickname for a swan he loved—he appropriated it for the bear, and Edward became Winnie the Pooh.

MARY, the classic nursery rhyme character ("Mary had a little lamb, its fleece was white as snow…").
Inspired by: An eleven-year-old girl in Boston, Massachusetts. In 1817, a young man named John Roulstone saw young Mary Sawyer on her way to school…followed by a pet lamb. He thought it was so amusing, he jotted down a little poem about it.

Thirteen years later, Mrs. Sarah Josepha Hale added 12 more lines to the poem and published the whole thing under her own byline. Today there's some controversy about the authorship of the poem…but not the inspiration.

OLIVER BARRETT IV, the romantic hero in *Love Story*, a #1 bestselling book by Erich Segal and a hit movie in the 1970s.
Inspired by: Two students Segal knew at Harvard in the 1960s. The side of Barrett that was "the tough, macho guy who's a poet at heart" was fashioned after Tommy Lee Jones (now an actor). The side that "had a controlling father and was pressured to follow in the father's footsteps" was inspired by Jones's roommate—Al Gore.

MICKEY MOUSE, the most famous cartoon character in history.
Inspired by: A real mouse…and maybe actor Mickey Rooney. The mouse, whom Disney called Mortimer, was a pet that the cartoonist kept trapped in a wastebasket in his first art studio in Kansas City. Rooney, a child movie star, says in his autobiography that *he* inspired the mouse's new name, in the early 1920s:

> One day I passed a half-open door in a dirty old studio and peeked in. A slightly built man with a thin mustache…looked up and smiled. "What's your name, son?"
> "Mickey,…What are you drawing?"
> "I'm drawing a mouse, son." Suddenly he stopped drawing, took me by the shoulders, and looked me in the eye. "Did you say your name was Mickey?"
> "Yes sir."
> "You know what I'm going to do?…I'm going to call this mouse Mickey—after you."

Do you talk to your car? According to polls, more women do than men.

COURT TRANSQUIPS

Here's more real-life courtroom dialogue.

Q: "Do you remember what shoes you were wearing?"
A: "You mean the day I fell down?"
Q: "Yes."
A: "The same shoes I'm wearing."
Q: "What do you call those shoes? Are they flats…or how would you describe them?"
A: "I'd describe them as 'these shoes.'"

Q: "Please review this document. Do you know what a fax is?"
A: "Yeah, I do, man. It's when you tell the truth, man, tell it like it is. That is what the facts is."

Q: "What is the relationship?"
A: "She's my aunt."
Q: "Who's brother or sister to whom here?"
A: My mother is his brother—is her—my mother is—what is it? By marriage, I guess you would say. My mother is her brother— is his brother by marriage, so she's just an aunt."

A: "You know, I don't know, but I mean, you know—you don't know but you know. You know what I'm saying?"
Q: "Do I? No. Do I know? No."

Q: "You assumed narcotics in reaching your opinions."
A: "Yes."
Q: "You didn't assume a Frito or a Chee-to or a banana. You assumed narcotics."
A: "It was a narcotics raid. It wasn't a Frito raid, counselor."

Q: "So you remember who the doctor was who performed that?"
A: "Yes. Very easy name to remember, Mee."
Q: "Martin?"(The witness's name.)
A: "No, Mee."
Q: "You?"
A: "That was his name."
Q: "Me?"
A: "Mee."
Q: "M-e?"
A: "M-e-e. That was his name, Dr. Mee"

Q: "Mr. Jones, do you believe in alien forces?"
A: "You mean other than my wife?"

Q: "Were you acquainted with the decedent?"
A: "Yes, sir."
Q: "Before or after he died?"

Q: "Did he ever kill you before?"
A: "Pardon me?"

ASPIRIN: THE MIRACLE DRUG

Here's more on the history of aspirin.
The first part of the story is on page 45.

MID-LIFE CRISIS

In 1950, aspirin earned a place in the *Guinness Book of World Records* as the world's best-selling painkiller. But if the medical community had paid attention to Dr. Lawrence Craven, an ear-nose-throat specialist, in 1948, aspirin would have been recognized as much more than that.

Dr. Craven had noticed that when he performed tonsillectomies, patients who took aspirin bled more than the ones who didn't. He suspected the aspirin was inhibiting the ability of blood to clot, something that might be useful in preventing strokes and heart attacks—both of which can be caused by excessive clotting of the blood.

Craven decided to test his theory. He put 400 of his male patients on aspirin, then watched them over several years to see how many had heart attacks. Not one did, so Craven expanded his research. He began following the histories of 8,000 regular aspirin-takers, to see if any of *them* had a heart attack. None of them did, either.

Dr. Craven published his findings in a medical journal. But nobody listened. "The medical community shunned his findings," says Dr. Steven Weisman. "He wasn't a cardiologist, he wasn't in the academic community and he was publishing in a lesser-known journal."

ASPIRIN SCIENCE

The biggest problem was that as late as 1970 nobody had any idea how aspirin worked. That year John Vane, a researcher with London's Royal College of Surgeons, discovered what Dr. Craven had known intuitively—that aspirin blocks an enzyme that causes blood platelets to stick together, which is what happens when blood clots.

By inhibiting clotting, aspirin helps to prevent strokes, heart attacks, and other cardiovascular ailments.

Not long afterward, researchers in Sweden discovered that aspirin also blocks the production of *prostaglandins*, hormone-like chemicals that affect digestion, reproduction, circulation, and the immune system. Excess levels of prostaglandins can cause headaches, fevers, blood clots, and a host of other problems. Scientists quickly began to discover that aspirin's ability to block the prostaglandin production makes it an effective treatment for many of these problems.

WONDER DRUG

For the first time in 70 years, researchers were beginning to understand aspirin's potential beyond reducing pain, fever, and inflammation. Thousands of studies have since been conducted to test aspirin's effectiveness against a number of diseases, and many more are planned.

The results have been astounding. In 1980, the U.S. Food and Drug Administration (FDA) recommended aspirin to reduce the risk of stroke in men experiencing stroke symptoms. In 1985, it recommended aspirin to heart attack patients as a means of reducing the risk of second heart attacks. One 1988 heart attack study was so successful that researchers shut it down five years early so that the test subjects who weren't taking aspirin could begin to take it. In 1996, the FDA recommended administering aspirin *during* heart attacks as a means of lowering the risk of death.

And that's only the beginning. Aspirin is believed to lower the risk of colon cancer by as much as 32%, and scientists are also exploring aspirin's ability to slow the progression of Alzheimers disease, cataracts, diabetes, numerous other forms of cancer, and even HIV, the virus that causes AIDS.

"No little white pill does everything, that's for sure," says the University of Pennsylvania's Dr. Garret Fitzgerald, one of the world's top aspirin experts. "But the strength of the evidence for aspirin working where it has been shown to work is probably greater than the strength of the evidence for any drug for human disease."

Bathroom Reader Warning: Aspirin isn't for everyone. Consult a doctor before taking aspirin regularly. Aspirin is still an acid, and it can irritate the lining of the stomach and cause pain, internal bleeding and ulcers. "'An aspirin a day' does not apply to everyone," says Dr. Paul Pedersen, a doctor of internal medicine. "It's not like apples."

• **Also:** In 1986, scientists established a link between aspirin and Reye's syndrome, a rare but sometimes fatal disease that strikes children suffering from acute viral infections like influenza and chicken pox.

ASPIRIN FACTS
• Americans take an estimated 80 million aspirin a day—about the same amount as the rest of the world combined. 30-50% of them are taken as preventative medicine for cardiac disease.
• How you take aspirin depends on where you live: Americans prefer pills; the English like powders that dissolve in water; Italians like fizzy aspirin drinks, and the French like aspirin suppositories.
• Roughly 6% of Americans cannot take straight aspirin because it irritates their stomachs. That's where coated or "buffered" aspirin comes in—each pill is treated with a special, slow-to-dissolve coating that prevents the aspirin from being absorbed by the body until it has left the stomach and gone into the intestines.
• One of the remaining unsolved aspirin mysteries is why it only works on you when you're sick. "If your body temperature is normal, it won't lower it," says Roger P. Maickel, a professor of pharmacology at Purdue University. "If you don't have inflammation, it doesn't have any antiarthritic effects on your joints. It's beautifully simple to work with, yet the damn thing does everything."

MIGRAINE MATERIAL
What did Felix Hoffman, inventor of aspirin, have to show for his work? Not much—aspirin made the Bayer family fabulously wealthy, and it earned Felix Hoffman's supervisor, Heinrich Dreser, enough money to retire early. Hoffman was not so lucky— he was entitled to royalties on anything he invented that was patented, but since aspirin was never successfully patented in Germany, the really big bucks eluded him.

INTERNATIONAL LAW

Believe it or not, these laws are real.

In England, it's illegal to name your pet "Queen" or "Princess" without the Queen's permission.

If you aren't a member of the royal family in Japan, it's illegal for you to own a maroon car.

In Equatorial Guinea, you can name your daughter anything you want—except Monica.

In India, women—but not men—are allowed to marry goats.

Old English law: if an object is smaller than a husband's little finger, he can beat his wife with it.

In Canada, if a debt is higher than 25¢, it's against the law for you to pay with pennies.

In Vancouver, British Columbia, the speed limit for tricycles is 10 miles per hour.

In Baluchistan, Pakistan, the law allows a man to "acquire" a wife by trading in his sister.

In Athens, Greece, driving on public roads while "unbathed" or poorly dressed can cost you your driver's license.

If a man is wearing a hat in Cheshire, England, the law requires him to raise it when a funeral passes.

You can keep cows in sheds in the Northern Territories of Canada, and you can keep chickens in sheds. But you can't keep cows *and* chickens in the same shed.

Makes sense: in London, England, it's illegal to operate a motor vehicle while sitting in the back seat.

In Australia, the pictures of convicted drunk drivers are published in newspapers with the caption, "He's drunk and in jail."

Cigarettes are legal in Nicaragua; cigarette *lighters* aren't.

Boxing is illegal in China (too brutal); capital punishment isn't.

Largest dinosaur: the Seismosaurus. They grew to 119 feet in length and weighed 90 tons.

NATURE'S REVENGE

What happens when we start messing around with nature, trying to make living conditions better? Sometimes it works...and sometimes nature gets even. Here are a few instances when people intentionally introduced animal or plants into a new environment...and regretted it.

Import: Kudzu, a fast-growing Japanese vine.
Background: Originally brought into the Southern U.S. in 1876 for use as shade. People noticed livestock ate the vine and that kudzu helped restore nitrogen to the soil. It seemed like a perfect plant to cultivate. So in the 1930s, the U.S. government helped farmers plant kudzu all over the South.
Nature's Revenge: By the 1950s, it was out of control, blanketing farmers' fields, buildings, utility poles and—often fatally—trees. Today, utility companies spend millions of dollars annually spraying herbicides on poles and towers to keep them kudzu-free. And instead of helping plant kudzu, the government now gives advice on how to get rid of it.

Import: The mongoose.
Background: The small Asian mammals famous for killing cobras were brought to Hawaii by sugar planters in 1893. Their reason: They thought the mongooses would help control the rat population.
Nature's Revenge: The planters overlooked one little detail: the mongoose is active in the daytime while the rat is nocturnal. "In Hawaii today," says one source, "mongooses are considered pests nearly as bad as rats."

Import: The starling, an English bird.
Background: In 1890, a philanthropist named Eugene Schieffelin decided to bring every type of bird mentioned in Shakespeare's plays to New York City's Central Park. He brought in hundreds of pairs of birds from England. Unfortunately, most (like skylarks and thrushes) didn't make it. Determined to succeed with at least one species, Schieffelin shipped 40 pairs of starlings to Central Park and let them loose just before the mating season on March 6, 1890.

Nature's Revenge: There are now more than 50 million starlings in the U.S. alone—all descendants from Schieffelin's flock—and they have become a major health hazard. They fly in swarms, littering roads and highways with their droppings, which carry disease-bearing bacteria that are often transmitted to animals and people. They've also become pests to farmers, screeching unbearably and destroying wheat and cornfields.

Import: The gypsy moth.
Background: In 1869, Leopold Trouvelot, a French entomologist, imported some gypsy moth caterpillars to Massachusetts. It was part of a get-rich-quick scheme: he figured that since the caterpillars thrive on oak tree leaves, which are plentiful there, he could crossbreed them with silkworm moths, and create a self-sustaining, silk-producing caterpillar. He'd make a fortune!

Unfortunately, the crossbreeding didn't work. Then one day, a strong wind knocked over a cage filled with the gypsy moth caterpillars. They escaped through an open window and survived.
Nature's Revenge: At first, the moths spread slowly. But by 1950, gypsy moths could be found in every New England state and in eastern New York. They've since spread to Virginia, Maryland, and beyond. Populations have become established as far away as Minnesota and California, probably due to eggs unknowingly transported by cars driven from the Northeast to those regions. They're not a major threat, but can cause severe problems: In 1981, for example, they were reported to have stripped leaves from 13 million trees.

Import: Dog fennel.
Background: At the turn of the 19th century, Johnny Appleseed wandered around the Ohio territory, planting apples wherever he went. It's not widely known that he also sowed a plant called *dog fennel*, which was believed to be a fever-reducing medicine.
Nature's Revenge: It's not only *not* medicine, it's bad medicine; farmers are sick of it. "The foul-smelling weed," says the *People's Almanac*, "spread from barnyard to pasture, sometimes growing as high as fifteen feet. Today, exasperated midwestern farmers still cannot rid their fields of the plant they half-humorously call 'Johnnyweed.'"

ODDBALL FOOD NAMES

Can you imagine being offered a nice, big helping of Burgoo? Sounds appetizing, doesn't it?

ANADAMA BREAD
A Gloucester, Massachusetts, fisherman was married to a woman named Anna and every night, she fed him corn-meal and molasses for dinner. He got so sick of it that one evening he stormed into the kitchen, threw some yeast into the mix, and baked a sodden, lumpy loaf...muttering "Anna, damn 'er" the whole time. His Yankee-accented phrase came out as *Anadama*, giving the bread its name.

This story first appeared in print in 1915—and though it sounds like a tall tale, it's cited so often that most food historians believe it.

BURGOO
Politics and Burgoo go hand in hand in Kentucky. This Southern beef and fowl stew was cooked for people at political rallies. There are several versions about how it was created, but this one is the most colorful: During the Civil War, a Yankee soldier managed to kill a number of wild birds which he promptly made into a stew, using a copper kettle normally used for mixing gunpowder. He invited his buddies to join him, and-having eaten nothing but hardtack and bacon for days—they jumped at the offer. The soldier suffered from a speech impediment. When he was asked what the dish was, he tried to say "bird stew," but it came out as "Burgoo."

JANSSON'S TEMPTATION
In 1846, Eric Jansson fled Sweden to escape religious persecution for his radical theology. He and his followers settled in Illinois. Jansson told his followers that eating was a sin that turned their thoughts away from God, and he allowed them only a starvation diet. His downfall came when they found him consuming a rich dish of potatoes, onions, and cream, now known as Jansson's Temptation.

It takes a drop of ocean water more than 1,000 years to circulate around the world.

BAPTIST CAKE

Many churches settle for a symbolic sprinkling of holy water during baptism, but Baptists insist on full immersion. When deep-fried doughnut-like confections were introduced in New England in the 1920s, they were named Baptist Cakes because they were "baptized" in hot oil.

HOPPIN' JOHN

A New Orleans dish of cowpeas and rice, traditionally served on New Year's Day to ensure good luck in the coming year. The name dates back to 1819 and is derived from a New Year's ritual of having the children hop around the table before being served.

LIMPING SUSAN

A variation on Hoppin' John, with red beans substituted for cowpeas.

JOHNNY CAKE

Blame the Yankee accent for Johnny Cakes, too. In Colonial America, travelers would bake a supply of cakes to take on trips, called Journey Cakes. "Journey" comes out as "johnny" when pronounced with a broad, New England accent. In 1940, the Rhode Island Legislature ruled that only cakes made from flint corn could carry the proud title of Johnny Cakes. There is a Johnny Cake Festival in Newport every October…as well as a Society for the Propagation of the Johnny Cake Tradition.

MONKEY GLAND

A cocktail made with "orange juice, grenadine, gin and an anise cordial." According to food historian John Mariani:

> It became popular in the 1920s, when Dr. Serge Voronoff, a Russian emigre to Paris and director of experimental surgery at the Laboratory of Physiology of the College de France, was promoting the benefits of transplanting the sex glands of monkeys into human beings to restore vitality and prolong life….

The cocktail, which facetiously promised similar restorative powers, may have been invented at Harry's New York Bar in Paris, by owner Harry MacElhone

DAMN YOU, STINK MAN!

*Until recently, all movies made in Hong Kong—including "chop sockey"
low-budget martial arts films—legally had to have English subtitles, because
it was a British colony. But chop sockey producers spend as little on
translations as possible—typically it might take only two days and $128
to translate a whole film. In Sex and Zen & a Bullet in the Head,
Stefan Hammond and Michael Wilkins list some of the most
ludicrous chop sockey subtitles. (These are real!)*

"You're a bad guy, where's your library card?"

"How can you use my intestines as a gift?"

"Quiet or I'll blow your throat up."

"Check if there's a hole in my underpants."

"No! I saw a vomiting crab."

"Damn you, stink man!"

"You're stain!"

"Bump him dead."

"Suck the coffin mushroom now."

"A big fool, with a gun, go to war. Surrendered and turned to a cake."

"You bastard, try this melon."

"Noodles? Forget it. Try my fist."

"Brother, my pants are coming out."

"Get out, you smurk!"

"Don't you feel the stink smell?"

"Take my advice or I"ll spank you without pants."

"You cheat ghosts to eat tofu?"

"I'm not Jesus Christ, I'm Bunny."

"You're bad. You make my busts up and down."

"He's Big Head Man, he is lousing around.

"She's terrific. I can't stand her."

"You daring lousy guy."

"Well! Masturbate in Hell!"

"The fart of God."

"What does it mean?"

"With a remarkable sound."

"Okay, I'll Bastare, show your guts."

"Suddenly my worm are all healed off."

"And you thought. I'm gabby bag."

Take your weight and divide by three. That's how much your legs weigh.

FLUBBED HEADLINES

*These are 100% honest-to-goodness headlines.
Can you figure out what they were trying to say?*

Kids Make Nutritious Snacks

ENRAGED COW INJURES FARMER WITH AXE

Red Tape Holds Up New Bridge

BILKE-A-THON NETS $1,000 FOR ILL BOY

PANDA MATING FAILS; VETERINARIAN TAKES OVER

School taxpayers revolting

Eye Drops Off Shelf

HELICOPTER POWERED BY HUMAN FLIES

Circumcisions Cut Back

POPE TO BE ARRAIGNED FOR ALLEGEDLY BUR-GLARIZING CLINIC

City wants Dead to pay for cleanup

MOORPARK RESIDENTS ENJOY A COMMUNAL DUMP

Montana Traded to Kansas City

Area man wins award for nuclear accident

International Scientific Group Elects Bimbo As Its Chairman

Storm delayed by bad weather

LEGISLATORS TAX BRAINS TO CUT DEFICIT

DEAD GUITARIST NOW SLIMMER AND TRIMMER

Study Finds Sex, Pregnancy Link

Include Your Children When Baking Cookies

Trees can break wind

RANGERS TO TEST PEETERS FOR RUST

Cockroach Slain, Husband Badly Hurt

Living Together Linked to Divorce

ECUADOR'S PRESIDENT DECLARES HE'S NOT DEAD

LACK OF BRAINS HIN-DERS RESEARCH

Two Sisters Reunited After 18 Years At Checkout Counter

Man, Shot Twice in Head, Gets Mad

MISSOURI WOMAN BIG WINNER AT HOG SHOW

Teacher Dies; Board Accepts His Resignation

PANTS MAN TO EXPAND AT THE REAR

Siberia means "sleeping land."

COMING UP SHORT

We feel like we're forgetting something in the lists below. It's on the tip of our tongues, darn it! There's one member of each set that we just can't remember! Can you?

The 9 Planets
Venus
Pluto
Saturn
Neptune
Mars
Mercury
Earth
Jupiter

**The 8 Members of
TV's Brady Family**
Mike
Cindy
Jan
Bobby
Greg
Carol
Marcia

The 5 Great Lakes
Erie
Superior
Huron
Michigan

**The 5 Original Members
of the Rolling Stones**
Bill Wyman
Mick Jagger
Brian Jones
Keith Richards

The 4 H's in the 4-H Club
Head
Hands
Health

The 13 Original U.S. Colonies
Delaware
Pennsylvania
New Jersey
Massachusetts
New York
Virginia
Connecticut
New Hampshire
Rhode Island
Maryland
North Carolina
South Carolina

The Life Savers' "5 Flavors"
Lemon
Lime
Orange
Cherry

The 4 Teletubbies
Laa-Laa
Po
Tinky Winky

ANSWER, PAGE 368

HOW A
MICROWAVE WORKS

Here's the story about the science that makes a microwave oven work.

WHAT ARE MICROWAVES?

Here's the first thing you should know about "microwaves": Like visible light, radio waves, and X-rays, they are waves of electromagnetic energy. What makes the four waves different from each other? Each has a different length (*wavelength*) and vibrates at a different speed (*frequency*).

• Microwaves get their name because their wavelength is much shorter than electromagnetic waves that carry TV and radio signals.

• The microwaves in a microwave oven have a wavelength of about four inches, and they vibrate 2.5 billion times per second—about the same natural frequency as water molecules. That's what makes them so effective at heating food.

• A conventional oven heats the air in the oven, which then cooks the food. But microwaves cause water molecules in the food to vibrate at high speeds, creating heat. The heated water molecules are what cook the food.

• Glass, ceramic, and plastic plates contain virtually no water molecules, which is why they don't heat up in the microwave.

MICROWAVE MECHANICS

• When the microwave oven is turned on, electricity passes through the magnetron, the tube which produces microwaves. The microwaves are then channeled down a metal tube (*waveguide*) and through a slow rotating metal fan (*stirrer*), which scatters them into the part of the oven where the food is placed.

• The walls of the oven are made of metal, which reflects microwaves the same way that a mirror reflects visible light. So when the microwaves hit the stirrer and are scattered into the food chamber, they bounce off the metal walls and penetrate the

---

The Netherlands used to be known as the United States.

food from every direction. Some ovens have a rotating turntable that helps food cook more evenly.

• Do microwave ovens cook food from the inside out? Some people think so, but the answer seems to be no. Microwaves cook food from the outside in, like conventional ovens. But the microwave energy only penetrates about an inch into the food. The heat that's created by the water molecules then penetrates deeper into the food, cooking it all the way through. This secondary cooking process is known as "conduction."

• The metal holes in the glass door of the microwave oven are large enough to let out visible light (which has a small wavelength), but too small to allow the microwaves (which have a larger wavelength) to escape. So you can see what's cooking without getting cooked yourself.

YOU CALL THAT COOKING?

According to legend, shortly after Raytheon perfected its first microwave oven in the 1950s, Charles Adams, the chairman of Raytheon, had one installed in his kitchen so he could taste for himself what microwave-cooked food was like. But as Adams's cook quickly discovered, meat didn't brown in the oven, french fries stayed limp and damp, and cakes didn't rise. The cook, condemning the oven as "black magic," quit.

When sales of microwave ovens took off in the late 1980s, millions of cooks discovered the same thing: Microwaves just don't cook some foods as well as regular ovens do. The reason: Because microwaves cook by exciting the water molecules in food, the food inside a microwave oven rarely cooks at temperatures higher than 212°F, the temperature at which water turns to steam.

Conventional ovens, on the other hand, cook at temperatures as high as 550°F. High temperatures are needed to caramelize sugars and break down proteins, carbohydrates, and other substances and combine them into more complex flavors. So microwave ovens can't do any of this, and they can't bake, either.

Some people feel this is the microwave's Achilles heel. "The name 'microwave oven' is a misnomer," says Cindy Ayers, an executive with Campbell's Soup. "It doesn't do what an oven does."

J, the youngest letter in the English alphabet, was not added until the 1600s.

"It's a glorified popcorn popper," says Tom Vierhile, a researcher with *Marketing Intelligence*, a newsletter that tracks microwave sales. "When the microwave first came out, people thought they had stumbled on nirvana. It's not the appliance the food industry thought it would be. It's a major disappointment."

Adds one cooking critic: "Microwave sales are still strong, but time will tell whether they have a future in the American kitchen." In the meantime, Uncle John isn't holding his breath—he's too busy heating up leftovers.

MICROWAVE FACTS

• Have you heard that microwave ovens are dangerous? In 1968 the Walter Reed Hospital tested them to see if the microwaves leaked out. They did—and the government stepped in to set the first federal standards for microwave construction. Today all microwaves sold in the U.S. must be manufactured according to federal safety standards.

• If you microwave your foods in a square container and aren't happy with the results, try cooking them in a round one. "Food cooks better in a round container than in a square one," says Jim Watkins, president of the company that makes Healthy Choice microwave food products. "No one really knows why."

• Irregularly shaped foods, such as a leg of chicken that is thick at one end and thin at the other end, cook unevenly.

• Food that has been cut up will also cook faster than a single, large piece of food, for the same reason: the microwaves penetrate completely through smaller pieces of food, but not through larger pieces.

• Aluminum foil reflects microwave energy the same way mirrors reflect light energy. That's why you can't use foil in a microwave...unless, for example, you're using it to shield some food items on a plate while others are being cooked. But be careful: if too much food is shielded with foil, the microwaves can overload the oven and damage the magnetron.

CLASSIC RUMORS

Some rumors have been around so long that they deserve a special place in the annals of gossip. Have you heard any of these?

ORIGIN: Mid-1940s.
RUMOR: The Harvard School of Medicine will buy your body for $500. All you have to do is let them tattoo the words "Property of Harvard Medical School" on the bottom of your feet. When you die, your body will be shipped C.O.D. to Harvard.
HOW IT SPREAD: By word of mouth, back when $500 was a lot of money.
THE TRUTH: Harvard says it has never paid people for their bodies, and only accepts donations from people who specify in their wills that they want their bodies to go to the school. Even then, surviving relatives have to agree with the bequest. To this day, the school receives several calls a week asking about the program.

ORIGIN: The 1950s, heyday of big hair.
RUMOR: A teenager got a beehive hairdo, and liked it so much that she didn't wash it out—not even after a couple of weeks. She sprayed it every morning with hair spray…and suddenly one morning got a terrible stabbing pain on the top of her head. She went to the doctor, who found a black widow that had stung the woman on her scalp. She died from the sting a few days later.
THE TRUTH: This story changes with fashion trends. In the 1960s, it was a mouse that tunneled into the brain of a "dirty hippie"; in the 1970s, a man died on the floor of a disco when the cucumber he stuffed down the front of his tight pants cut off circulation to his legs. Most versions have two morals: 1) bathe regularly; and 2) avoid loony fashion fads.

ERA: The 1970s, during the energy crisis
RUMOR: The oil companies have a pill that can make a car go 100 miles on one gallon of gas. But they're sitting on it to keep gasoline sales high. (Similar stories abounded about super-carburetors and experimental cars that went 1,000 miles on a gallon of gas.)

Einstein couldn't read until the age of nine.

HOW IT SPREAD: Word of mouth, perhaps as an explanation for the fuel crisis, and/or a manifestation of public fear and suspicion of huge corporations.

THE TRUTH: Oil companies scoff at the idea, and no one has ever produced a shred of evidence. The story can be traced to an old gas station con, when hucksters would pull into a gas station, fill a fake gasoline tank with water, and then convince the gas station owner that the car ran on water and a magic pill. The con man then sold the owner a jar of the pills for all the cash he had.

ORIGIN: Late 1930s.

RUMOR: If the wrapper of your Tootsie Roll Pop has a picture of the Indian aiming his bow and arrow at a star (called "Shooting Star" by the company) on it, you can send it in for a free bag of candies.

HOW IT SPREAD: From one kid to another since the Tootsie Roll Pop was introduced in 1936.

THE TRUTH: The Tootsie Roll Company has never redeemed an Indian wrapper for bags of candy. Even if it wanted to, it could not afford to, since nearly half of all Tootsie Roll Pops have the Indian on the label. The company responds to such requests with a legend of its own: in a special form letter, it explains that Shooting Star is the one who invented the process of putting the Tootsie Pop inside the lollipop. Every once in a while, Shooting Star returns to the factory and inspects the candy to make sure the company is following his instructions. The Indian on the wrapper is Shooting Star's seal of approval: it shows that he has personally inspected that piece of candy himself.

ORIGIN: The 1960s.

RUMOR: It's against the law to kill a praying mantis. If you're caught, you can be fined.

THE TRUTH: Praying mantises are good for gardens, but there's no law protecting them—they're not endangered. (In fact, this rumor predated the Endangered Species Act by many years.) The tale was probably invented years ago by a gardener trying to keep kids from destroying the weird-looking, but beneficial, bugs.

If an octopus is hungry enough, it will eat its own arms.

BUILDING A BETTER SQUIRT GUN

When Uncle John was a kid, he had squirt guns that shot 5 to 10 feet at most, and that was only if you pulled the trigger so hard it hurt. Today, there are water toys that shoot 50 feet or more. Here's the story.

BOY WONDER

Lonnie Johnson loved to tinker. As a kid, he used to take his brothers' and sisters' toys apart to see how they worked. By high school, he'd graduated to mixing rocket fuel in the family kitchen. One year he used scrap motors, jukebox parts, and an old butane tank to create a remote-controlled, programmable robot…which won first prize in the University of Alabama science fair. Not bad for a kid from the poor side of Mobile, Alabama.

UNDER PRESSURE

Johnson got an engineering degree from Tuskeegee Institute and wound up working at the Jet Propulsion Lab in Pasadena, California. But he still spent his spare time tinkering. He recalls that one evening in 1982, "I was experimenting with inventions that used water instead of freon as a refrigeration fluid. As I was shooting water through a high-pressure nozzle in the bathtub, I thought "Wow, this would make a neat water pistol."

He built a prototype squirt gun out of PVC pipe, plexiglass, and a plastic soda bottle. Then he approached several toy companies…but none of them thought a squirt gun with a 50-foot range would sell. Johnson even looked into manufacturing the toys himself, but couldn't afford the $200,000 molding cost.

BREAKTHROUGH

In March 1989, he went to the International Toy Fair in New York and tried to sell his invention again. This time, the Larami Corporation was interested. They arranged a meeting with Johnson at their headquarters in Philadelphia. When everyone was seated, Johnson opened his suitcase, whipped out his prototype, and shot a burst of water across the entire room. Larami bought the gun on the spot. Within a year, the "Super Soaker" was the best-selling squirt gun in history.

The firefly is the official insect of the state of Pennsylvania.

THE EIFFEL TOWER

It's hard to believe now, but when the Eiffel Tower was proposed in the late 1800s, a lot of Parisians—and French citizens in general—opposed it. Here's a look at the story behind one of the most recognizable architectural structures on earth.

REVOLUTIONARY THINKING
In 1885, French officials began planning the Great Exposition of 1889, a celebration of the 100th anniversary of the French Revolution. They wanted to build some kind of monument that would be as glorious as France itself.

The Washington Monument, a masonry and marble obelisk, had recently been completed. At 557 feet high, it was the tallest building on earth. The French decided to top it by constructing a 1,000-foot-tall tower right in the heart of Paris.

Now all they had to do was find somebody who could design and build it.

OPEN SEASON
On May 2, 1886, the French government announced a design contest: French engineers and architects were invited to "study the possibility of erecting on the Champ de Mars an iron tower with a base 125 meters square and 300 meters high."

Whatever the contestants decided to propose, their designs had to meet two other criteria: 1) the structure had to be self-financing—it had to attract enough ticket-buying visitors to the exposition to pay for its own construction; and 2) it had to be a temporary structure that could be torn down easily at the end of the Exposition.

MERCI...BUT NON, MERCI
More than 100 proposals were submitted by the May 18 deadline. Most were fairly conventional, but some were downright weird. One person proposed building a huge guillotine; another suggested

---

U.S. kids leave an estimated 812 million cookies out for Santa on Christmas Eve.

erecting a 1,000-foot-tall sprinkler to water all of Paris during droughts; a third suggested putting a huge electric light atop the tower that—with the help of strategically placed parabolic mirrors—would provide the entire city "eight times as much light as is necessary to read a newspaper."

NO CONTEST
The truth was, none of them had a chance. By the time the contest was announced, Alexandre-Gustave Eiffel—a 53-year-old structural engineer already considered France's "master builder in metal" had the job sewn up. (He would later become known as *le Magicien du Fer*—"the Iron Magician.")

Weeks earlier, he had met with French minister Edouard Lockroy and presented plans for a wrought iron tower he was ready to build. Eiffel had already commissioned 5,329 mechanical drawings representing the 18,038 different components that would be used. Lockroy was so impressed that he rigged the contest so only Eiffel's design would win.

JOINT VENTURE
In January 1887, Eiffel signed a contract with the French government and the City of Paris. Eiffel & Company, his engineering firm, agreed to contribute $1.3 million of the tower's estimated $1.6 million construction cost. In exchange, Eiffel would receive all revenues generated by the tower during the Exposition...and for 20 years afterward. (The government agreed to leave the tower up after the Exposition.) Afterward, full ownership reverted to the City of Paris. They could tear it down if they wanted.

MONEY MACHINE
Unlike other public monuments, the Eiffel Tower was designed to make money from the very beginning. If you wanted to take the elevator or the stairs to the first story, you had to pay 2 francs; going all the way to the top cost 5 francs (Sundays were cheaper). That was just the beginning: restaurants, cafes, and shops were planned for the first story; a post office, telegraph office, bakery, and printing press were planned for the second story. In all, the tower was designed to accommodate up to 10,416 paying customers at a time.

GROUNDBREAKING
Construction began on January 26, with not a moment to spare. With barely two years left to build the tower in time for the opening of the Exposition, Eiffel would have to build the tower more quickly than any similar structure had been built before. The Washington Monument, just over half the Eiffel Tower's size, had taken 36 years to complete.

PARISIAN PARTY POOPERS
A 1,000-foot tower would dwarf the Parisian skyline and overpower the city's other landmarks, including Notre Dame, the Louvre, and the Arc de Triomphe. When digging started on the foundation, more than 300 prominent Parisians signed a petition protesting the tower. They claimed that Eiffel's "hollow candlestick" would "disfigure and dishonor" the city. But Eiffel and the city ignored the petition, and work continued uninterrupted.

OTHER FEARS
The tower still had its critics. A French mathematics professor predicted that when the structure passed the 748-foot mark, it would inevitably collapse; another "expert" predicted that the tower's lightning rods would kill all the fish in the Seine.

The Paris edition of the New York *Herald* claimed the tower was changing the weather; and the daily newspaper *Le Matin* ran a headline story claiming "The Tower Is Sinking." "If it has really begun to sink," *Le Matin* pontificated, "any further building should stop and sections already built should be demolished as quickly as possible." As the tower's progress continued unabated, however, a sense of awe began to replace the fear.

* * * *

INTERESTING SIDELIGHT
August Eiffel also designed and built the iron skeleton that holds up the Statue of Liberty.

FORGOTTEN HISTORY

A few tidbits of obscure history from Keep Up
with the World, *a 1941 book by Freling Foster.*

X-RAY-PROOF UNDERWEAR

"A short time after X-rays were discovered in 1895 and news of their penetrating power had spread throughout the world, the women of England believed—and were horrified by—the rumor that a British firm was about to make X-ray spectacles that would enable the wearer to look right through clothing. Within a few months, a manufacturer and a London department store made a small fortune with their new 'X-ray-proof underwear.'"

APE HANGED AS A FRENCH SPY

"In 1705, during Queen Anne's War between France and England, a small vessel was wrecked in the North Sea off the English coast village of West Hartlepool and the sole survivor, a pet ape belonging to the crew, was washed ashore on a plank and captured by fishermen. The villagers had never before seen such a peculiar character, but they were not to be fooled by his hairy disguise and outlandish chatter. The following day, the monkey was tried by court martial, found guilty and hanged as a French spy."

THE FIRST MOVIE STAR

"The first film star was John Bunny of New York City, who made approximately 100 one-reel comedies for the Vitagraph Company between 1911 and his death in 1915. As his pictures were shown in numerous countries, Bunny's short fat figure soon became more widely known than that of any other living individual. When he went on a world tour in 1913, he became the first movie star ever to be recognized and surrounded by huge crowds in every city he visited."

THE AMPERSAND

"The oldest symbol representing a word is "&," known as the *ampersand*. Originally, it was one of the 5,000 signs in the world's first shorthand system, invented by Marcus Tiro in Rome in 63 B.C."

Average annual income in the United States at the start of World War II: $1,070.

THE FIRST COMPUTER PROGRAMMERS

Uncle John was sitting in the bathroom, thumbing through the
Wall Street Journal *(surprisingly good bathroom reading, on
occasion), when he came across this historical tidbit.*

This, in brief, is the story of the first computer programmers
—how much they gave to history, [and] how little history
gave back to them....

FOR WOMEN ONLY

The year was 1945. The clacking of adding machines and clouds
of cigarette smoke filled a university-owned row house along
Walnut Street [in Philadelphia]. Inside, dozens of women calculat-
ed trajectories to help wartime artillery gunners take aim. Men,
the Army reasoned, lacked the patience for such tedium—a single
problem might require months of work.

The army called the women "computers." One of them, Jean
Bartik, was a 20-year-old math prodigy recruited from the farms of
Missouri. Another, Betty Holberton, was the granddaughter of an
astronomer who spent her childhood steeped in classical literature
and language. The women formed a tight fellowship, drawn
together by youth, brains, and the war effort...

THE COMPUTER AGE

One day word spread that the brightest "computers" were needed
to work on a new machine called the Electronic Numerical Inte-
grator and Computer, or *ENIAC*—a steel behemoth, 100 feet long
and 10 feet high, built of 17,480 vacuum tubes in an engineering
building at the University of Pennsylvania. It was the first electronic computer, intended to automate the trajectory calculations
the female computers performed by hand.

Running the ENIAC required setting dozens of dials and plug-
ging a ganglia of heavy black cables into the face of the machine,
a different configuration for every problem. It was this job—"programming," they came to call it—to which just six of the young

women were assigned: Marlyn Meltzer, Ruth Teitelbaum, Kay Antonelli, and Frances Spence, as well as Ms. Bartik and Ms. Holberton. They had no user's guide. There were no operating systems or computer languages, just hardware and human logic. "The ENIAC," says Bartik, "was a son of a bitch to program."

HOW THEY DID IT
The first task was breaking down complex differential equations into the smallest possible steps. Each of these had to be routed to the proper bank of electronics and performed in sequence…. Every datum and instruction had to reach the correct location in time for the operation that depended on it, to within 1/5,000th of a second.

Yet despite this complexity, the Army brass considered the programming to be clerical work; that it was women stringing the cables only reinforced this notion. Their government-job rating was SP, as in "subprofessional." Initially they were prohibited as security risks even from *entering* the ENIAC room, forcing them to learn the machine from wiring diagrams. When finally admitted, they sometimes had to straighten the clutter of gear the engineers left overnight.

Finally, in February 1946, the scientists were ready for the ENIAC official unveiling. A test problem involving the trajectory of a 155-millimeter shell was handed to Jean Bartik and Betty Holberton for programming. The machine performed flawlessly, calculating the trajectory in less time than it would take the bullet to land. After the demonstration, the men went out for a celebratory dinner. The programmers went home.

LIFE ISN'T FAIR
In the 50 years since, their legacy is confined mainly to Movietone footage and sepia photos—women standing alongside the machine, as if modeling a Frigidaire. Why was history so ungenerous? Partly because in the awe surrounding the machine itself, the hardware was seen as the whole story. In addition, three of the programmers married engineers with top jobs on the ENIAC, making them wives first in the eyes of the history makers and history writers.

A copious, definitive history of the ENIAC, written by the Army ordnance officer who commanded the project, merely lists the programmers' names (misspelling one of them) and identifies which of the engineers they married.

The greater injustice is not history's treatment of the women but its resistance to revision....[For example,] until [an enthusiastic historian] made an issue of it, most of the programmers had not even been invited to the gala dinner...celebrating the 50th anniversary of the ENIAC.

* * * *

MOTHERS OF INVENTION
*Here are two women you may never have heard
of, but who may have affected your life.*

Mother of Invention: Kate Gleason, a New York architect in the 1920s.
The Invention: Tract housing
Background: After watching engines being put together on a Cadillac assembly line, Gleason decided to try using mass production techniques to build affordable housing for soldiers who'd returned from World War I. Her first development was "Concrest," a 100-unit concrete housing project. Its six-room homes sold for $4,000 each.

Mother of Invention: Ruth Wakefield, owner of the Toll House Inn and restaurant in Whitman, Massachusetts, in the 1930s.
The Invention: Chocolate chip cookies
Background: One afternoon Wakefield was baking a batch of "chocolate butter drop" cookies for her restaurant. She decided to smash a semisweet chocolate bar into tiny chunks and dump the pieces into the batter, rather than take the time to melt the bar first. She figured the chunks would melt into the batter in the oven, and the cookies would be indistinguishable from her regular ones. She was wrong—and her customers loved the difference. Today Americans consume more than 150 million pounds of chocolate chip cookies every year.

LUCKY FINDS

In our last Bathroom Reader, we included a section about valuable things people have found. Since then we've found many more stories. Hey— maybe it's not such a rare occurrence. It could happen to you!

GARAGE SALE TREASURE
The Find: Two Shaker "gift" paintings
Where They Were Found: Inside a picture frame
The Story: In 1994, a retired couple from New England bought an old picture frame for a few dollars at a garage sale. When they took the frame apart to restore it, two watercolor drawings—dated 1845 and 1854—fell out.

A few months later, the couple was traveling in Massachusetts and noticed a watercolor on a poster advertising the Hancock Shaker Village Museum. It was similar to the two they'd found. Curious, they did some research and found out the works were called "gift paintings."

It turns out that the Shakers, a New England religious sect of the 1800s, did not allow decorations on their walls; Shaker sisters, however, were permitted to paint "trees, flowers, fruits and birds...to depict the glory of heaven." The paintings were then "gifted" to other sisters and put away as holy relics. And one of the couple's paintings was signed by the most famous of all "gift" artists, Hannah Cohoon.

They called a curator of the Hancock Museum with the news, but he didn't believe them. Only 200 Shaker "gift" paintings still exist...and very few are of the quality they described. Moreover, all known paintings were in museums—none in private hands. Nonetheless, in January 1996, the couple brought the paintings to the museum, where they were examined and declared authentic. A year later, in January 1997, Sotheby's sold them for $473,000.

BIZARRE BITE
The Find: A diamond
Where It Was Found: In a plate of pasta
The Story: In October 1996, Liliana Parodi of Genoa, Italy, went to her favorite restaurant for some pasta. The meal was unevent-

---

The market value of the raw materials in a 170-lb. man's body, at 1997 prices: About $25.

ful…until she bit down on something hard and it wedged painfully between her teeth. She complained to the management, then left. The next morning, she went to a dentist, who extracted the object—a one-carat, uncut diamond worth about $3,000. Parodi took it to a jeweler and had it set in a ring. How it got into the pasta is still a mystery.

A BEATLE'S LEGACY
The Find: Dozens of sketches by John Lennon
Where They Were Found: In a notebook
The Story: In 1996, a man named John Dunbar—who'd been married to British singer Marianne Faithfull in the 1960s—was going through some old belongings and came across a notebook he hadn't seen in over 25 years. He'd had it with him at a London party in 1967, on a night when he and his friend John Lennon were taking LSD together. But he'd stashed it away and forgotten about it.

During that week in 1967, Lennon had seen an ad in the newspaper offering "an island off Ireland," for about $2,000. At the party, the drugged-out Beatle suddenly decided to buy it. He and Dunbar immediately flew to Dublin, traveled across Ireland in a limousine, and hired a boat to get there. "The island was more like a couple of small hills joined by a gravelly bar with a cottage on it," Durbar recalled. "When we got there, John sat down and started drawing." The pair stayed on the island for a few days. Lennon did buy it, but never lived there. (In fact, he gave it away a few years later, to a stranger who showed up at Apple Records.)

Dunbar kept the notebook as a memento of the trip, and today, experts estimate the drawings at about $165,000. The incredulous Dunbar can always look at it as a belated "thank you"—he was the fellow, it turns out, who introduced Lennon to Yoko Ono.

LOTTERY TICKET
The Find: A wallet with $224.
Where It Was Found: On a street in Adelaide, Australia
The Story: In the 1970s, Joan Campbell found a wallet and tracked down the owner, hoping for a nice reward. She was disappointed—all the man gave her was a 55¢ lottery ticket. Later, she cheered up: the ticket paid $45,000.

Gadsby, a 50,000-word novel by Ernest Wright, contains no words with the letter "e."

THE BEST BUSINESS DEAL IN U.S. HISTORY

*The early days of the auto industry were like today's Internet boom—
people could make huge fortunes by investing in the right car company.
But no high-tech rags-to-riches story quite matched the return on investment that the Dodge brothers got for their $7,000 in auto parts
and $3,000 in cash. It's a great, little-known business tale.*

RAGS TO ROADSTERS
In 1901, the early days of the automobile, Ransom Eli
Olds was looking for subcontractors who could manufacture parts for his Curved Dash Oldsmobile. The best machine
shop in the Detroit area was a company called Leland and
Faulconer, but they were already committed to supplying parts for
the new Cadillac Automobile Company (see page 474). So Olds
turned to the second-best machine shop in town, owned and operated by John and Horace Dodge.

Experience Counts
The brothers Dodge were only in their mid-30s, but they already
had more than 20 years' experience working with internal com-
bustion engines. Their father owned a machine shop on the river
that connected Lake Huron with Lake Erie, and the brothers
spent much of their childhood helping him repair and rebuild ship
engines.

By the time John and Horace were in their 20s, both were
working as machinists in Detroit. They spent the next several
years perfecting their skills at various companies, and in 1897
opened a bicycle company to manufacture an "improved" bicycle
they'd designed themselves. Two years later, they sold the company and used the money—$7,500 in cash and $10,000 worth of
machine tools—to open the Dodge Brothers Machine Shop in
Detroit.

SHIFTING GEARS
Dodge Brothers started out manufacturing parts for all different
types of products, including firearms, bicycles, automobiles, and

steam engines. But they got so much business from Olds that they dropped everything else and began manufacturing auto parts exclusively. Olds sold 2,000 cars in 1902, more than any other carmaker in the country, and every one of them had a Dodge transmission. As production continued to climb, Dodge Brothers moved to a newer, larger shop and spent tens of thousands of dollars on new machine tools to keep up with the demand.

Then in 1903, the Dodge brothers took a huge risk: they dumped the Olds Motor Works account and agreed to begin manufacturing engines, transmissions, and chassis for the Ford & Malcomson Company—which, unlike Olds, had only recently opened for business and had yet to manufacture a single car.

HARD BARGAIN

Why would the Dodge brothers abandon Olds for Ford–Malcomson? Part of the reason was that Henry Ford, the company's co-founder, had showed them the plans for his Model A "Fordmobile," and the Dodges were impressed. They thought it had a good chance of succeeding.

But there was an even bigger incentive: Ironically, Henry Ford's track record of failure (he had already run two companies into the ground) actually made doing business with him more lucrative for the Dodge brothers than if he had been a success. His credit rating was so bad that he had to offer the brothers a sweeter business deal than they could have gotten anywhere else in town.

Normally, in the machine parts industry, an auto company like Ford-Malcomson would have 60 days to pay for auto parts after delivery. But since the Dodges weren't sure if Ford would still be in business in 60 days, they demanded cash up front on the first shipment of parts, and payment within 15 days on each subsequent delivery. If Ford couldn't pay, ownership of all unsold parts automatically reverted to the Dodge brothers. The terms were tough, but Ford had to agree.

HOWDY, PARDNER

There was one more perk. When Henry Ford and Alex Malcomson, Detroit's leading coal merchant, set out to found an auto company together, they had hoped to finance the entire venture with their own savings. But they soon realized they didn't have enough money: Malcomson's credit was so overstretched that he took his name off of Ford & Malcomson (renaming it the Ford Motor Company), so his bankers wouldn't find out he had money tied up in the business. (Plus, if the company went under, as Malcomson feared it might, he worried his name would become associated with failure.)

Henry Ford's financial position wasn't much better: he had very little money of his own, and had already alienated Detroit's business community with his two earlier business failures. Nobody wanted to invest in a company run by a two-time loser like Ford.

With so few people willing to invest in Ford, Malcomson pushed the company's stock onto friends and colleagues who owed him favors. He also pitched the shares to people who had a direct financial stake in the company's survival, two of whom were John and Horace Dodge. Malcomson offered them a 10% stake in the Ford Motor Company, in exchange for $7,000 worth of auto parts and $3,000 in cash.

Now you know what the deal is. Turn to page 93 for the rest of the story.

* * * *

HOLY BAT FACTS!

• Most species of bats live 12 to 15 years, but some live as long as 30 years. Some species can fly as fast as 60 miles per hour and as high as 10,000 feet.

• Bats are social animals and live in colonies in caves. The colonies can get *huge:* Bracken Cave in Texas contains an estimated 20 million Mexican free-tailed bats.

• Vampire bats drink blood through a "drinking straw" that the bat makes with its tongue and its lower lip. The bats' saliva contains an anticoagulant that keeps blood flowing by impeding the formation of blood clots.

• It's not uncommon for a vampire bat to return to the same animal night after night, weakening and eventually killing its prey.

Honeybees can fly as fast as 30 mph.

THE ORIGIN OF BASKETBALL, PART I

Unlike baseball and football, which trace their roots to games that have been played for centuries, basketball was invented by one man— a Canadian named James Naismith—in a couple of days in 1891. It is the only major sport considered native to the U.S. Here's its history.

SOMETHING NEW

Today the YMCA is synonymous with sports, but that hasn't always been the case. In the mid-1880s, it was primarily a missionary group. "In fact," Ted Vincent writes in *The Rise and Fall of American Sport*, "the Young Men's Christian Association condemned almost all sports, along with dancing, card playing, and vaudeville shows, on the grounds that these activities were 'distinctly worldly in their associations, and unspiritual in their influence,' and therefore 'utterly inconsistent with our professions as disciples of Christ.'"

Good Sport

Then, at the YMCA's national convention in 1889, 24-year-old Dr. Luther Gulick started a revolution when he suggested that "good bodies and good morals" might actually go together. He insisted that keeping physically fit could make someone a better person, rather than inevitably leading them down the path of sin....And he proposed that the YMCA use organized athletics to reach out to youngsters who might otherwise not be interested in the Y's traditional emphasis on religion.

His proposal met with heavy opposition from conservatives, who argued that a "Christian gymnasium teacher" was a contradiction in terms. But when Gulick's idea was put to a vote, he won. Gulick was put in charge of a brand-new athletics teaching program at the YMCA School for Christian Workers in Springfield, Massachusetts.

CHANGING TIMES

Gulick's ideas were actually part of a larger social movement. For decades, America had been making the transition from a largely

Attention Pentagon! The United States has never lost a war in which mules were used.

rural, farm-based society to an industrialized economy, in which much of the population lived and worked in cities. Americans who had once labored in fields from sunup to sundown were now spending much of their working lives cooped up inside a factory, or behind a desk or sales counter.

"Middle-class Americans in particular reacted to the growing bureaucracy and confinement of their work lives, and to the remarkable crowding of their cities, by rushing to the outdoors, on foot and on bicycles," Elliot Gorn writes in *A Brief History of American Sports*. "Hiking, bird-watching, camping, rock-climbing, or simply walking in the new national parks—participation in all of these activities soared in the years around the turn of the century.

MASS APPEAL
Middle-class Americans who embraced physical activity as the answer to their own yearnings also began to see it as an answer to some of society's ills. The repeal of child labor laws and high levels of immigration meant that the tenement districts in America's major cities were full of immigrant youths who had little or nothing to do. Leaders of the "recreation movement," like Dr. Gulick, felt that building public playgrounds and bringing organized play programs into the slums would help the kids stay out of trouble and make it easier for them to assimilate into American life.

"Reformers thought of themselves as being on an exciting new mission, Americanizing children by helping them to have fun," Gorn says. "Playground reformers sought to clean up American streets, confine play to designated recreational spaces, and use their professional expertise to teach 'respectable' athletics." In an era in which public playgrounds were virtually unheard of, the facilities and athletic programs that organizations like the YMCA were beginning to offer often provided the only positive outlet for urban kids' energies.

BACK TO SCHOOL
As Gulick set up his program to train YMCA physical education instructors, he also decided to require men training to be "general secretaries" (the official title for men who ran local YMCA chapters) to take phys ed classes.

These students were older and more conservative than other students. They hadn't been sold on Gulick's newfangled sports

ideas and, left to their own devices, would avoid physical education classes entirely. Gulick feared that if he didn't bring these
future YMCA leaders around to his point of view while they were
in Springfield, they wouldn't implement his programs when they
got back home...and his efforts would be fruitless.

Cold Shoulder

Working with the general secretaries was a snap at first: in the
early fall they just went outside and played football or soccer. But
when the weather turned cold and they were forced indoors,
things got difficult. The best recreation Gulick could come up
with was a schedule of military drills...followed by German,
French, and Swedish gymnastics. Day after day, the routine was
the same, and the students became thoroughly bored.

THE INCORRIGIBLES

Within weeks, the class was in open rebellion, and two successive
physical education instructors resigned rather than put up with
their abuse. They told Gulick that he might as well give up on
"The Incorrigibles," as the class had become known.

Gulick wasn't ready to quit yet. For weeks, an instructor named
James Naismith had been arguing that The Incorrigibles weren't
to blame for the situation. "The trouble is not with the men," he
said, "but with the system we are using. The kind of work for this
class should be of a recreative nature, something that would
appeal to their play instincts." At one faculty meeting, he even
proposed inventing a new indoor game. So when Gulick put Naismith in charge of the class, he commented pointedly: "Now
would be a good time for you to work on that new game that you
said could be invented."

For Part II, turn to page 95.

* * * *

*"I cannot imagine any condition which could cause this ship to founder.
I cannot conceive of any vital disaster happening to the vessel.
Modern shipbuilding has gone beyond that."*
—**E.I. Smith, captain of the Titanic**

WE AIN'T LION: THE MODERN ZOO IS BORN

It wasn't that long ago that seeing an elephant at the London Zoo was about as shocking to the average person as meeting a Martian would be today. Here's the story of how zoos got their start.

OLD-TIME MENAGERIES
People have "collected" exotic animals for more than 5,000 years. Priests in ancient Egypt raised lions, tigers, and other sacred animals in and around temples, and as early as 1100 B.C., China's Zhou Dynasty established what was called the "Garden of Intelligence," a 900-acre preserve filled with deer, antelope, birds, fish, and other animals that were studied as well as hunted.

Exotic animals were also popular in ancient Rome, where they were collected by wealthy families and used in gladiator games.

Sometimes the lions, tigers, bulls, bears, and other creatures fought each other to a bloody death for public amusement; other times they were pitted against Christians, heretics, or condemned criminals (or, if none were available, ordinary criminals). Sometimes the Romans even filled their coliseums with water, so gladiators in boats could hunt water animals like hippos and crocodiles.

These games were so popular—and killed so many animals—that by the time they finally came to an end in the 6th century A.D., numerous species in the Roman empire, including the elephants of North Africa, the hippopotami of Nubia, the lions of Mesopotamia, and the tigers of Hycrania, had all been driven to extinction.

THE DARK AGES
When Rome fell in the 5th century A.D., interest in animals declined, and it wasn't until the 13th century that nobles and other wealthy Europeans began collecting animals on a large scale again. They even exchanged them like trading cards.

King Frederick II of Sicily was a typical collector of the era: his menagerie included hyenas, elephants, camels, lions, monkeys, cheetahs, and a giraffe...and when he got tired of the giraffe, he traded it to the sultan of Egypt for a polar bear.

THE LONDON ZOO

In 1235 King Henry III of England moved his grandfather's animal collection to the Tower of London. The collection included camels, lions, leopards, and lynx...and King Louis IX of France contributed an elephant—the first one ever seen in Great Britain. The animals were put on display for the royal family and its guests, but were also occasionally pitted against one another—tigers vs. lions, bears vs. dogs—to entertain royal visitors. However, the novelty eventually wore off, and the animals became neglected.

Then, in 1445, Margaret of Anjoy, wife of Henry VI, received a lion as a wedding gift...which inspired her to have the entire Royal Menagerie—what was left of it—restored. But when the royal family moved out of the Tower in the early 1700s, they left their animals behind. That created a problem: if the royal family wasn't going to support the menagerie, who was? Finally, someone came up with the idea of opening the collection to the public, and charging them admission. Price: three half-pence, or if you preferred, a dog or cat to feed to the lions.

CHANGING TIMES

As the British Empire expanded to the far corners of the globe in the early 1800s, interest in exotic animals grew beyond mere curiosity. In 1826 an explorer named Sir Stamford Raffles founded the London Zoological Society, which took its name from the ancient Greek word *zoion*, which means "living being."

Two years later, the Society moved the royal family's animal collection from the Tower of London to a new site in Regent's Park. It was a big hit with members of the royal family, many of whom contributed animals.

But unlike the Tower of London, the Zoological Park was closed to the public—the animals were "objects of scientific research," Raffles explained, "not of vulgar admiration." Only members of the Zoological society and their guests were allowed to

What do grape juice and the blesbok antelope have in common? Same color.

visit. (A written voucher would allow a nonmember to enter, and these became very common and were even traded in pubs.)

The public was officially excluded from the "zoo," as it had become known, until 1846, by which time the novelty had worn off and attendance had fallen dramatically. So the Zoological Society opened its doors to anyone with a penny, and hundreds of thousands of new visitors streamed into the park. "For the city dweller," Linda Koebler writes in *Zoo*, "[it] provided a place of greenery that was a relief from the ugly, dirty cities of this period."

The term "zoo" entered mainstream culture a year after the London Zoological Garden opened to the public, thanks to the popularity of one particular song: "Walking in the Zoo is an Okay Thing to Do."

ZOOS IN EUROPE

In the early 1800s, having a public zoo became a status symbol for any European city that considered itself modern and sophisticated.

If they still had royal collections of animals available, they quickly converted them to zoological parks. If they didn't, they created new zoos. Zoos in Dublin, Berlin, Frankfurt, Antwerp, and Rotterdam were among the best known.

Le Zoo

In France, however, the development of public zoos was slowed by the Revolution of 1789. Common people saw private collections of captive animals as a way for the rich to flaunt their wealth. According to one account, when a mob of revolutionaries arrived at the Ménagerie du Parc to free the animals, "The crowd wanted the animals set free so that others could catch them and eat them, outraged that these animals grew fat while the people starved. But once the zoo director explained that some of the creatures would eat the crowd rather than vice versa, the du Parc revolutionaries decided to liberate only the more edible captives."

Cat got your tongue? Did someone call you a cheetah?
Don't monkey around, turn to page 102
for more wild facts about zoos.

Female cigar store Indians once outnumbered male ones by four to one.

THE BEST BUSINESS DEAL IN U.S. HISTORY, PART II

When the Dodge Brothers put $3,000 in cash and $7,000 in parts into the Ford Motor Company, they made history. Here's what happened next. (Part I of the story is on page 84.)

TURNAROUND

Four weeks after the Dodge brothers made their deal with Malcomson, the Ford Motor Company was on the verge of bankruptcy. With $223.65 in the bank, not a single car sold, and payroll for the Ford workers due the next day, it looked like the company's stock would be worthless.

Then, on July 15, 1903, a dentist named Dr. E. Pfennig became Ford's first customer, paying $850 cash for a Model A. "Dr. Pfennig's payment of the full cash price through the Illinois Trust and Savings Bank represented a turning point in the fortunes of the Ford Motor Company," Robert Lacey writes in *Ford: The Men and the Machine.* "From $223.65 onwards, its cash flow went one way only."

UP, UP, AND AWAY

When it opened for business in 1903, the Ford Motor Company could only build a few cars at a time. But as orders increased, Henry Ford and his assistants knew that the key to success was to find ways to speed production.

They did. In the year ending September 1906, the company made 1,599 cars; the following year, production more than quadrupled to 8,000; and by 1912, Ford was manufacturing 78,000 cars per year. That was only the beginning: production more than doubled the following year and then more than doubled again in 1914, until Ford was manufacturing over 300,000 cars per year, or 1,000 cars for every work day, a production increase of 4,000% in just over a decade.

Oh, Brother

About the only thing that grew faster than the Ford Motor Company's production and sales figures was the value of Ford stock,

10% of which belonged to the Dodge brothers. They'd earned back their entire $10,000 in the first year's dividends alone, and since then their Ford stock had paid out millions more.

In addition, since they were still manufacturing most of Ford's mechanical components at their own Dodge Brothers factory (at the time the largest and most modern such manufacturing plant in the world), they profited twice: first by supplying parts to Ford and second, by owning shares in the company.

T-TIME

That changed in 1914, when Henry Ford built his own parts manufacturing plant to replace the one owned by the Dodge brothers. Until then, the Ford Motor Company, like most other auto companies, had focused on assembling cars, leaving the actual manufacturing of the parts to subcontractors. Now that Ford could afford to finance his own manufacturing plant, he didn't need the Dodge brothers any more.

With their business relationship with Ford coming to an end, the brothers had to figure out what do with their plant. Henry Ford had offered to lease the plant and run it himself, and the Dodges gave it serious thought…but then they had another idea.

DON'T CHANGE A THING

When it went on sale in October 1908, the Ford Model T was the most advanced car of its day. As the years passed, automotive technology improved, but Henry Ford refused to make any changes to it, stylistically or even mechanically. Unlike other cars, you still had to start the Model T using a hand crank, and since it didn't come with a fuel gauge, the only way to tell how much gas you had was by dipping a stick into the gas tank. Having been with Ford from the beginning, the Dodge brothers knew all of the car's weaknesses, but when they suggested improvements, Ford ignored them.

In the end, the Dodge brothers decided to use their factory to manufacture the car that Henry Ford refused to build: one that was better than the Model T.

Turn to page 100 for Part III.

Turn to page 100 for Part III.

THE ORIGIN OF BASKETBALL, PART II

*Here's more on how the game of basketball
was invented. Part I starts on page 87.*

PROMISES, PROMISES...
As James Naismith admitted years later in his memoirs, the
new game he had in mind was an indoor version of an exist-
ing sport, like baseball or rugby. And when Dr. Gulick put him in
charge of The Incorrigibles' physical education classes, he set out
to find one he could adapt.

Naismith spent two weeks experimenting with different games,
but something always seemed to get lost in the translation: Indoor
soccer, for example, was fun—but too many windows were broken.
And rugby turned out to be too dangerous on the gymnasium's
hardwood floors. Other sports were safer...but they were so boring,
The Incorrigibles refused to play them.

Outdoor games were meant to be played outdoors, Naismith
concluded, and that was that.

BACK TO THE DRAWING BOARD
Time was running out. With only 24 hours left till his deadline for
reporting to the faculty on the success of his efforts, Naismith
decided to try a different approach: he would analyze a number of
different games systematically, and figure out what made them
challenging and fun. Then he would incorporate many of those
elements into a new game that would be, as he put it, "interesting,
easy to learn, and easy to play in the winter and by artificial light."

Do Unto Others
Naismith's new game would also have to walk a political
tightrope: it had to be physically challenging enough to sustain
the interest of The Incorrigibles, but not so rough or violent that
it would offend conservatives within the YMCA movement. They
had opposed getting involved with sports in the first place...and
Naismith didn't want to give them any excuse to declare the
experiment a failure.

HE GOT GAME

Amazingly, Naismith then sat down and, step-by-step, invented one of the most popular games in sports history.

Step 1. He figured that since nearly all popular sports have balls, his game should have one, too. But should it be small or large? Small balls like baseballs and lacrosse balls required bats, sticks, and racquets. Naismith was afraid players might use them to hit each other. He chose a big ball.

Step 2. Naismith felt that running with a ball would invariably lead to tackling the person carrying it—and tackling was too violent for the YMCA (not to mention too dangerous on a wood floor). So in the new game, the person who had the ball wouldn't be allowed to run with it; they wouldn't even be allowed to move. Instead, the player with the ball would have to stand in one place and pass it to the other players. That was the key to the game. "I can still recall how I snapped my fingers and shouted, 'I've got it!'" Naismith recalled years later.

Step 3. And what about the shape of the ball? It would either have to be round or shaped like a rugby ball (the predecessor of the football). Rugby balls were easier to carry under the arm, but that would encourage tackling. Round balls were easier to throw, which made them perfect for a passing game. Naismith decided to use a soccer ball.

Step 4. Naismith figured that there should be a goal at each end of the gymnasium...but what kind of goal? A huge one, like a soccer goal, would make scoring too easy—so the goal would have to be smaller. But a tiny goal would be easy to block...and blocking the goal would lead to pushing and shoving. So he decided to put the goal high over people's heads, where it would be impossible to block.

Step 5. This led to another consideration: if the goal was vertical, like the goalposts in football, players would throw the ball at it as hard and as fast as they could—which would be dangerous indoors. It would also reward force over skill, which was the antithesis of what Naismith wanted.

Naismith suddenly remembered a game he'd played as a child, called Duck on the Rock. The object was to knock a "duck" off of a rock by throwing stones at it. The best players always threw their rocks in an arc rather than directly at the duck, so that if they missed, they wouldn't have to run as far to retrieve the rock.

That inspired Naismith to use a horizontal goal, parallel to the ground. That way, players wouldn't be able to score just by throwing the ball as hard as they could: they'd have to throw it in an arc to get it in.

SERENDIPITY STRIKES

Naismith figured a wooden box nailed to the balcony that ran around the gym would work pretty well as a goal, and asked the janitor if he had any boxes lying around.

"No," the janitor told him, "but I have two old peach baskets down in the store room, if they will do you any good." "Thus," Robert Peterson writes in *Cages to Jump Shots*, "did the game miss being called box ball."

Naismith nailed one peach basket to the balcony at one end of the gym, and one at the other end. The balcony of the YMCA in Springfield just happened to be 10 feet off the floor—which is why, today, a regulation basket is 10 feet high.

THE FIRST GAME

Naismith typed up a list of 13 rules and posted them on the gym's bulletin board. The following morning, he read The Incorrigibles the rules; then he divided the 18-man class into two teams of 9 and taught them to play the game.

He promised to change any rules that didn't work out. "It was the start of the first basketball game," he recounted in his memoirs years later, "and the finish of the trouble with that class."

* * * *

"Women want mediocre men, and men are working hard to be as mediocre as possible." **—Margaret Mead**

Until 1937, the referee tossed a jump ball after every basket in basketball.

WOULD WE LIE
TO YOU?

Every chance we get. In this quiz, we explain some everyday phe-
nomena that may have long puzzled you...the only trouble is, once
again, we're offering too many explanations. Can you find the one
true answer in each set?

1. In cartoons, moonshine jugs are always labeled XXX. Where
   does this come from?
   a) During the 1800s, breweries in Britain marked their bottles
      X, XX, or XXX as a sign of alcohol content. The number of
      X's corresponded to the potency of the drink. Naturally, hard
      alcohol such as corn whiskey would earn the XXX rating.
   b) Nineteenth-century reading primers contained woodcuts
      showing the evils of drink. To hammer the point home, bot-
      tles or kegs in the picture were marked XXX—an old sym-
      bol for poison.
   c) Small-scale whiskey brewers in rural America simply used
      whatever jugs were at hand when bottling their liquor for
      market—and if the jug in question was already labeled, say,
      "Molasses," he brewer simply X'ed the label out to avoid
      confusion.

2. Why is pink the standard color for bubble gum?
   a) Bubble gum is made from chicle, and chicle is naturally
      pink. Any bubble gum that isn't pink has been dyed by the
      manufacturer.
   b) When the first commercial batch of bubble gum was made,
      the manufacturer only had pink food coloring on hand. The
      gum was an instant hit, and other manufacturers copied it...
      including the color.
   c) Early bubble gum was much stickier. If a bubble popped in
      your face, it took a long time to remove it. So manufacturers
      made their gum pink.

3. Why are there buttons on coat sleeves, when there's nothing to button them to?
   a) Coat makers were tired of having customers come in and ask for replacement buttons, so they began sewing replacement buttons onto each sleeve.
   b) Those buttons were added only after the advent of dry cleaning. Dry cleaners use them to hold the sleeves away from the coat during cleaning.
   c) Believe it or not, those buttons are there to keep you from wiping your nose on your sleeve. Napoleon Bonaparte supposedly spotted a soldier using his coat sleeve as a hankie. Disgusted, he ordered new jackets for his army—this time with buttons on the sleeves, to prevent a recurrence.

4. Why is it believed that walking under a ladder brings bad luck?
   a) To early Christians, any triangle was symbolic of the Holy Trinity—including the triangle formed by leaning a ladder up against a building. Walking beneath a ladder was seen as a violation of this holy symbol.
   b) "Climbing the ladder" has been a metaphor for success since ancient Roman times. A Roman man who chose to walk past the "unclimbable" side of a ladder was indicating to the gods that he wasn't interested in being successful—a "wish" that the gods were always grimly happy to grant.
   c) In its original form, this only applied to ladders with workmen at the top of them, a safety device so that you wouldn't get hit by anything the workman happened to drop.

5. How do you dig a tunnel underwater?
   a) You dig using scuba equipment and waterproof machinery. Then, when the tunnel's finished, you pump out all the water.
   b) You dig a trench underwater, and assemble a lightweight but watertight "frame" in it. Once you've pumped all of the water out of your frame, you can begin strengthening it—from the inside, where it's dry.
   c) You dig really deep beneath the water, so you never have to deal with a flooded tunnel.

ANSWER, PAGE 368

THE BEST BUSINESS DEAL IN U.S. HISTORY, PART III

Here's the last installment of the story. (Part II is on page 93.)

C AR WARS
On November 14, 1914, the first Dodge rolled off the assembly line. It had a bigger engine than the Model T and a modern stick-shift transmission, as well as features like a speedometer, an electric starter, electric headlights, a windshield, and a spare tire. And it only cost $100 more than the Model T.

THE EMPIRE STRIKES BACK
Naturally, Henry Ford was not amused that Ford dividends were being used to bankroll his competition. But when the Dodge brothers offered to sell him their Ford stock, he refused...and instead announced in 1916 that the Ford Motor Company would no longer pay dividends and would instead plow all of its profits back into the business.

The Dodge brothers sued to force Ford to pay dividends, and in 1919 they won: Ford was required to pay $19 million in back dividends (most of which went directly back to Henry Ford, since he owned the lion's share of the stock anyway), but Ford would not give in. On December 1918, he announced that he was "retiring" from Ford and turning control over to his son Edsel.

Henry left for an extended vacation in southern California. Then on March 5, 1919, the *Los Angles Examiner* broke a story that shook the automobile industry:

HENRY FORD ORGANIZING HUGE NEW COMPANY TO BUILD A BETTER, CHEAPER CAR

According to the report, while his old company had employed 50,000 workers, the new company would hire as many as 250,000 and would have automobile plants all over the world. The scale of production would make it possible to sell cars for between $250 and $350, cheaper than they had ever been sold before. No other auto manufacturer would be able to match the price.

GETTING OUT

The Dodge brothers were in a bind—if Ford was serious, it would probably drive both Dodge Brothers and the Ford Motor Company out of business. Their own company and their Ford stock would be worthless.

"But the Dodge brothers and the other minority shareholders found themselves mysteriously approached in the following weeks by would-be Ford share purchasers," Robert Lacey writes. "It became clear that the threads all led back to Henry, working through Edsel in Detroit. The bidding started at $7,500 per share (the Dodge brothers owned 2,000 shares). The Dodge brothers responded with their $12,500 price—and $12,500, in the end, became the price that Ford had to pay." The "huge new company," it turned out, was just a ploy that Ford used to depress the value of the Dodge brothers stock so that he could buy them out on the cheap.

SO LONG, FELLAS

The Dodge brothers received $25 million for their Ford stock, which came on top of the $9.5 million they had received in dividends between 1903 and 1919, for a total return of $34.5 million on their original $10,000 investment. Even though Ford had gotten the better of the bargain, the Dodges (along with the other original investors in Ford) made so much money that business historians now consider it the most profitable investment in the history of American commerce.

Note: Less than a year later, the Dodge brothers were attending the 1920 New York Auto Show when Horace suddenly fell ill with pneumonia. His condition was so grave that John maintained a round-the-clock bedside vigil, only to catch pneumonia himself and die 10 days later. Horace lingered for just a few more months before he died. In 1925 their widows sold the Dodge Brothers Motor Car Company to a New York banking syndicate for $146 million in cash—at the time the largest cash transaction in auto history. In May 1929, the bankers sold Dodge Brothers to automaker Walter Chrysler for $170 million...just in time for the Great Depression.

THE MODERN ZOO, PART II

Every year more than 120 million people visit zoos, aquariums, oceanariums, and wildlife parks in the United States and Canada—a greater attendance than that of football, baseball, and hockey games combined! The story of the origin of the modern zoo is on page 90.

STATUS SYMBOL

In the late 1850s, Philadelphian Dr. William Camac visited the London Zoo. Inspired by what he saw, he founded the Philadelphia Zoological Society. His goal: To build a world-class zoological garden and the first scientific zoo in America.

By the late 1850s, major cities all over Europe either had zoos or were in the process of establishing them. They were status symbols: The citizens of Madrid, Hamburg, and Dublin, for example, regarded zoos as a means of communicating to the rest of world that their cities were to be taken as seriously as London or Paris.

Dr. Camac wanted the same thing for Philadelphia: "When we see cities such as Amsterdam, Frankfurt, and Dublin—cities not so large as Philadelphia—supporting first-class zoological gardens," he wrote, "we see no reason why Philadelphia, with all its taste, wealth, enterprise, and advantages, should not in time possess one of the finest institutions in the world."

SIDESHOW

The United States lagged far behind Europe in the development of zoos. Westward expansion brought pioneers in contact with animals they had never seen before...and many animals were captured and brought back to cities to be exhibited to curious crowds. But as late as the 1870s, most animal viewing was limited to spectacles like a bear chained up in the corner tavern, or traveling carnivals put on by sea captains to show off exotic animals captured overseas.

EARLY AMERICAN ZOOS

New York

By 1861 New York City had a menagerie in Central Park, but this jumble was little more than a dumping ground for private collections and carnivals, including a black bear, two cows, deer, monkeys, raccoons, foxes, opossums, ducks, swans, eagles, pelicans, and parrots. No rational thought was put into the collection; the keepers just accepted whatever animals people gave them.

Still, the menagerie was a popular attraction. "By the late 1800s," Linda Koebner writes in *Zoo*, "it was a center of entertainment both for wealthy Fifth Avenue strollers and for the poor who were looking for a break from their daily working lives. Newly arrived immigrants lived in dark, crowded tenements on the Lower East Side of New York. A trip up to the green of Central Park to see the menagerie was well worth the walk or the nickel fare on the trolley."

Chicago

The menagerie in Chicago's Lincoln Park wasn't much better than the one in Central Park. It got its start when the Central Park menagerie presented them with a gift of two swans. This prompted similar "gifts," and by 1873 the park had 27 mammals and 48 birds.

GENUINE ARTICLE

While these zoos were popular attractions, neither Central Park nor Lincoln Park knew anything about animals or bothered to hire anyone who did; care and feeding of the creatures was left to the parks department, whose main concern was picking up garbage and raking leaves.

As Dr. Camac proposed it, the Philadelphia Zoological Garden would be something completely different: a well-funded, intelligently planned collection of animals housed in permanent facilities and run by a professional, full-time staff. The public would be admitted into the zoo, but it would also serve a more serious purpose: scientists at the University of Pennsylvania, the Academy of Sciences, and other organizations would be able to study and observe the animals up close.

Planning for the facility began in March of 1859, but the outbreak of the Civil War interfered with construction, so it was not completed until 1873.

Big year: Dr. Pepper, Coca-Cola, and Hires Root Beer were all invented in 1886.

THE TOILET ERA

When it opened to the public on July 1, 1874, the Philadelphia Zoo was a state-of-the-art facility, complete with a monkey house, bird house, prairie dog village, and sea lion pool. But the early zookeepers had a lot to learn about caring for animals. Hunters and trappers who captured the animals knew next to nothing about how the animals lived in the wild or what they ate, and thousands died before they could be delivered to the zoo. The zookeepers didn't know much more, and animals that made it to the zoo didn't live much longer.

Because animal behavior was so poorly understood, animals that lived in social or family groups in the wild were often acquired one at a time and lived alone in bare cages—no attempt was made to simulate their natural environment. Animals frequently had nowhere to hide, and climbing animals like monkeys and wildcats had nowhere to go to get off the floor. The emphasis in cage design was on preventing disease by making them easy to clean: enclosures were usually made of concrete and tile and looked so much like bathrooms, Koebner writes, that "this manner of keeping the animals gave rise to the term 'the toilet era.'"

Visitors to the zoos were similarly shortchanged: displays did little to educate the public other than give the name of the animal and the feeding schedule. Scientific aspects of the zoo were played down; the garden's staffers themselves were poorly informed and so could do little to shed light on any of the exhibits.

Where the public was concerned, the emphasis was on entertainment. Elephants paraded, bears danced, and chimpanzees wore clothes and ate with silverware at dinner tables, part of the zoology garden's attempt to show how "humanlike" they were.

A NEW ERA

Things began to improve at the turn of the century, thanks in large part to a German circus trainer named Carl Hagenbeck, considered the "father of modern zoos." For years Hagenbeck had made his living catching and training exotic animals for zoos. In 1907 he expanded his business by opening his own zoo, which he named the Hagenbeck Tierpark.

As an animal catcher, Hagenbeck had seen animals in the wild and was determined that the animals in his zoo would never live in cages that looked like restrooms. "I wished to exhibit them not as captives, confined to narrow spaces and looked at between bars, but as free to wander from place to place within as large limits as possible."

Hagenbeck put his experience as an animal trainer to work, testing the animals to see how high and how far they could jump, and then dug moats so deep and wide that the animals would not try to escape. He also tried to give the exhibits an authentic appearance so that the animals would be as comfortable as possible.

Optical Illusion

Hagenbeck also arranged the exhibits to give them as natural an appearance as possible; it even seemed as if predators and their prey were part of the same exhibit. The lion exhibit was located just in front of the zebra, antelope, and ostriches (safely separated by a moat that was concealed behind bushes and landscape.) All of the animals appeared to be together, just as they would be in their natural habitat in Africa. As a result, Koebner writes, "the public could see the interrelationship of animals, begin to picture what the African landscape looked like and learn about predators, prey and habitats."

The advantages of Hagenbeck's reforms were obvious, and most zoos began adopting his ideas to improve their exhibits. Still, his enclosures had drawbacks: They were expensive, took up more space than cages, and increased the distance between animals and the viewing public from 5 feet to as much as 75 feet. And some zoo directors felt they were too revolutionary. Dr. William Hornaday of the Bronx Zoo, for example, criticized the new enclosures as "a half-baked German fad." But Hornaday was in the minority. Zookeepers from all over the world began making pilgrimages to the Hagenbeck Tierpark to learn as much as they could.

CHANGING TIMES

Hagenbeck's reforms were part of a broader zoological trend: all over the world, zoos were beginning to take better care of their animals. In the old days, the supply of animals in the wild seemed inexhaustible—if an animal in a zoo died, they could just send a hunter into the jungle to get another one. Life was cheap, and animals were expendable.

By the early 1900s, zoos were already beginning to look different. Many animals had been driven to extinction or close to it. And foreign governments—realizing how valuable the surviving animals were—started charging zoos for the privilege of hunting in their territories. As the supply of animals went down and the cost of obtaining them went up, zoos became more interested in preserving and extending the lives of the animals they had.

But the practical aspects of running and maintaining a zoo didn't change as fast as the philosophy. "Even with increased difficulties in capture and export, it would still be many decades before capture in the wild slowed significantly," Koebner writes in *Zoo*. Until about the early 1960s, zoos still obtained the majority of their animals from well-funded expeditions into the wild, which amounted to little more than raids upon wildlife areas in Africa and Asia. Barbaric practices, such as killing a mother elephant or hippopotamus in order to capture its child, were still commonplace and widely accepted.

ZOOS TODAY

In the 1960s and 1970s, however, zoos began to make substantive shifts toward conservation—not just of the animals in the zoo, but also those still in the wild. And instead of competing against one another, they began working together to accomplish these goals. This is critical in the case of endangered species that are extinct, or practically so, in the wild…and survive only in zoos today.

In cases where only a few dozen animals survive and their numbers are scattered among several zoos, the only way to bring the species back from extinction is to manage the animals as one population.

"Today's zoos have a very specific message to preach," writes Allen Nyhuis in *The Zoo Book*. "By introducing the public to the world's enormous variety of animals and their native habitats, they hope that people will better appreciate the animals and want to help preserve them."

* * * *

Since 1984, America's zoos have spent more than
$1 billion on upgrading and improvements.

Your fingernails are made from the same substance as a bird's beak.

THE MINIATURE GOLF CRAZE

Most of us have played this "sport" at least once, but today we can't imagine how popular it was in the late 1920s. Here's the story of one of the most popular American fads of all time.

LILLIPUTIAN LINKS

It all started in 1927 at a hotel perched on Tennessee's Lookout Mountain, the picturesque site of a major Civil War battle. The owner, Garnet Carter, wanted to find a way to promote his resort and golf course. He decided to build a new golf course that anyone could play—a cheap version of the tiny courses which used to appear in front of English Inns. The hazards on the course—tree roots, sand traps, and water hazards—were arranged so that even the most pathetic golfer could handle them. His plan worked so well that the mini-links soon eclipsed the resort's other attractions, and he had to charge a "greens fee" to keep the massive crowds down.

BOOM

Carter was an astute businessman—he immediately recognized the potential profits in miniature golf. So he founded the Fairyland Manufacturing Company and began constructing "Tom Thumb" courses all over Tennessee, and eventually, the entire South.

In the fall of 1929, the pygmy links invaded California and New York, and then the rest of the nation. For only $2,000, Carter's company would lay down a course that would be operational in less than a week, and they proved so popular (and profitable) that many courses would earn back their initial investment in only a few days. The game was the first of many recreational fads of the Great Depression, successful mainly because it was so inexpensive to play.

Within a year, you could find mini golf courses everywhere—from highway filling stations to vacant city lots. And by the mid-1930s, 20 million Americans were regular players. On any given night, there were close to four million people flooding over 40,000

Q. Who invented Daylight Savings Time? A. Benjamin Franklin.

courses nationwide. People joked that the only industry still hiring during the Depression was miniature golf, which in 1930 employed 200,000 workers and generated profits of over $225 million in a single year.

Not only that, the fad helped bolster the flagging Depression-era cotton and steel industries. How? Crushed cotton seed hulls were used as a surfacing material for the greens and steel pipes were used for trick shots and hazards.

IT'S A SIN

Even a pastime as harmless as miniature golf was not without controversy. The courses were banned within 50 feet of churches, hospitals, and public schools, and the nongolfing element of the population complained nightly that the late night revelry of reckless young golfers—who would spike their sodas with bootleg liquor—disturbed their sleep. The game also sparked a debate between physicians and pastors. Doctors liked it—miniature golf took young folks out of stuffy movie theaters at night and put them in the fresh outdoor air for some healthy activity. But church officials claimed that playing on the Sabbath—the most popular day for recreation—was a sin. Ironically, a few churches around the country saw a chance to help pay off their debts and went over to the dark side, encouraging one and all to come and play (but never on the Sabbath.)

BUST

In the end, too many entrepreneurs saw a cheap, profitable Tom Thumb course as their road out of financial hardship. The fatal combination of market saturation and dwindling interest in the game brought about its swift end. In 1931 *Miniature Golf Management*, a one-year-old publication, noted that every California course was in the red financially.

But its shrewd inventor survived the fall. In 1929, he had the foresight to sell out to a Pennsylvania pipe manufacturer and settle for royalties from future miniature courses. At the end of the tiny sport's three year heyday, he emerged unscathed. A half-century later, the game retains a small following in more than one sense of the word—it has been bequeathed to children.

WHY ASK WHY?

Sometimes the answer is irrelevant—it's the question that counts.
These cosmic queries have been sent in by BRI readers.

Why isn't there mouse-flavored cat food?

Shouldn't there be a shorter word for *monosyllabic*?

Why is *dyslexic* so hard to spell?

Why are they called *stands* when they're made for sitting?

Why are there flotation devices under plane seats instead of parachutes?

If it's illegal to drink and drive, why do bars have parking lots?

Do you need a silencer if you are going to shoot a mime?

How does the guy who drives the snowplow get to work in the mornings?

If nothing sticks to Teflon, how do they make Teflon stick to the pan?

Why do they call it a *building*? Why isn't it a *built*?

Why is *verb* a noun?

Are there seeing-eye humans for blind dogs?

What does Geronimo say when he jumps out of a plane?

Do pediatricians play miniature golf on Wednesdays?

How can a house burn up while it burns down?

Why is the third hand on the watch called the *second hand*?

Is it good if a vacuum really sucks?

Why do we sing "Take me out to the ball game" when we're already there?

Why is it called *after dark* when it really is *after light*?

Why do we press harder on the buttons of a remote control when we know the batteries are dead?

Before drawing boards, what did they go back to?

How many stars in the Seven Sisters (also called the Pleiades)? About 250.

UNCLE JOHN'S STALL OF FAME

You'd be amazed at the number of newspaper articles BRI members send in about the creative ways people get involved with bathrooms, toilets, toilet paper, etc. So we've created Uncle John's "Stall of Fame."

Honoree: David Garza of Henrietta, Texas
Notable Achievement: Owns "The Toilet of Mystery"
True Story: Between 1991 and 1993, Garza fished more than 75 Papermate ballpoint pens out of his toilet—sometimes as many as 5 pens a day—and still has no idea how they got there. It has made him into a local celebrity. "Everywhere I go people say to me, 'Hey, have you got a pen?'"

Honoree: Ann Landers
Notable Achievement: Demonstrated how passionate people are about even the most trivial bathroom issues
True Story: In the mid-1980s, Landers innocently printed a letter raising the issue of whether toilet paper should come off the top or the bottom of the roll, in her advice column. A flood of letters ensued. In fact, Landers revealed in 1986 that, "in 31 years, this question has been the most controversial" of all the issues ever raised in the column. Her own conclusion: The paper should come over the top. Why? "Fine quality toilet paper has designs that are right side up," she explained.

Honorees: Paul and Virginia Alee of Boulder, Colorado
Notable Achievement: Solved—once and for all—the "top or bottom" toilet paper issue (see above)
True Story: The couple couldn't agree. So, "when we built our house," they told the *Rocky Mountain News*, "we had the builder put two dispensers in each bathroom, with one unrolling in one direction, and the other rolling in the other direction. The builder told us he got more contracts as a result of showing our home to the public than any other 'show home' they'd ever put on display."

Honoree: A Halifax bar called "Number 15"
Notable Achievement: The only pub in England built in a public restroom
True Story: Halifax is considered the pub capital of Britain. According to news reports, there are more pubs per household than anywhere in the country. "The local paper, the *Evening Courier*, even boasts its own Pub Correspondent." The demand for pubs is so strong that when an underground public lavatory became available, someone bought it and converted it into a pub called W.C.'s. When it was recently sold, the name was changed to Number 15. (*Ed. note:* Why not Number 2?)

Honoree: Edmond Rostand (1868–1918)
Notable Achievement: Author of the most famous play ever written in a bathroom
True Story: Rostand didn't like to be rude to his friends, but didn't like to be interrupted when he was working either. Rather than risk having to turn away any friends who might drop by to visit, "he took refuge in his bathtub and wrote there all day." His biggest bathroom success: *Cyrano de Bergerac.*

Honoree: Yang Zhu, a young mother in China
Notable Achievement: Gave birth in a train bathroom...and lost the baby down the toilet (she got it back).
True Story: Yang Zhu was nine months pregnant and headed home by train on May 4, 1999, when she began to suffer stomach pains. Her husband took her to the washroom where, "to her great surprise," she gave birth to her first child into the toilet "as soon as she squatted down....The panic-stricken and screaming Yang ripped off the umbilical cord with her hands, and the baby immediately slipped down through the toilet and fell onto the rails."

Three security guards spotted the baby, covered in blood and lying in the middle of the tracks, but before they could reach him, another train sped by right over him. Miraculously, he only had slight bruises and a small cut on his head that needed three stitches.

The Arctic tern flies as far as 10,500 miles when it migrates.

THE ORIGIN OF THE FORK

Of the three eating utensils we normally use, only forks have a modern origin. Knives and spoons are prehistoric—but as recently as 1800, forks weren't commonly used in America. Some food for thought...

KNIVES, BUT NO FORKS

Centuries ago, few people had ever heard of a "place setting." When a large piece of meat was set on the table (sometimes on a platter, sometimes directly on the table), diners grabbed the whole thing with their free hand...then pulled out a knife and sliced off a piece with the other hand. Most eating was done with fingers: Common people ate with all five, while nobles—who understood sophisticated table manners—ate with only three (thumb, forefinger, and middle).

At that time, there were no utensils. In fact, most men owned just one multipurpose blade, which, in addition to carving food, was used for fighting, hunting, and butchering animals. But wealthy nobles had always been able to afford a different knife for each purpose, and by the Middle Ages, they had developed a setting of *two* knives, for very formal dining. One knife was thrust into a large piece of meat to hold it in place on a plate, while the second was used to cut off a smaller piece, which the eater speared and placed in his mouth.

FORKS

One of the drawbacks of cutting a piece of meat while holding it in place with a knife is that the meat has tendency to "rotate in place like a wheel on an axle," Henry Petroski writes in *The Evolution of Useful Things*. "Frustration with knives, especially their shortcomings in holding meat steady for cutting, eventually led to the development of the fork." The name comes from *furca*, the Latin word for a farmer's pitchfork.

The first fork commonly used in Europe was a miniature version of the big carving fork used to spear turkeys and roasts in the kitchen. It had only two "tines" or prongs, spaced far enough apart

---

King George I of England (1714–1727) was German. He couldn't speak a word of English.

to hold meat meat in place while cutting it; but apparently it was not something you stuck in your mouth and ate with—that was still the knife's job.

A FOOLISH UTENSIL
These first table forks probably originated at the royal courts of the Middle East, where they were in use as early as the seventh century. About A.D. 1100 they appeared in the Tuscany region of Italy, but they were considered "shocking novelties," and were ridiculed and condemned by the clergy—who insisted that "only human fingers, created by God, were worthy to touch God's bounty." Forks were "effeminate pieces of finery," as one historian puts it, used by sinners and sissies but not by decent, God-fearing folk.

"An Italian historian recorded a dinner at which a Venetian noblewoman used a fork of her own design," Charles Panati writes in *The Extraordinary Origins of Everyday Things*, "and incurred the rebuke of several clerics present for her "excessive sign of refinement.' The woman died days after the meal, supposedly from the plague, but clergymen preached that her death was divine punishment, a warning to others contemplating the affectation of a fork."

FORK YOU
Thanks to these derogatory associations, more than 250 years passed before forks finally came into wide use in Italy. In the rest of Europe they were still virtually unheard of. Catherine de Medici finally brought them to France in the 1500s when she became queen. And in 1608 an Englisman named Thomas Coryate traveled to Italy and saw people eating with forks; the sight was so peculiar that he made note of it in his book *Crudities Hastily Cobbled Up in Five Months:*

The Italians...do always at their meals use a little fork when they cut their meat....Should [anyone] unadvisedly touch the dish of meat with his fingers from which all at the table do cut, he will give occasion of offense unto the company, as having trangressed the laws of good manners, insomuch that for his error he shall be at least browbeaten if not reprehended in words....The Italian cannot by any means indure to have his dish touched with fingers, seeing all men's fingers are not alike clean.

Coryate brought some forks with him to England and presented one to Queen Elizabeth, who was so thrilled by the utensil that she had additional ones made from gold, coral, and crystal. But they remained little more than a pretentious fad of the royal court.

Forks became more common during the late 17th century, but it wasn't until the 18th century that they were widely used in continental Europe as a means for conveying food "from plate to mouth." The reason: French nobles saw forks as a way to distinguish themselves from commoners. "The fork became a symbol of luxury, refinement, and status," writes Charles Panati. "Suddenly, to touch food with even three bare fingers was gauche." A new custom developed—when an invitation to dinner was received, a servant frequently was sent ahead with a fine leather case containing a knife, fork, and spoon to be used at dinner later.

Making a New Point
But before this revolution took place, the fork had to be redesigned. The first forks were completely useless when it came to scooping peas and other loose food into the mouth—the gap between the two tines was too large. So cutlery makers began adding a third tine to their forks, and by the early eighteenth century, a fourth. "Four appears to have been the optimum [number]," Henry Petroski writes in *The Evolution of Useful Things*. "Four tines provide a relatively broad surface and yet do not feel too wide for the mouth. Nor does a four-tined fork have so many tines that it resembles a comb, or function like one when being pressed into a piece of meat."

Coming to America
One of the last places the fork caught on in the Western world was colonial America. In fact, forks weren't commonly used by the average citizen until the time of the Civil War; until then, people just ate with knives or their fingers. In 1828, for example, the English writer Frances Trollope wrote of some generals, colonels, and majors aboard a Mississippi steamboat who had "the frightful manner of feeding with their knives, till the whole blade seemed to enter the mouth." And as late as 1864, one etiquette manual complained that "many persons hold forks awkwardly, as if not accustomed to them."

MODERN MYTHOLOGY

*These mythological characters may be as famous
in our culture as Hercules or Pegasus were in ancient Greece.
Here's where they came from.*

NIPPER (THE RCA DOG). Nipper, a fox terrier, was originally owned by the brother of English painter Francis Barroud; when the brother died, Francis inherited the dog. According to legend, when a recording of the brother's voice was played at his funeral, the dog recognized his master's voice and looked into the horn of the phonograph. "Barroud depicted this incident in a painting that showed his brother's coffin, with the dog sitting on top listening to the Victrola. The image (minus the coffin, of course) became the symbol of RCA Victor."

PAUL BUNYAN. Paul Bunyan is commonly thought to be a character from traditional folklore, but he is actually what is known as "fakelore"—"an ersatz creation developed to meet the American need for instant homegrown folk heroes." Paul Bunyan was actually created in 1920 by an advertising agent named W.B. Laughead, to serve as a fictional spokesperson for the Red River Lumber company. "As such," Richard Shenkman writes in *Legends, Lies and Cherished Myths of American History*, "Paul is about as authentic a folk hero as Mr. Clean or the Jolly Green Giant— that is to say, not very authentic at all."

SPUDS MacKENZIE. "Some guy in our Chicago agency drew a rough sketch of a dog called the Party Animal, for a Bud Light poster," Anheuser-Busch's marketing director told *Sports Illustrated*. "So we had to find a real dog that looked like this drawing." They picked Honey Tree Evil Eye, a female English bull terrier. The poster was only supposed to be distributed to college students, but "orders for the poster of this strange-looking dog were monumental. We still can't explain it. It's like everything else in advertising. You just hope you get it right, but you never know for sure." After Spuds made his (her) TV debut during the 1987 Super Bowl, Bud Light sales shot up 20%. But Spuds was retired in controversy a few years later when Anheuser-Busch was accused of using him (her) to encourage underage drinking.

THE TACO BELL CHIHUAHUA. The most famous fast-food character of the 1990s was invented by chance, when two advertising executives named Chuck Bennett and Clay Williams were eating lunch at the Tortilla Grill in Venice, California. "We saw a little Chihuahua run by that appeared to be on a mission," Bennett says. "We both looked at each other and said, 'That would be funny.'"

THE CALIFORNIA RAISINS. In 1986 California raisin growers were facing a double whammy: declining raisin sales *and* a bumper raisin harvest coming—which would depress prices. So the California Raisin Board asked their ad agency, Foote, Cone & Belding, to come up with a campaign to help increase sales. The agency turned the assignment over to two young copywriters, Seth Werner and Dexter Fedor…who couldn't think of anything. One evening they confessed their worries to some friends. "We'll probably do something stupid like have raisins sing 'Oh, I Heard it Through the Grapevine,'" Werner told the friends. That got a laugh…so the next morning Werner and Fedor began thinking about really doing the commercial that way—never realizing what a huge hit the characters would become. "No one can really explain the idea," Werner says. "In fact, the more people try to put their finger on it, the stupider it sounds."

Our Little Secret: In most press reports, Claymation pioneer Will Vinton, who filmed the ads, is credited with creating the raisin characters. But the truth is—and you'll never read this anywhere but here—by the time Vinton was hired, the raisins were already designed. The artist who designed them, Michael Brunsfeld, has also created every *Bathroom Reader* cover.

Fedor and Werner didn't have any idea what the raisins should look like, and Brunsfeld, a director at Colossal Pictures, submitted a design for an animated test commercial. "Raisins were difficult to make into appealing characters," Michael recalls. "It was like putting eyes on a wrinkled blob." The solution: Drawing them in the "rubber hose" style of the '30s and giving them oversized sneakers for balance. "That made them feel loose and funky." By the time the test ad was done, everything was in place. Vinton could just copy it. Everyone else got rich from the ads—but all Brunsfeld got were the original drawings—which are mounted on his wall today.

HONK IF YOU LOVE PEACE AND QUIET

Every year, BRI member Debbie Thornton sends in a list of real-life bumper stickers. Have you seen the one that says...

When everything's coming your way, you're in the wrong lane and driving against traffic.

A DAY WITHOUT SUNSHINE IS LIKE NIGHT.

You never really learn to swear until you learn to drive.

If you think nobody cares, try missing a couple of payments.

Originality is the art of concealing your sources.

You have the right to remain silent.

Shin—Device for finding furniture in the dark

WHICH IS THE NONSMOKING LIFEBOAT?

COLE'S LAW: Thinly sliced cabbage.

Experience is something you don't get until just after you need it.

I CAN RESIST ANYTHING BUT TEMPTATION

No sense being pessimistic. It wouldn't work anyway.

I intend to live forever. So far, so good.

You're just jealous because the voices only talk to me.

DYSLEXICS OF THE WORLD, UNTIE.

Beauty is in the eye of the beer holder.

Be nice to your kids. They'll choose your nursing home.

Clones are people two.

Does the name Pavlov ring a bell?

EVER STOP TO THINK, AND FORGET TO START AGAIN?

If you can read this, I can slam on my brakes and sue you.

It's all relative: Belgium is about the same size as New Jersey.

TRUTH IN ADVERTISING

Did you laugh when you read this title? Well, okay, we agree—it is an oxymoron. And here's some proof.

THE AD SAID: The Coors Brewing Company was launching its "Pure Water 2000 Campaign" in the late 1980s, "Because it was the right thing to do." The company's 1990 annual report stated: "Pete Coors [great-grandson of company founder Adolph Coors] personally kicked off the Coors Pure Water 2000 program, a national commitment to help clean up America's rivers, streams, and lakes." TV and print ads showed him "standing streamside, extolling the virtues of clean water."

IN THE REAL WORLD: The *Denver Post* reported that Coors "officially became a toxic criminal on October 12, 1990, when they pleaded guilty to violating state environmental law by illegally pumping industrial solvents into Clear Creek from 1976 to 1989."

• And when a massive Coors beer spill wiped out all of the fish in a 5.2-mile stretch of the creek in 1991, company head Bill Coors told shareholders it was no big deal—the fish were only "junk fish," and Clear Creek "was not a prime fishing stream."

THE ADS SAID: 140 different retailers—including cruise lines, expensive stores, chic gift boutiques, and resort destinations "don't take American Express." So bring your Visa card.

IN THE REAL WORLD: "Some of the featured partners, Carnival Cruise Lines among them, took American Express until just before they appeared in Visa's commercials," The *Wall St. Journal* reported in 1999. "And, after reaping the national publicity at Visa's expense, quietly resumed taking American Express. Others didn't even go that far: 'We never really stopped taking Amex fully,' says Les Otten, chairman of American Skiing Company."

THE AD SAID: In 1999 American Express ran a "reality" TV commercial featuring a man named Robert H. Tompkins, identi-

---

If any of the heads of Mt. Rushmore had a body, it would be nearly 500 feet tall.

fied as a card member since 1958. "Do you know me?" he asks
viewers, then answers, "Probably not." The ad goes on to give
viewers a glimpse of his life story: Tompkins moved to Paris 40
years ago to learn about wine, where he fell in love and became a
vintner. In a voiceover, he thanks American Express for being
there "even in the worst of times," as an air raid siren sounds and
black-and-white footage of a tank rolling through the streets fills
the screen. "Not to worry," an American Express representative
tells him over the phone, "We've found a way to get you out."
IN THE REAL WORLD: "While there really is a Mr. Tompkins, he really is an American Express card holder, and he gave his
consent to use his name in the ad, American Express later admitted that...none of the events depicted in the commercial had
actually happened to him, not even one."

...Well, then, what was Mr. Tompkins' life really like? Hard to
say—according to news reports, American Express "declined to
give any further information about Mr. Tompkins."

AND MORE CLASSIC MOMENTS OF TRUTH...
• "Green Giant was ordered to tell consumers its 'American Mixture' variety of frozen vegetables is a product of Mexico."

• "Fabergé Company was fined because its ad campaign promising
'Now: More Brut!' was for a product containing less Brut than
previous versions."

• "Allstate Insurance apologized for sending letters praising an
agent as a winner of Allstate's 'Quality Agent Award' when the
man had just been banned from the business in the largest agent
misconduct case in California history."

• The John Hancock insurance company launched an advertising
campaign featuring "real people in real situations." When a journalist asked to speak to these real people, a company spokesperson
conceded that they were actors and 'in that sense they are not real
people.'"

• "A New Jersey company was charged with fraud because its
'secret' hair replacement technique turned out to be sewing
toupees to men's scalps."

—The San Francisco Examiner

Most destructive car chase ever filmed: *The Junkman* (1982); 150 cars were destroyed.

MILITARY SURPLUS: THE STORY OF CARROT CAKE

Our good friend Jeff Cheek has been writing about food ever since he left the CIA (the spy agency, not the food institute—no kidding!). He wrote this column for a local newspaper; we decided it was worth sharing with all our BRI members.

THE FRUIT MAN

George C. Page was a Nebraska farm boy who arrived in Los Angeles in the mid-1920s with a dream…and $2.30 in his pocket. He found a job as a busboy/dishwasher and worked double shifts until he'd saved $1,000. Then he rented a vacant store and founded Mission-Pak, shipping exotic Southern California fruits as holiday gifts. It was an overnight success. Ten years later, he was a millionaire, with eight packing plants and over a thousand workers.

In 1941, after the Japanese bombed Pearl Harbor, Page volunteered for active duty. He discovered, however, that the government had classified him as an "essential industrialist," and wouldn't let him serve in the military. Instead, they arranged for him to go to the University of California at Berkeley to learn how to dehydrate vegetables. With German submarines sinking our ships, every shipload had to count. Dehydration, and rehydration after delivery, seemed like the answer.

WAR SURPLUS

When the atomic bomb brought the Pacific war to an end, Page's government contracts were canceled. He was left with thousands of five-gallon cans of dehydrated carrots…and no place to sell them.

Page went back to his old boss at the restaurant where he'd started out. They tried everything. Baked carrots. Stewed carrots. Fried carrots. No luck; customers sent these tasteless dishes back. Finally, they dumped a few cups of shredded dried carrots into a cake mix. It was an instant hit. Other restaurants and bakeries wanted to add carrot cake to their menus. Page sold them five-gallon cans of dehydrated carrots, along with a printed recipe for carrot cake. Within a few months he'd gotten rid of his surplus carrots, and carrot cake was being served as dessert all over America.

IT'S A WEIRD, WEIRD WORLD

Proof that truth really is stranger than fiction.

THAT VOODOO THAT YOU DO

"When her seventh-grade students refused to calm down, Monique Bazile, a substitute teacher in Irvington, New Jersey, threatened to burn down their houses and performed voodoo, causing some children to complain of itching."

—*Esquire,* **January 1993**

BEAN COUNTER

"A Nairobi physician, after removing a bean from a young girl's ear, jammed it back in when her parents came up short on cash for the $6 operation."

—**"The Edge,"** *Oregonian*

DUCK, DUCK, GOOSE

"A Tulsa, Oklahoma, physician, writing in a 1992 issue of the *Irish Journal of Psychological Medicine*, reported on a 32-year-old woman whose neighbors had a large satellite dish installed in their yard. The woman became convinced she was being wooed by Donald Duck and that the dish was put there to facilitate his communicating with her. After 'hovering' around the dish, she eventually undressed and climbed into it...where she later said she consummated marriage to Mr. Duck."

—*News of the Weird*

JUST CALL ME DAFFY

"A Wisconsin psychiatrist was accused of malpractice by one of his patients, Nadean Cool, who claimed he had convinced her that she had 120 separate personalities, including that of a duck, and then billed her health-care provider $300,000 for group therapy."

—**TV** *Guide*

"THE BLAST BLASTED BLUBBER BEYOND ALL BELIEVABLE BOUNDS"

We at the BRI are always on the lookout for great urban legends. For years the tale of the Exploding Whale has floated around the Internet. But it's not an urban legend—it's 100% true. Here's the story:

A WHALE OF A PROBLEM

How do you get rid of a 45-foot-long stinking dead whale? That was the bizarre question George Thornton had to answer on the morning of November 12, 1970. A few days earlier, an eight-ton rotting sperm whale carcass had washed ashore on a Florence, Oregon, beach, and the responsibility fell on Thornton—assistant highway engineer for the Oregon State Highway Division—to remove it. His options were limited. He couldn't bury the rapidly decomposing corpse on site because the tides would soon uncover it, creating a health hazard for beachgoers. And because of the whale's overpowering stench, his workers refused to cut it up and transport it elsewhere. He also couldn't burn it. So what could he do? Thornton came up with an unbelievable solution: blow the whale up with dynamite.

WHALE WATCHING

Thornton's expectation was that the whale's body would be nearly disintegrated by the explosion, and he assumed that if any small chunks of whale landed on the beach, scavengers like seagulls and crabs would consume them. Indeed, many seagulls had been hovering around the corpse all week.

Thornton had the dynamite placed on the leeward side of the whale, so that the blast would hopefully propel the whale pieces toward the water. Thorton said, "Well, I'm confident that it'll work. The only thing is we're not sure how much explosives it'll take to disintegrate the thing." He settled on 20 cases—half a ton of dynamite.

As workers piled case upon case of explosives underneath the whale, spectators swarmed around it to have their pictures taken—

upwind, of course—in front of the immense carcass, right near a massive gash where someone had hacked away the beast's lower jaw. Even after officials herded the crowds a full quarter of a mile away for safety, about 75 stubborn spectators stuck around, most of them equipped with binoculars and telephoto lenses. After almost two hours of installing explosives, Thornton and his crew were finally ready to blow up a whale. He gave the signal to push in the plunger.

THAR SHE BLOWS!

The amazing events that followed are best described through the eye of a local TV news camera that captured the episode on tape. The whale suddenly erupts into a 100-foot-tall plume of sand and blubber. "Oohs" and "aahs" are heard from the bystanders as whale fragments scatter in the air. Then, a woman's voice breaks out of the crowd's chattering: "Here come pieces of…*WHALE!*" Splattering noises of whale chunks hitting the ground grew louder, as onlookers scream and scurry out of the way. In the words of Paul Linnman, a Portland TV reporter on the scene, "The humor of the entire situation suddenly gave way to a run for survival as huge chunks of whale blubber fell everywhere."

For several minutes after the blast, it rained blubber particles. Fortunately, no one was hurt by the falling chunks, but everyone—and everything—on the scene was coated with foul-smelling, vaporized whale. The primary victim of the blubber was an Oldsmobile owned by Springfield businessman Walter Umenhofer, parked well over a quarter of a mile away from the explosion. The car's roof was completely caved in by a large slab of blubber. As he watched a highway worker remove the three-by-five foot hunk with a shovel, a stunned Umenhofer remarked, "My insurance company's never going to believe this."

THE AFTERMATH

Down at the blast site, the only thing the dynamite had gotten rid of were the seagulls. They were either scared away by the blast or repulsed by the awful stench, which didn't matter because most of the pieces of blubber lying around were far too large for them to eat. The beach was littered with huge chunks of ripe whale, including the whale's entire tail and a giant slab of mangled whale meat that never left the blast site. And the smell was actually worse than before.

Thornton had hoped his work was done, but it was just beginning—he and his workers spent the rest of the day burying their mistake. His blunder drew the attention of news stations all over the country, but amazingly, he was promoted just six months later.

Twenty-five years later, the tale of the exploding whale is documented all over the Internet. And the Oregon Highway Division still gets calls about it today—many callers hoping to get their hands on the video. The whale is still dead, but the story took on a life of its own.

* * *

ASK THE EXPERTS

The Heart Was Taken
Q: *Why do people cross their fingers for good luck?*
A: "The practice may have evolved from the sign of the cross, which was believed to ward off evil." (From *The Book of Answers*, by Barbara Berliner)

Yee-Haw!
Q: *In movie Westerns, people fire guns straight up into the air as warning shots or just to make noise during a celebration. But those bullets have to come down somewhere. How dangerous will they be if they hit somebody?*
A: "Physics tells us that when it hits the ground the bullet will have the same velocity it had when it left the muzzle of the pistol, 700 to 800 mph. But that ignores air resistance. Realistically, the bullet's landing speed can be around 100 to 150 mph. That's more than enough speed to do serious or lethal damage to a cranial landing site.

"And by the way, the jerk who fires the bullet isn't very likely to be hit by it. In one experiment, out of 500 machine-gun bullets fired straight upward, only 4 landed within 10 feet (3 meters) of the gun. Wind has a great effect, since bullets can reach altitudes of 4,000 to 8,000 feet (1,200 to 2,400 meters) before falling back down. (From *What Einstein Told His Barber*, by Robert. L. Wolke)

BOX-OFFICE BLOOPERS

We all love bloopers. Here are a bunch of movie mistakes to look for in popular films. You can find more in a book called Roman Soldiers Don't Wear Watches: 333 Film Flubs, *by Bill Givens.*

Movie: *Terminator 2: Judgment Day* (1991)
Scene: As Arnold Schwarzenegger's cyborg character heads toward a bar, he passes a parked car.
Blooper: Arnie's cranial read-out says the car he's scanning is a Plymouth sedan. It's actually a Ford.

Movie: *Forrest Gump* (1994)
Scene: In a sequence set around 1970, someone is shown reading a copy of *USA Today*.
Blooper: The newspaper wasn't created until 1982.

Movie: *Camelot* (1967)
Scene: King Arthur (Richard Harris) expounds on the joys of his mythical kingdom.
Blooper: The 6th-century king has a 20th-century Band-Aid on the back of his neck.

Movie: *Wayne's World* (1992)
Scene: Wayne and Garth are filming their cable access show.
Blooper: The exterior shot of the house shows it's night. Look out the window of the interior shot: it's daytime.

Movie: *The Invisible Man* (1933)
Scene: Claude Rains, in the title role, strips completely naked and uses his invisibility to elude police.
Blooper: The police track his footprints in the snow. But check out the footprints—they're made by feet wearing shoes.

Movie: *Field of Dreams* (1989)
Scene: Shoeless Joe Jackson is shown batting right-handed.
Blooper: The real Shoeless Joe was left-handed.

Movie: *The Wizard of Oz* (1939)

Scene: Before the Wicked Witch of the West sends her flying monkeys to capture Dorothy and friends in the Haunted Forest, she tells the head monkey that she has "sent a little insect on ahead to take the fight out of them." What does she mean by that? She's referring to a song-and-dance sequence featuring "The Jitterbug," a bug that causes its victims to dance wildly until they are exhausted.

Blooper: The sequence was cut from the film before its release.

Movie: *Face-Off* (1997)

Scene: The hero (John Travolta) learns that a bomb is about to go off somewhere. But where? He's got six days to pry the information from the villain. We then see the bomb—it shows 216 hours.

Blooper: Do the math: 216 hours equals *nine* days. Did someone forget to tell us we've gone to 36-hour days?

Movie: *Entrapment* (1999)

Scene: Catherine Zeta-Jones's character says she needs 10 seconds to download computer files that will steal billions of dollars from an international bank. She states further that after 11:00 p.m. her computer will steal 1/10th of a second every minute, totaling ten seconds by midnight.

Blooper: More Hollywood math: One-tenth of a second per minute for 60 minutes equals only six seconds...four shy of the required ten.

Movie: *The Story of Robin Hood* (1952)

Scene: In one scene, Maid Marian (played by Joan Rice) wears a dress with a zipper in the back.

Blooper: Did they have zippers in the 12th century?

Movie: *Wild Wild West* (1999)

Scene: After thwarting the plans of the evil Loveless (Kenneth Branagh), Jim West (Will Smith) and Artemus Gordon (Kevin Kline) ride off into the sunset heading back to Washington, D.C.

Blooper: A romantic notion, but impossible: Washington is in the east and the sun sets in the west.

CELEBRITY GOSSIP

Here's our cheesy tabloid section—a
bunch of gossip about famous people.

LUCIANO PAVAROTTI

When Pavarotti performs for the public, he only does so under very strict conditions. His contract states that during sound check, "there must be no distinct smells anywhere near the artist." In his dressing room, he demands that all sofas be mounted on six-inch risers and that "soft toilet paper" be provided. As for his hotel accommodations, he insists that "the master bedroom must always be kept in total darkness." He refuses to go onstage for a performance before he finds a bent nail somewhere on the stage and pulls it out.

MARLON BRANDO

While filming the 2001 movie *The Score*, Brando refused to be on the set at the same time as director Frank Oz. Brando referred to Oz as "Miss Piggy" (Oz provided the voice of Muppet Miss Piggy many years ago) and teased him with lines like "Don't you wish I was a puppet, so you could control me." Robert De Niro was forced to direct Brando instead, with Oz giving him instructions via headset.

WALT DISNEY

Before Walt Disney's 35th birthday, his brother Roy encouraged employees to throw the boss a surprise party. Two of the animators thought it would be hilarious to make a short movie of Mickey and Minnie Mouse "consummating their relationship." When Disney saw the animation at the party, he feigned laughter and playfully asked who made it. As soon as the two animators came forward, he fired them on the spot and left.

SERENA WILLIAMS

According to London's *Metro* newspaper, tennis star Serena Williams claims to have a six-hour-a-day online shopping addiction. Even while competing in the French Open, she was "stuck" online buying things she didn't need. The source of her compulsion: fame has forced her to avoid shopping in public.

During WWII, the Oscar statue was made of plaster—metal was an essential wartime material.

WIDE WORLD OF BATHROOM NEWS

Here are bits and pieces of bathroom trivia we've flushed out of the newspapers of the world over the past couple of years.

GERMANY

Germany's Defense Ministry, which is looking for ways to reduce the country's military costs, has asked soldiers to use less toilet paper. "Lavatory paper is not always used just in the lavatory, it is often also used to wipe things up," a spokespeson explained. "We are asking people to think before they wipe."

UNITED STATES ABROAD

Haliburton, the oil services company that Dick Cheney headed before resigning to run for vice president, admitted during the 2000 presidential campaign that the company "maintains separate restrooms overseas for its American and foreign employees." The company defended its separate-but-equal restroom policy, saying it was done for "cultural reasons," and that Cheney was "unaware" of the practice during his five years as chief executive.

ENGLAND

• The Westminster City Council has decided to erect open-air urinals next to the National Gallery in Trafalgar Square. "Nighttime revelers, waiting at a bus stop outside the gallery, have been relieving themselves against the new wing," the council said in a press release. "The gallery now fears that the stone of the building is being affected by uric acid. Urinals will be placed in problem areas where 'wet spots' have been identified."

• From Scotland Yard: "The Department of Professional Standards is investigating an incivility charge arising from the search of a home under the Misuse of Drugs Act. An allegation has been received from a person in the house that one of the male officers broke wind and did not apologize to the family for his action. The complainant felt it was rude and unprofessional."

Weird coincidence: Ex-presidents Thomas Jefferson and John Adams both died on July 4, 1826.

CHINA

Archaeologists exploring the tomb of a king of the Western Han dynasty (206 B.C. to 24 A.D.) have unearthed what they believe is the world's oldest flush toilet, one that predates the earliest European water closet by as much as 1,800 years. The toilet, which boasts a stone seat, a drain for running water, and even an armrest, "is the earliest of its kind ever discovered in the world," the archaeologists told China's official Xinhua news agency, "meaning that the Chinese flushed first."

MEXICO

In June 2001, the *Milenio* daily newspaper revealed Mexican president Vicente Fox, who was elected on an anticorruption platform, has furnished the Los Pinos presidential palace with "specially embroidered" bath towels that cost $400 apiece. But they're just a tiny part of the more than $400,000 worth of household items that Fox has purchased during his first six months in office. President Fox admitted to the expenditures and even praised their disclosure by *Milenio*, citing the article as "evidence of progress in bringing transparency to government spending." (The minimum wage in Mexico, where 40 million people live in poverty, is about $132 a month.)

NIGERIA

A Nigerian housewife has reported seeing an apparition of the Virgin Mary in the window of her bathroom in the city of Lagos. "I walked into the bathroom at about five a.m. and was shocked and overwhelmed by fear with the visible appearance of the Virgin Mary," Christiana Ejambi told reporters. Since then the Blessed Virgin has reappeared several times and has given Ejambi messages on a number of subjects, including religious faith and how to control the crowds that have gathered to witness the miracle. Per the instructions of the Virgin Mary, only three people are allowed into the restroom at a time; everyone else has to wait their turn.

*   *   *

"Red meat is *not* bad for you. Now blue-green meat, *that's* bad for you." —Tommy Smothers

On any given day, half the people in the world will eat rice.

TIMOTHY DEXTER: AMERICA'S LUCKIEST IDIOT

Have you ever thought about someone: "How could anybody so stupid be so successful?" If not, you will after you read this story from Zanies: The World's Greatest Eccentrics, *by Jay Robert Nash.*

KING MIDAS

Born in Malden, Massachusetts, on January 22, 1747, Timothy Dexter worked first as a farmer, and then, in Boston, became an apprentice leather tanner. At age 20, with his life's savings in his pocket, all of nine dollars, he moved on to the thriving town of Newburyport, where he met and married a wealthy widow, 31-year-old Elizabeth Frothingham.

Dexter fancied himself a shrewd businessman. Using his wife's money, he copied what other businessmen were doing—he bought stocks. With no understanding of which stocks to buy, he simply bought cheap ones. Somehow, their values rose and Dexter was able to sell at a profit.

Competitors laughed at the semi-illiterate Dexter and amused themselves by giving him lunatic business tips. One merchant told Dexter that the West Indies, where colonization was booming, was sorely in need of warming pans, mittens and Bibles.

Having no idea of the extremely hot weather in the West Indies, Dexter took the tip and proceeded to buy more than 40,000 warming pans, 40,000 pairs of mittens, and 40,000 Bibles and shipped them out. He then waited for fortune to smile on him.

DUMB LUCK

By incredible luck, when Dexter's shipments arrived in the West Indies, there was a religious movement beginning, and his Bibles were purchased at a 100% profit. More luck: A fleet of Russian trading ships visiting ports in the West Indies had their agents immediately buy up the mittens to the last pair. The warming pans sat idly in a warehouse until some inventive planter discovered that they made ideal skimmers with which molasses could be ladled into vats—each and every pan was sold for a profit. These

---

What did Christopher Columbus look like? No one knows—his portrait was never painted.

incredible sales brought Dexter an estimated $150,000, making him enormously wealthy.

CARRYING COAL TO NEWCASTLE

Jealous of Dexter's dumb luck, merchants in his town purposely sought to ruin him by urging him to invest every dime he possessed in shipping coal to Newcastle, England. The unschooled Dexter, not knowing that Newcastle was the center of England's coal-mining industry, hired scores of sailing ships, filled their holds with soft Virginia coal and sent the cargoes to England.

But instead of becoming an international laughingstock, Dexter's amazing good fortune held; a massive strike in Newcastle had left mines empty and there was a shortage of coal in the area. When Dexter's ships arrived, his coal was purchased at enormous profits, making him twice as rich as he had been.

INCREASING ODDITIES

As he grew older, Dexter became more and more eccentric. His wife, Elizabeth, constantly nagged him about his foolish ways. Instead of arguing with her, Dexter pretended that she had died and that her presence in his sprawling mansion was no more than an apparition. When visitors arrived, Dexter would point to her and say: "This is Mrs. Dexter, the ghost that was my wife."

The zenith of Dexter's eccentricities was reached when he decided to publish his memoirs, entitled *A Pickle for the Knowing Ones, or Plain Truths in a Homespun Dress*. The book was, from beginning to end, one long, incoherent sentence, without a single punctuation mark.

Dexter ordered the printing of thousands of copies and had them widely distributed. Few read the book and those who did ridiculed Dexter as a rich buffoon, a self-indulgent idiot who naively destroyed the English language in an expensive fit of egomania. The lack of punctuation in the memoirs was repeatedly pointed out to Dexter as the crowning glory of his moronic gestures.

REVISIONIST

Dexter answered his critics in a revised edition of *A Pickle for the Knowing Ones* some years later. He had the following page reproduced in the second edition:

mister printer the Nowing ones complane of my book the fust
edition had no stops I put in A Nuf here and thay may peper
and solt it as they plese

,,,;;;;;;

;;

....!!!!!!!!!!!!!!!!!!!!!!!!!!!!...

....!!!!!!!!!!!!!!!!!!!!!!!!!!!!!!..

....!..

....................,,

,,,,,,,,,,,,,,,,,...............................????????????????????????????..................

....

As a final display of Dexter's golden touch, the book is now considered a valuable collector's item.

*　　　*　　　*

MENCKEN'S OBSERVATIONS ON DEMOCRACY

*H.L. Mencken (1880–1956) was a writer, editor, and critic
for Baltimore newspapers and one of America's wittiest,
and most opinionated political commentators.*

1. Democracy is the theory that intelligence is dangerous. It
assumes that no idea can be safe until those who can't understand
it have approved it.

2. Democracy is the theory that two thieves will steal less than
one.

3. It is a bit hoggish, but it might be worse. It will be centuries
before we are ready for anything better.

4. The principal virtue of democracy is that it makes a good
show—one incomparably bizarre, amazing, shocking, and obscene.

5. Democracy is the liberty of the have-nots. Its aim is to destroy
the liberty of the haves.

6. Democracy is a sort of laughing gas. It will not cure anything,
perhaps, but it unquestionably stops the pain.

7. The Fathers who invented it, if they could return from Hell,
would never recognize it. It was conceived as a free government of
free men; it has become simply a battle of charlatans for the votes
of idiots.

TRUE CONFESSIONS

Confessions so obviously true, they're kind of embarrassing.

ACROSS

- **1** City transport
- **4** Actress Lara Flynn ___
- **9** Not frazzled
- **13** Razor brand
- **15** Painter's prop
- **16** SSS designation
- **17** He said: "I never wanted to be famous; I only wanted to be great."
- **19** Duo
- **20** On cloud nine
- **21** Casual kind of room
- **23** Loose
- **24** Opera's male lead, usually
- **25** Date
- **27** TMC alternative
- **29** He said: "I'm not smart enough to lie."
- **34** Bilko, for one (abbr.)
- **37** Astronaut Slayton
- **38** Prominent

39 Tigger's pal
41 Candlelight watch
43 Membership fees
44 Use sandpaper
46 Billy and Daniel's more famous brother
48 Harden
49 He said: "Sometimes, at the end of the day when I'm smiling and shaking hands, I want to kick them."
52 ___ radio
53 Polished off
54 Reggae fan, perhaps
58 Cooling machines, fo short
60 Pick up the tab
62 Island off the coast of China
63 Splotch
65 He said: "I left high school a virgin."
68 Sweater Girl Turner
69 It may cause tears in the kitchen
70 Jib, for one
71 Nervous
72 Had in mind
73 AAA suggestion

DOWN
1 Insertion symbol
2 "And thereby hangs ___"
3 Singer Adams
4 Droplet
5 Boathouse item
6 Fashion monogram
7 Looked lasciviously
8 Otherwise
9 Swipe
10 Comparable
11 *Star Wars* princess

12 Chico or Karl
14 Thespian
18 King of Judea
22 Wolfgang Puck, e.g.
25 H.H. Munro's pen name
26 Adjective for Grace Kelly
28 Brass or rubber follower
30 When pigs fly
31 Pricey timepiece
32 Suit to ___
33 Digs made of twigs
34 Practice punching
35 Desert in Mongolia
36 Chanteuse's offering
40 A couple of laughs
42 Tennis ace Nastase
45 Humid
47 Kind of reef
50 The start of something new
51 Carpenter's mouthful, maybe
55 Say "*%#$&!"
56 Unspoken but understood
57 It's at risk in stiletto heels
58 Competent
59 Dressed (in)
61 Speck
62 It may be pitched at night
64 ___ of Pigs
66 Soon-Yi's mom
67 Junior

ANSWER, PAGE 369

UNUSUAL INVENTIONS

*Here's living proof that the urge to invent something—anything—
is more powerful than the urge to make sure that the invention
will be something that people will actually want to use.*

The Invention: Personal Sound Muffler
What It Does: Have you ever wanted to scream in the
middle of a crowded room? With this device, you can...
without disturbing others. About the size of a dust mask, the
muffler's interior is made of sound-absorbing foam, with a saddle-
shaped opening that seals tightly to the user's face. Extra bonus:
"A microphone mounted at the bottom of the muffler activates a
light, giving the user immediate visual feedback as to the intensity
of sound produced."

The Invention: Bulletproof Dress Shirt
What It Does: Just what every well-dressed gangster needs. Wear
this with a tie or over a turtleneck, and no one will ever know
you're actually wearing a bulletproof garment. Main features:
removable bulletproof pads made of "an ultrahigh-molecular-
weight extended chain polyethylene fabric for superior bullet-
stopping power."

The Invention: Self-Dusting Insecticide Boot Attachment
What It Does: Like a flea collar for people, only you wear it
around your boot, not around your neck. It's supposed to prevent
ticks and other crawling insects from creeping up your leg.

The Invention: Tool for Imprinting on Hot Dogs
What It Does: No home should be without one. This amazing
invention is actually a branding iron for imprinting messages on
hot dogs ("Happy Birthday to Frank").

The Invention: Flushable Vehicle Spittoon
What It Does: Designed for use in a car or truck, this device is for
anyone who likes to drive and spit at the same time. Mount the
cylindrical receptacle anywhere on the dashboard with a conven-

ient Velcro tab. Your "fluids" flow into the funnel-shaped bottom of the spittoon, out a drainage tube, and onto the ground under the car. Then flip a switch and windshield washer fluid is automatically pumped to a spray nozzle that rinses the interior of the spittoon receptacle. You're ready to start spitting again.

The Invention: Life Expectancy Timepiece

What It Does: It looks like a watch and you wear it like a watch, but this timepiece actually displays the approximate time remaining in your life. The wearer determines his or her own life expectancy by referring to a combination of actuarial and health factor tables. How much time do you have left? Just check your watch.

The Invention: Toilet Seat Clock

What It Does: These days people like to know the time every minute of the day, even when they're in the bathroom. But where do you put a clock in the bathroom? This waterproof digital clock is mounted in the front of a U-shaped toilet seat. And the seat cover has a rectangular cutout, so the clock can be seen even when the lid is down. The clock can be reversed, so you can read it either sitting on the seat, or standing facing the toilet.

The Invention: Electrofishing Pole

What It Does: For the modern fisherman, this device is an electrified stainless-steel loop with an insulated fiberglass handle. The user wears a battery-backpack, which is connected to the loop and has another wire in the water, completing the electrical circuit. When a fish swims within the electric field created by the electrodes, ZAP! The fish quickly loses consciousness and can be easily plucked from the water. We recommend using rubber gloves.

The Invention: Electrified Tablecloth

What It Does: Plagued by picnic pests? This tablecloth has a pair of built-in electrical strips, powered by a 9-volt DC battery. An insect trying to cross the strips will get an electrical shock strong enough to discourage further travel across the table, making the world safe for potato salad. Good news: The strips are not strong enough to shock a person who accidentally touches them.

THE DUSTBIN OF HISTORY

*Think your heroes will go down in history for something they've done?
Don't count on it. These folks were VIPs in their time…but they're
forgotten now. They've been swept into the Dustbin of History.*

FORGOTTEN FIGURE: Vaughn Meader, a comedian and
impersonator in the early 1960s

CLAIM TO FAME: In 1961 Meader mimicked President
John F. Kennedy while kidding around with friends. His impersonation was so good that they encouraged him to incorporate it into
his act. So Meader put a five-minute "press conference" at the end
of his routine, taking questions from the audience and responding
in Kennedy's Boston accent. The JFK shtick got him a mention in
Life magazine, which helped him land a contract to record *The
First Family*, an entire album of his Kennedy parodies.

The First Family sold more than 10 million copies, making it
at the time the most successful record in history. Meader became
a superstar overnight. When he appeared in Las Vegas, he pulled
in $22,000 a week—not bad for a guy who'd been making $7.50 a
night just a few months earlier.

Then on November 22, 1963, a year after *The First Family*
made him the biggest name in comedy, Meader climbed into a
taxicab in Milwaukee. The driver asked him if he'd heard about
Kennedy's trip to Dallas. "No, how's it go?" Meader replied, thinking the driver was setting up a joke. No joke—in an instant Meader went from being one of the most popular acts in show business
to being a pariah. No one could bear to watch him perform, even
after he stopped doing JFK, the memories were just too painful.

INTO THE DUSTBIN: Meader's career never recovered; by
1965 he was broke. "That was it," Meader told a reporter in 1997.
"One year, November to November. Then boom. It was all over."

FORGOTTEN FIGURE: Lucy Stone, mid-19th-century feminist, suffragist, and abolitionist

CLAIM TO FAME: When Stone married abolitionist Henry Blackwell in 1855, she became the first woman in U.S. history to keep her own surname. Not a big deal these days, but in 1855 it was shocking. In those days, marriage laws in many states effectively awarded "custody of the wife's person" to the husband, as well as giving him sole control over the wife's property and their children. Stone and Blackwell intended the gesture as a protest against these laws, declaring that "marriage should be an equal partnership, and so recognized by law," not an institution in which "the legal existence of the wife is suspended."

Stone consulted several lawyers before taking the step; they all assured her there was no law specifically requiring her to take her husband's name. But the move was highly controversial, and in 1879 it cost Stone the thing she had fought for years to obtain: her right to vote. That year the state of Massachusetts allowed women to vote in school board elections for the first time, but the registrar refused to register her as anything other than "Mrs. Blackwell." Rather than surrender on principle, Stone chose not to vote.

INTO THE DUSTBIN: Stone died in 1893, 27 years before passage of the 19th Amendment guaranteed women's suffrage.

FORGOTTEN FIGURES: The Dionne quintuplets

CLAIM TO FAME: Born on May 28th, 1934, Yvonne, Annette, Emilie, Cecile, and Marie Dionne became world-famous as the first documented quintuplets. Their miraculous birth and survival, coming in the depths of the Great Depression, captivated the public and provided a welcome distraction from the economic troubles of the day.

What's not as well known is that the "quints" were also five of the most cruelly exploited children of the 20th century. Born to an impoverished French Canadian farm couple who already had six children, the girls were taken from their parents within weeks of birth and made wards of the government under the care of Dr. Alan Dafoe, the doctor who had delivered them. He raised them in "Quintland," a specially constructed "hospital" that was little more than a zoo with five tiny human residents.

Over the next nine years, more than four million tourists— up to 6,000 a day—visited Quintland to view the children from behind two-way mirrors, pumping $500 million into the Ontario economy and turning Dafoe into one of the most famous doctors in the world. The only people who were discouraged from visiting were parents Oliva and Elzire Dionne; they weren't even allowed to photograph their own children because the rights to their image had been sold off and used to advertise products like Puretest Cod Liver Oil, Lysol, and Palmolive.

INTO THE DUSTBIN: In 1954 one of the quints, Emilie, died during an epileptic seizure. Four surviving quints weren't nearly as interesting as a complete set of five, so their fame began to fade. In 1997 the surviving women wrote an open letter to the parents of the newborn McCaughey septuplets pleading with them not to make the same mistakes.

"Multiple births should not be confused with entertainment, nor should they be an opportunity to sell products," the letter read. "Our lives have been ruined by the exploitation we suffered."

*   *   *

ANIMALS FAMOUS FOR 15 MINUTES

THE STAR: A blind cod living in a fjord in Norway

THE HEADLINE: *For Blind Fish, A Light At End Of Tunnel*

WHAT HAPPENED: In March 2000, Norwegian fisherman Harald Hauso caught a cod in one of the nets he uses to catch crabs and starfish. When Hauso saw that the cod was blind, he let it go out of pity.

A week later the cod was back. He let it go again, but it came back again and again...and again: Hauso estimates that the cod came back and deliberately got himself caught in the net on 35 different occasions. "He's found an easy place to find food," Hauso told reporters. "And he knows I let him go every time." As word of the cod's story spread, he became a local celebrity.

THE AFTERMATH: In January 2001, a marine park in Aalesund, Norway, learned of the cod's plight and gave it a home in their aquarium. Bad news, though: After two months of luxurious aquarium living, the cod suddenly and inexplicably rolled over and died.

FIRSTS

*Here are some more stories of when and how things
we take for granted came to be created, from
The Book of Firsts, by Patrick Robertson.*

THE FIRST TOOTHPASTE TUBE
Date: 1892

Background: The first collapsible metal toothpaste tube
was devised by Dr. Washington Sheffield, a dentist of New London, Connecticut, and manufactured by his Sheffield Tube Corp.

THE FIRST LAWN MOWER
Date: 1830

Background: The first mower was invented by Edwin Budding of
Stroud, Gloucestershire, England. He signed a contract for the
manufacture of machinery for the purpose of cropping or shearing
the vegetable surface of lawns. Previously Budding had been
employed at a textile factory, and is said to have been inspired
with the idea of the lawn mower from using a machine designed
to shear the nap off cloth.

The first recorded customer for the new contraption was Mr.
Curtis, head gardener of Regent's Park Zoo, who bought a large
model in 1831. A smaller mower was available for the use of
country gentlemen, who, said Budding, "will find in my machine
an amusing, useful, and healthful exercise." Just how "amusing"
anyone found the heavy and inefficiently geared machine is open
to doubt, but it was clearly an improvement on cutting the lawn
with scythes. The growth of the new industry was slow, until the
advent of lawn tennis in the 1870s, which brought an influx of
mowers into backyards all over games-loving Victorian England.

THE FIRST NEWSPAPER PHOTOGRAPH
Date: March 4, 1880

Background: The first daily newspaper photograph was actually a
halftone illustration by Stephen H. Horgan, from Henry J.
Newton's photograph of New York's Shantytown, which appeared
in the *New York Daily Graphic.*

STRANGE LAWSUITS

These days, it seems that people will sue each other over practically anything. Here are a few more real-life examples of unusual legal battles.

THE PLAINTIFF: Janette Weiss

THE DEFENDANT: Kmart Corporation.

THE LAWSUIT: Weiss was shopping for a blender. But the blenders were stacked on a high shelf, just out of her reach. Ignoring the laws of gravity, Weiss jumped up and grabbed the bottom box. Predictably, when she yanked it out, the three blenders on top came crashing down on her head. Claiming to be suffering from "bilateral carpal-tunnel syndrome," Weiss sued Kmart for "negligently stacking the boxes so high on the upper shelf."

THE VERDICT: Not guilty. After Weiss admitted on the stand that she knew the boxes would fall, it took the jury half an hour to find in favor of Kmart.

THE PLAINTIFF: Dr. Ira Gore

THE DEFENDANT: BMW America

THE LAWSUIT: In 1990, Gore purchased a $40,000 BMW. After he got it home, he discovered that the dealer had touched up a scratch in the paint on a door and never bothered to tell him he was buying damaged goods. Outraged, Gore sued.

THE VERDICT: The jury awarded Gore $4,000 compensation, even though the actual repair cost only $600. And then they slapped BMW with an unbelievable $2 million in punitive damages.

THE PLAINTIFF: Jeffrey Stambovsky

THE DEFENDANT: Helen V. Ackley

THE LAWSUIT: Stambovsky purchased Ackley's house in Nyack, New York, for $650,000. When he later discovered that the house was "haunted," he sued Ackley for failing to disclose the presence of poltergeists.

THE VERDICT: Guilty. Unfortunately for her, Ackley had bragged to friends for years that the place was spooked. She was even interviewed by *Reader's Digest* for an article on haunted houses. The judge found that Ackley should have told Stambovsky everything about the house, noting that the existence of ghosts meant that she had actually broken the law by not leaving the house vacant.

THE PLAINTIFF: Chad Gabriel DeKoven
THE DEFENDANT: Michigan Prison System
THE LAWSUIT: DeKoven, a convicted armed robber who goes by the name "Messiah-God," sued the prison system, demanding damages that included thousands of trees, tons of precious metals, peace in the Middle East, and "return of all U.S. military personnel to the United States within 90 days."
THE VERDICT: Case dismissed. While noting that all claims must be taken seriously, the judge ultimately dismissed the suit as frivolous. DeKoven, the judge said, "has no Constitutional right to be treated as the 'Messiah-God' or any other holy, extra-worldly or supernatural being."

THE PLAINTIFF: Louis Berrios
THE DEFENDANT: Our Lady of Mercy Hospital
THE LAWSUIT: Berrios, a 32-year-old quadriplegic, entered the hospital complaining of stomach pains. Doctors took X-rays to determine the cause of his pain and then called the police when the film revealed what they thought were bags of heroin in Berrios's stomach. The police interrogated Berrios and kept him handcuffed to a gurney for 24 hours, only to discover that the "bags of heroin" were actually bladder stones. Berrios, "shamed, embarrassed and extremely humiliated," sued the hospital for $14 million.
THE VERDICT: Unknown.

THE PLAINTIFF: Judith Richardson Haimes
THE DEFENDANT: Temple University Hospital
THE LAWSUIT: Haimes claimed to have had psychic abilities... until a CAT scan at the Philadelphia hospital "destroyed her powers." The hospital's negligence left her unable to ply her trade as a clairvoyant, she said.
THE VERDICT: Amazingly, the jury awarded Haimes $986,465. The judge disagreed and threw out the verdict.

11% of the planet—5.8 million square miles—is covered by glaciers.

UNCLE JOHN'S
MEDICINE CABINET

*There's a story behind every item in your
medicine cabinet. Here are a few.*

• Before World War I, "Aspirin" was a registered trademark of the German company, Bayer. When Germany lost the war, Bayer gave the trademark to the Allies as a reparation in the Treaty of Versailles.

• Why do men wear fragrances? Isn't that a little "girly?" It used to be. But thanks to some clever marketing during World War II, Old Spice aftershave became part of the soldier's standard-issue toiletry kit and changed the smell of things.

• Hate taking care of your contact lenses? It could be worse. Early contacts were made from wax molds (wax was poured over the eyes). The lenses, made of glass, cut off tear flow and severely irritated the eyes. In fact, the whole ordeal was so painful that scientists recommended an anesthetic solution of cocaine.

• On average, each person uses 54 feet of dental floss every year. That may sound like a lot, but dentists recommend the use of a foot and a half of dental floss each day. That's equal to 548 feet a year.

• In the late 1940s, aerosol hairspray was a growing fad among American women. The only problem was that it was water insoluble, which made it hard to wash out. Why? The earliest fixative was shellac, more commonly used to preserve wood.

• Women ingest about 50% of the lipstick they apply.

• Ancient Chinese, Roman, and German societies frequently used urine as mouthwash. Surprisingly, the ammonia in urine is actually a good cleanser. (Ancient cultures had no way of knowing that.)

• Almost half of all men who have dyed their hair were talked into it the first time by a woman.

A recent check of 62 police cars in Atlanta, Georgia, found that 27 had expired tags.

CAUGHT IN THE ACT

*Things aren't always as they seem, and savvy
marketers can turn lying into an art form.
But sometimes they get caught.*

THE PRODUCT: Heinz Ketchup

YOU ASSUME: When you buy a bottle of ketchup that says "20 oz." on it, you get 20 ounces of ketchup.

WOULD THEY LIE TO US? Bill Baker of Redding, California, bought a 20-ounce bottle of ketchup for his wife's meatloaf. The recipe called for 20 ounces exactly, but when they poured it in the measuring cup, it was an ounce and a half short.

EXPOSED: Bill got ticked off. "If it says 20 ounces, it should be 20 ounces," he said. He called the state's Division of Measurement, setting off a five-year statewide investigation of H. J. Heinz Co. What did they find? Heinz's bottled products, from the 20-ounce to the 64-ounce size, were regularly 0.5% to 2% short. That may not seem like much, but officials estimated that Californians had been cheated out of 10 million ounces—78,124 gallons—of the red stuff. That's $650,000 worth of ketchup. Heinz was ordered to pay $180,000 in civil penalties, and agreed to overfill their bottles for one year—by about 10 million ounces.

THE PRODUCT: Used cars

YOU ASSUME: When you buy a used car from big-name automaker's dealership, you're getting a safe, reliable car.

WOULD THEY LIE TO US? Auto manufacturers buy back about 100,000 cars every year because of defects. Under federal "lemon laws," if they can't fix a car's problem, they have to buy it back. Where does it go from there? For years automakers claimed they would never resell a defective car; it would either be destroyed or studied by their engineers.

EXPOSED: In March 2001, in a lawsuit over a "laundered lemon" sold to a North Carolina couple, DaimlerChrysler was forced to reveal some incriminating facts: Between 1993 and 2000, the auto

---

giant had paid $1.3 billion to buy back more than 50,000 vehicles—and resold nearly all of them, recouping two-thirds of the buyback cost. They had been sold to Chrysler dealers who then resold them to the public. And, most damaging to the company, many of the legally required disclosure forms were unsigned, meaning buyers were told nothing about the cars' histories.

In July 2001, Chrysler settled with the couple for an undisclosed amount, but the company was still facing a class-action suit inspired by the case. In December 2001, another couple in California won a similar case against Ford Motor Co., who, the jury ruled, had knowingly resold them a lemon. Amount the jury ordered Ford to pay: $10 million.

THE PRODUCT: Movie reviews

YOU ASSUME: The movie reviews you read in newspapers and magazines are from authentic, unbiased movie critics.

WOULD THEY LIE TO US? In 2001 several advertisements for Sony-made films featured quotes from reviews by "David Manning" of "*The Ridgefield Press*," a small paper in Connecticut. Manning always seemed to give Sony's movies high praise. His take on *A Knight's Tale* star Heath Ledger: "This year's hottest new star!"

EXPOSED: After *Newsweek* reporter John Horn questioned the authenticity of the ads in June 2001, and the state of Connecticut investigated, Sony admitted they'd written the reviews themselves. David Manning didn't exist, and the real *Ridgefield Press* knew nothing about it. The investigation also revealed that people appearing in Sony's TV commercials—who seemed to be genuine moviegoers—were actually Sony employees. "These deceptive ads deserve two thumbs down," said state Attorney General Richard Blumenthal. In February 2002, Sony was fined $325,000 and agreed to stop the practice. After the case, Universal Pictures, 20th Century Fox, and Artisan Entertainment all admitted that they, too, had used employees and actors posing as moviegoers in their TV ads.

OVEREXPOSED: Shortly after the fake reviewer was revealed, two men in California filed a class-action lawsuit against Sony for "deliberately deceiving consumers." By July, 10 more had been filed against all of Hollywood's major movie studios over deceptive advertising practices. The verdict? Coming soon to a courthouse near you.

Face facts: In a standard deck of cards, the king of hearts is the only king with no moustache.

PENNY WISE

Some people collect coins; Uncle John collects trivia about coins.

Abraham Lincoln was the first president to be depicted on a U.S. coin, a penny issued in 1909. The penny is the only U.S. coin where the person faces right instead of left.

Why was the Lincoln penny issued beginning in 1909? To commemorate the 100th anniversary of Abraham Lincoln's birth.

When the Citizens Bank of Tenino, Washington, closed on December 5, 1931, the town was without ready cash to do business, so denominations of 25 cents, 50 cents, and $1 were printed on three-ply Sitka spruce wood, the first wooden money issued as legal tender in the U.S.

Spanish doubloons were legal tender in the United States until 1857.

Until 1965, pennies were legal tender only up to 25 cents. A creditor couldn't be forced to accept more than 25 pennies in payment of a debt. Silver coins were legal tender for amounts not exceeding $10 in any one payment.

The 1921 Alabama Centennial half-dollar was the first U.S. coin designed by a woman, Laura Gardin Fraser.

During World War II, the United States minted pennies made of steel to conserve copper for making artillery shells.

Booker T. Washington was the first African American to be depicted on a U.S. coin, a half-dollar issued in 1946.

Codfish were depicted on many of the early coins of the infant United States from 1776 to 1778.

The first U.S. cent, which was the size of today's 50-cent piece, was coined in 1793. In 1856 the Mint produced the first penny of today's size.

In 1932 Congress issued a commemorative coin—the Washington quarter—to celebrate the 200th birthday of George Washington. The quarter was intended to be used for only one year, but it was so popular that it was continued as a regular-issue coin from 1934 on.

Rule of thumb: your thumbnail grows more slowly than any of your fingernails.

IT SLICES! IT DICES!

This puzzle has everything! It has seven products—but wait! There's more! If you order now, you'll also receive seven examples of hype like the world has never seen—at no cost to yourself! All you need to do is match each classic commercial product to the claim it's famous for. If you need the answers, allow 6 to 8 weeks for delivery.

_____ 1. GLH#9 (Hair-in-a-can)
_____ 2. Inside the Eggshell Scrambler
_____ 3. The Miracle Mop
_____ 4. The Pocket Fisherman
_____ 5. The Ronco Bottle and Jar Cutter
_____ 6. The Ronco Rhinestone and Stud Setter
_____ 7. The Veg-O-Matic

a. "It lets you wring out the head without putting your hands into the dirty water!"

b. "It changes everyday clothing into exciting fashions!"

c. "Attaches to your belt, or fits in the glove compartment of your car!"

d. "A hobby for Dad, craft for the kids, a great gift for Mom!"

e. "You'll use it a lot and every time you do, you'll save washing a bowl and fork!"

f. "No one likes dicing onions...the only tears you'll shed will be tears of joy!"

g. "You can use it on your dog!"   **ANSWER, PAGE 370**

TAKING DEBATE

In 1986, Ann Landers revealed that in the 31 years she'd been writing her advice column, there was one subject that had been the most controversial of them all. What was it?

    a. The in-laws
    b. Abortion rights
    c. The amount of time husbands spend watching sports on TV
    d. The amount of money wives spend shopping
    e. Whether toilet paper should come off the top or the bottom of the roll

ANSWER, PAGE 370

UNCLE JOHN'S "CREATIVE TEACHING" AWARDS

*Another round of the BRI's Creative Teaching Awards,
because we're just so proud of teachers who continue to
ake education an exciting and creative experience.*

SUBJECT: Animal care

WINNER: Leslie Davis, of Savannah, Georgia

APPROACH: In May 2002, Davis assembled her elementary school students and took them to a nearby park—where they stole a duck from the pond. Then they went back to the school, where they planned to release the duck as a prank.

REACTION: The 23-year-old teacher was charged with public drunkenness, obstruction, and contributing to the delinquency of minors.

SUBJECT: Fashion

WINNER: Vice Principal Rita Wilson, Rancho Bernardo High School, Poway, California

APPROACH: During the 2002 April Dance, Ms. Wilson wanted to make sure that female students were following the dress code. So, as they were entering the building, she lifted up the girls' skirts to see if they were wearing thong underwear, which was prohibited. According to a source, she even did so in front of male students.

REACTION: The Poway Unified School District investigated and concluded that the vice principal "used poor judgment"…then demoted her to a classroom teaching job.

SUBJECT: Civics

WINNER: School administrators at Hamilton High School, in Chandler, Arizona

APPROACH: As part of a law-enforcement training class, four students took part in a "gun drill," storming school hallways with fake guns, shouting "Don't make me do it!" But apparently someone had failed to warn the faculty about the drill.

REACTION: Panicked students and teachers locked down the classrooms until they were sure they were safe. The instructor who planned the drill—Police Officer Andy McIlveen—was asked not to return to the school district. Said Assistant Principal Dave Constance, "This is not an appropriate way to teach school safety."

SUBJECT: Humanities
WINNER: Ronald Cummings, of Santa Ana, California
APPROACH: For some reason, Cummings drove a group of students—a 14-year-old boy and two 18-year-olds—to a gang fight and then gave them a cigarette lighter that looked exactly like a pistol.
REACTION: Immediately put on leave from the school, he was charged by police with contributing to the delinquency of minors, making terrorist threats, and using a fake firearm in a threatening manner. He faces eight years in prison.

SUBJECT: History
WINNER: School officials in West Palm Beach, Florida
APPROACH: To make sure students would fulfill state requirements in history, the officials developed a 100-question test—and then required that students answer only 23 of them correctly to pass.
REACTION: Not much. Some teachers complained, but the school board defended the low grade scale...and the test went on anyway. Bottom line: The students can get three-quarters of the answers wrong and still pass.

SUBJECT: Ethics
WINNER: Third-grade teacher Betty Bettis and gym teacher Thomas L. Sims, of Kansas City, Missouri
APPROACH: When a lunch money collection in Bettis's class came up $5 short, the teacher strip searched the students. She took the girls into a restroom, had them strip to their underwear, and then had them check each others' panties. Sims took the boys into a gym and had them strip and then shake their underwear.
REACTION: Outraged parents made the story international news. One student even went on a talk show to describe the incident. By the way, they found the missing money in a rest room...but not as a result of the strip search.

OLD HISTORY, NEW THEORY

Here's another example of new findings that may change history books.

The Event: On May 6, 1937, the German blimp *Hindenburg* exploded over a New Jersey airfield, killing 36 people, and effectively ending the age of passenger airships.

What the History Books Say: The explosion was caused when the highly volatile hydrogen gas that kept the airship afloat was ignited, most likely by a static electric charge.

New Theory: Two boards of inquiry couldn't explain how the hydrogen escaped from sealed gas cells, which it had to do before it could explode. Yet investigators still determined that hydrogen was the cause of the explosion. According to Dr. William Van Vorst, a chemical engineer at UCLA, they were wrong.

A frame-by-frame analysis of film footage suggests that whatever it was that first ignited, it wasn't the hydrogen. "The picture indicates a downward burning. Hydrogen would burn only upward," Van Vorst says, "with a colorless flame." Eyewitnesses described the explosion as more like "a fireworks display."

So what caused the explosion? Van Vorst says it was the *Hindenburg*'s skin. The ship's cotton shell was treated with chemicals so volatile that they "might well serve as rocket propellant," he says. And the way it was attached to the frame allowed for the buildup of large amounts of static electricity, which, when discharged, were enough to ignite the fabric.

Smoking Gun: It turns out that the Zeppelin Company quietly conducted its own investigation after the disaster...and concluded the same thing. The *Hindenburg*'s sister ship, *Graf Zeppelin,* was reconstructed using new methods and materials, and went on to fly more than a million miles without incident.

Publicly, however, the company blamed hydrogen. Why? Politics. The United States controlled the world supply of helium, which is nonflammable, but refused to sell any to Nazi Germany. So Zeppelin had to use explosive hydrogen gas...which made the United States look bad when the *Hindenburg* went down in flames.

THE MAGIC SCREEN

"As new as 1960!" That was the slogan on Uncle John's first Etch A Sketch. It provided hours of mindless fun (just like TV), even though he couldn't figure out how it worked (he still can't).

A HUMBLE BEGINNING

In 1958 a 37-year-old Parisian garage mechanic named Arthur Granjean invented an amazing new toy. He called it *L'Ecran Magique*—Magic Screen.

The Magic Screen was an unusual toy for its time—it didn't have a lot of little pieces that could get lost and didn't need batteries. Granjean felt sure his creation would interest someone at the International Toy Fair in Nuremberg, Germany. But everyone passed on it...until executives from a small American toy firm, the Ohio Art Company, convinced their boss to take a second look. That did it. Ohio Art bought the rights for $25,000 and renamed it Etch A Sketch. Then they advertised it on TV—just in time for the 1960 Christmas season—and sales took off. The response was so great that they kept the factory open until noon on Christmas Eve desperately trying to fill orders.

A CLASSIC TOY

How does Etch A Sketch work? There's a stylus, or pointer, mounted on two rails behind the screen. Using a system of wires and pulleys connected to the knobs on front, one rail moves back and forth, and the other moves up and down. The gray stuff is powdered aluminum mixed with tiny plastic beads. The powder sticks to the glass screen because aluminum powder sticks to *everything*. The beads help the powder flow easily. When the stylus moves, it touches the glass and scrapes the aluminum powder off. Shake it, and the aluminum is redistributed evenly. To prevent it from breaking, a clear plastic film covers the glass.

The basic Etch A Sketch design hasn't changed since 1960, although variations have been introduced:

• Pocket-sized models, travel-sized models, and glow-in-the-dark models (only the frame glows).

• The new Zooper model makes weird noises—beeps, boops, squeaks, and squawks—as the knobs turn.

• There's also an Etch A Sketch "action pack," which offers various puzzles and games printed on overlays placed on top of the screen.

• To celebrate the toy's 25th anniversary in 1985, Ohio Art came out with an Executive model made of silver. The drawing knobs were set with sapphires and topaz. Price: $3,750.

ETCH A SKETCH TRIVIA

• **How many?** Eight thousand Etch A Sketches are sold every day.

• **World's largest Etch A Sketch.** Steve Jacobs created it at the Black Rock Arts Festival in California in 1997. He placed 144 regulation-sized Etch A Sketches in a huge square and surrounded them with a huge red Etch A Sketch frame, including huge white knobs. It qualified for a Guinness World Record.

• **Robot Etch A Sketch.** A Canadian computer programmer named Neil Fraser pulled the knobs off a standard Etch A Sketch and hooked it up to two motors that were attached to the port of his computer. The motors worked by remote control, enabling Fraser to draw pictures without ever touching the toy. Other robotic components tilt the Etch A Sketch upside down and shake it.

• **Extreme Etch A Sketch.** George Vlosich was ten years old in 1989 when, on a long drive from Ohio to Washington, D.C., he brought along his Etch A Sketch. On the way home, he drew a sketch of the Capitol that was so good his parents photographed it. An artist was born. He soon began sketching portraits of his favorite sports heroes, then waited after games to get them to autograph his Etch A Sketch. The "Etch A Sketch Kid" started getting so much media attention that in 2000, Ohio Art sent someone to his home to see if he lived up to his reputation. They were so impressed by his talent that they've been supplying him with free Etch A Sketches ever since.

It takes George between 40 and 60 hours to complete a single Etch A Sketch masterpiece. After it's done, he carefully unscrews the back and removes the excess aluminum powder to preserve the picture forever. His Etch A Sketch artworks sell for up to $5,000 each.

THE VIDEO GAME
HALL OF FAME

*Today most video games are played in the home, but in the 1970s and
1980s, if you wanted to play the newest, hottest games,
you went to an arcade. Here are the stories of a few of the
classics we played back in the golden age of arcade games.*

SPACE INVADERS (Taito, 1978)

Object: Using a laser cannon that you scroll back and
forth across the bottom of the screen, defend yourself from
wave after wave of aliens descending from the top of the screen.

Origin: Space Invaders started out as a test that was used to measure the skill of computer programmers, but someone decided that
it might also work well as an arcade game. They were right—the
game became a national craze in Japan.

Introduced to the U.S. market by Midway in October 1978,
Space Invaders became the biggest hit of the year. It made so
much money—a single unit could earn back its $1,700 purchase
price in as little as four weeks—that it helped arcade games break
out of arcades and smoky bars into nontraditional venues like
supermarkets, restaurants, and movie theaters.

TEMPEST (Atari, 1981)

Object: Shoot the moving shapes—red brackets, green spikes, yellow lines, and multicolored balls, before they climb up and out of
the geometrically shaped "well" they're in and get you.

Origin: Atari game designer Dave Theurer needed an idea for a new
video game, so he went to the company's book of potential themes
compiled from brainstorming sessions. The idea he chose to develop
was "First Person Space Invaders"—Space Invaders as seen from the
perspective of the laser cannon at the bottom of the screen.

Theurer created a game and showed it to his superiors...and
they told him to dump it unless he could "do something special
with it." Theurer told them about a nightmare he'd had about
monsters climbing out of a hole in the ground and coming to get
him. "I can put it on a flat surface and wrap that surface around to

make a cylinder, and rotate the cylinder," Theurer suggested. As he conceived it, the cylinder would move while the player stood still…but he abandoned that idea when the rotating cylinder started giving players motion sickness. "I switched it so the player moved around," Theurer says. "That fixed it."

PAC-MAN (Namco, 1980)

Object: Maneuver Pac-Man through a maze and eat all 240 dots without getting caught by one of the four "ghosts"—Inky, Blinky, Pinky, and Clyde.

Origin: In 1979 a game designer named Toru Iwatani decided to make a game that would appeal to women, who were less interested in violent, shoot-the-alien games like Space Invaders. Iwatani thought that eating things on the computer screen would make a good nonviolent alternative to shooting them. He came up with the idea for the Pac-Man character over lunch. "I was having pizza," he says. "I took one wedge and there it was, the figure of Pac-Man." Well, almost: Pac-Man was originally supposed to be called Puck-Man, because the main character was round like a hockey puck…but the name was changed to Pac-Man, because Namco officials "worried about American vandals changing the 'P' to an 'F'."

DONKEY KONG (Nintendo, 1980)

Object: Get the girl.

Origin: One of Nintendo's first video games was a Space Invaders knockoff called Radarscope. It flopped in the United States, nearly bankrupting the distributor—who wanted to stop doing business with Nintendo. What could Nintendo do? They promised to ship new chips to American distributors so the unsold Radarscope games could be turned into new games.

There was just one problem—they didn't have any new game chips. So Nintendo president Hiroshi Yamauchi told the company's staff artist, Shigeru Miyamoto, to come up with something, *fast.*

Miyamoto had never made a game before, and he hated tennis games, shooting games, and most games that were popular at the time. So he invented a game about a janitor who has to rescue his girlfriend from his pet ape, who has taken her to the top of a construction site. Miyamoto wanted to name the game after the ape,

---

If you plant bamboo today, it may not sprout flowers and produce seeds for 100 years.

so he looked up the words for "stubborn" and "ape" in his Japanese/English dictionary... and found the words "donkey" and "Kong." Donkey Kong went on to become one of the most successful video games in history, giving Nintendo the boost it needed to build itself into a multibillion-dollar company and an international video game juggernaut. And it might never have succeeded if Radarscope hadn't failed.

DEFENDER (Williams Electronics, 1980)

Object: Use your spacecraft to shoot hostile aliens while saving humanoids from being kidnapped and turned into mutants.

Origin: Another game helped along by a dream: Defender was supposed to make its debut at the 1980 Amusement & Music Operators of America (AMOA) convention, but less than two weeks before his deadline, creator Eugene Jarvis had only the rough outlines of a game—the name, Defender, and a spaceship attacking aliens, all against a planetary backdrop dotted with humanoids who didn't really do anything. What was the defender defending?

"The answer came to him in a dream," Nick Montfort writes in *Supercade*. "Those seemingly pointless little men, trapped on the surface below, *they* were the ones to be defended."

Jarvis made his deadline, but the AMOA was afraid the game was too complicated. They were wrong. Defender became one of the most popular games of the year and made so much money that in 1981 the AMOA voted it Video Game of the Year.

LEGENDARY FLOP: LUNAR LANDER (Atari, 1979)

Object: Find a flat spot on the lunar surface and use your booster engines to slow your spaceship (without running out of fuel) and land it safely on the moon.

Origin: The game was adapted from a computer simulation used in college physics courses to teach students about lunar gravity. Atari had high hopes for the game, even designing a special two-handled lever that controlled the booster engines. It flopped. So did the special lever: "Springs on the lever made it snap back in place when it was released," Steven Kent writes in *The Ultimate History of Video Games*. "Unfortunately, some younger players got their faces too close to the lever, resulting in complaints about children being hit in the face."

Odds of being killed by a bolt of lightning are about the same as being killed falling out of bed.

PLAY D'OH!

Homer Simpson, America's favorite animated dad, lets fall a few gems. Drop the letters from each vertical column, but not necessarily in the order in which they appear, into the empty squares below them to spell out Homer's homilies, reading from left to right. Words may wrap around from one line to the next; black squares signify the spaces between words.

1.

T	M		E		T	N	N		V	E			E				P		R		N	
O	H	S	N	O	T	N	N	B	R	T	M	I	F	Y	U	A	E	R	M	A	I	G
I	U	E	R	M	A	S	A	O	U	M	A	L	L	S	Y	O	U	R	E	L	U	P	I

2.

	T	D			O	U		F	A	I		I			M	I	R		R		S	R		
A	O	N		Y	L	E		T	O	N	E	E	S		O	E	S		R	R	E	T	L	Y
S	N	H	E	Y	O	U	S	S	R	I	L	D	D	Y	N	U	V	E	B	A	B	T	Y	Y

3.

H	E							L		T					I					A		R	S
I	F		G		H	H	E	R	A		S	O	L	R	F			U	O	O	B		E	U
U	N	N	E	T	T	W	R	E	H	O	L	T	O	U	Y	T	N	N	S	O	B	N	E	N	U
V	E	C	T	T	I	E	Y	R	K	I	F	Y	E	W	T	I	N	O	M	B	W	N	H	O
I	I	T	Y	O	U	N	O	T	E	L	A	B	R	I	A	E	T	Y	U	M	Q	M	H	A	Q	T

ANSWER, PAGE 370

AROUND THE HOUSE

The next time you're doing some home improvement, chances are you'll use one at least one of these three products.

TAKES THE CAKE

In 1894 Theodore Witte was applying putty around a window frame with a butter knife—and it was a messy job. Sometime later, while waiting in line at a bakery shop, he noticed a baker squeezing icing onto a cake from a tube attached to a nozzle...with complete precision. Witte went straight home and designed a "puttying tool." He patented his idea of "using a ratcheted piston to force window putty through a nozzle to effect a smooth, weatherproof seal." Witte never made much money for his invention, but to his credit, he got it right the first time; very little about the caulking gun has changed since then.

SOMETHING'S FISHY

After someone spilled raw fish oil on his metal deck, a Scottish fishing boat captain named Robert Fergusson noticed that—over time—the deck stopped rusting. So after he landed in New Orleans, Fergusson spent many years trying to formulate a fish-oil based paint that would inhibit rust and corrosion. His biggest problem wasn't getting it to work, but getting it to work without smelling fishy. Finally in 1921, after working with more fish oil than any person should ever have to, Fergusson unveiled a new paint that stopped rust, dried overnight, and left no lingering aroma: Rust-Oleum.

ROCKET SCIENCE

Norm Larsen, a chemist at the Rocket Chemical Company, had unsuccessfully tested 39 compounds that would prevent corrosion and eliminate water from electrical circuitry. He finally got it right in 1953 and labeled the compound Water Displacement Formula 40. Other workers snuck the stuff home and discovered that in addition to preventing corrosion, it also stopped squeaks and unstuck locks. So the Rocket Chemical Company marketed it for home use. The product, now called WD-40, hit store shelves in 1958. Today more than a million cans are sold every week.

Q: What do Eskimos use for toothpicks? A: Walrus whiskers.

LUCKY FINDS

*Ever found something really valuable? It's one of the
best feelings in the world. Here's an installment
of a regular* Bathroom Reader *feature.*

HONEST STAN
The Find: $20,000
Where It Was Found: In a drawer

The Story: On January 29, 2002, home inspector Stan Edmunds
was checking out a house in Hinsdale, New Hampshire, for a
prospective buyer. To get to the attic, he had to go through a
closet, and an odd wooden shelf support kept catching his eye.
The third time through, he pulled on it—and out slid a hidden
drawer. Inside it: $20,000 in $100 bills.

Edmunds could have put it in his pocket and walked away, but
he didn't—he called the real-estate agent. The agent contacted
the heirs of the homeowner, who divided the money up. And one
of them sent Edmunds a check for his honesty...for $50. He said
he would be donating it to charity.

CHICAGO HOPE
The Find: Superbowl Championship ring
Where It Was Found: In a couch

The Story: In 1996 retired Hall of Fame running back Walter
Payton was coaching a high school basketball team outside of
Chicago. As an exercise in trust, he gave one of the boys, Nick
Abruzzo, his 1986 Superbowl ring—complete with his name and
41 diamonds—to hold for a few days. Nick and his friends passed
it around in awe...and then lost it.

Five years later, college student Phil Hong bought an old couch
for his dorm room from his friend Joe Abruzzo—Nick's younger
brother. One day, while looking in the couch for a lost dog toy, he
found the ring. The longtime Chicago fan knew what it was immediately. "Growing up, Walter Payton was my idol," he said. Unfortunately, Payton died of cancer in 1999, but Hong returned the ring
to his widow, Connie Payton. "This ring was what he worked for
his whole life," he said. "It needs to be back in the family."

HANGING IN PLAIN SIGHT

The Find: Masterpiece painting

Where It Was Found: Hanging on a wall

The Story: In July 2001, an elderly couple in Cheltenham, England, decided to sell an old painting that had been hanging on a wall in their house for decades. They figured it was worth a few thousand dollars. They wrapped it in a blanket and took it to Christie's auction house. "They arrived in their van and I came outside to look at what they had," said appraiser Alexander Pope. "It was a classic valuation moment." It turned out to be a masterpiece by 17th-century French artist Nicolas Poussin. Sale price at auction: $600,000.

GIVE ME A RING SOMETIME

The Find: Diamond ring

Where It Was Found: In a bar in Vancouver, British Columbia

The Story: In 1998 a man selling costume jewelry approached 21-year-old Tanya Tokevich while she was sitting in a Vancouver bar. She ended up buying a ring for $20. "It didn't look like much," she said. "It was dull, but I just thought it was nice." She decided to have it appraised to find out whether she'd gotten a good deal. She had. It wasn't costume jewelry—it was an antique engagement ring with a 2.05-carat diamond worth $11,000.

THE CASE OF THE MISSING LIST

The Find: Famous list

Where It Was Found: In a suitcase in Germany

The Story: When a Stuttgart couple found an old suitcase in their parent's loft after they died in 1999, they didn't think much of it—until they saw the name on the handle: O. Schindler. Inside were hundreds of documents—including a list of the names of the Jewish slave-laborers and their fake jobs that factory owner Oskar Schindler gave to the Nazis during WWII. The bold move saved 1,200 Jews from extermination and inspired the movie *Schindler's List*. Apparently, friends of Schindler's had used the loft as a storage space decades earlier and then forgot about it. The couple gave the suitcase and all the documents to a newspaper, but asked for no money in return. It now resides in Yad Vashem Holocaust Museum, in Jerusalem.

Makes sense: *Radish* comes from the Latin *radix*, meaning "root."

THE PROFESSOR'S "INVENTIONS"

It's one of TV's eternal mysteries: Here he was stranded on Gilligan's Island with no tools and no power. Yet the Professor was such a genius that he could invent virtually anything... except a boat. Stupefying. Well, here's a list of some of the things he did invent.

- Lie detector (made from the ship's horn, the radio's batteries, and bamboo)

- Bamboo telescope

- Jet pack fuel

- Paralyzing strychnine serum

- "Spider juice" (to kill a giant spider)

- Nitroglycerine

- Shark repellent

- Helium balloon (rubber raincoats sewn together and sealed with tree sap)

- Coconut-shell battery recharger

- Xylophone

- Soap (made from plant fats, it's not really so far-fetched)

- Roulette wheel

- Geiger counter (*that's* far-fetched)

- Pedal-powered bamboo sewing machine

- Pedal-powered washing machine

- Keptibora-berry extract (to cure Gilligan's double vision)

- Pedal-powered water pump

- Pedal-powered telegraph

- Hair tonic

- Pedal-powered generator

- Various poisons and antidotes

- Pool table (for Mr. Howell)

- Lead radiation suits and lead-based makeup (protection against a meteor's cosmic rays)

Seawater is about 800 times more dense than air.

THE WHO?

Ever wonder how bands get their names? So do we. After some digging around, we found the stories behind these famous names.

GENESIS. Named by producer Jonathan King, who signed the band in 1967. He chose the name because they were the first "serious" band he'd produced and he considered signing them to mark the official beginning of his production career.

HOLE. Named after a line in the Euripedes play *Medea*: "There's a hole burning deep inside me." Singer Courtney Love chose it because she says, "I knew it would confuse people."

THE BLACK CROWES. Originally a punk band called Mr. Crowe's Garden (after singer Chris Robinson's favorite kid's book). They later shortened the name and switched to southern rock.

AC/DC. Chosen because it fit the band's "high-voltage" sound.

CREAM. Eric Clapton, Jack Bruce, and Ginger Baker chose the name because they considered themselves the cream of the crop of British blues musicians.

THE CLASH. A political statement to demonstrate the band's antiestablishment attitude? No. According to bassist Paul Simonon: "I was looking through the *Evening Standard* with the idea of names on my mind, and noticed the word *clash* a few times. I thought The Clash would be good."

GUNS N' ROSES. The band chose Guns N' Roses by combining the names of two bands that members had previously played in: L.A. Guns and Hollywood Rose.

ELTON JOHN. Born Reginald Kenneth Dwight, he joined the backing band for blues singer Long John Baldry. Dwight later changed his name by combining the first names of John Baldry and saxophonist Elton Dean.

THE O'JAYS. Originally the Triumphs, they changed their name to the O'Jays in 1963 to honor Eddie O'Jay, a Cleveland disc jockey who was the group's mentor.

JANE'S ADDICTION. According to band legend, Jane was a hooker and heroin addict whom the band members met (and lived with) in Hollywood in the mid-1980s.

THEY MIGHT BE GIANTS. Named after an obscure 1971 B-movie starring George C. Scott and Joanne Woodward.

DAVID BOWIE. David Robert Jones changed his last name to Bowie to avoid being mistaken for Davy Jones of the Monkees. He chose Bowie after the hunting knife he'd seen in American films.

BAD COMPANY. Named after the 1972 Western starring Jeff Bridges.

THE POGUES. Began as Pogue Mahone, which is Gaelic for "kiss my arse."

ELVIS COSTELLO. Born Declan MacManus, he changed his name at the urging of manager Jake Riviera. According to Costello: "It was a marketing scheme. Jake said, 'We'll call you Elvis.' I thought he was completely out of his mind." Costello is a family name on his mother's side.

THE B52S. Not named after the Air Force jet. *B52* is a southern term for tall bouffant hairdos, which the women of the band wore early in the band's career.

THE POLICE. Named by drummer Stewart Copeland as an ironic reference to his father, Miles, who had served as chief of the CIA's Political Action Staff in the 1950s.

MÖTLEY CRÜE. Comes from Motley Croo, a band that guitarist Mick Mars worked for as a roadie in the early 1970s. According to bassist Nikki Sixx, they changed the spelling and added the umlauts because they "wanted to do something to be weird. It's German and strong, and that Nazi Germany mentality—'the future belongs to us'—intrigued me."

RADIOHEAD. Originally called On A Friday (because they could practice only on Fridays), EMI signed them in 1992. But EMI execs feared that On A Friday might be confusing to some. So the band quickly chose a new name. Their inspiration: an obscure Talking Heads song called "Radio Head."

UNCLE JOHN'S PAGE OF LISTS

Some random facts from our files.

5 Roman Delicacies, circa 200 A.D.
1. Parrot tongue
2. Ostrich brain
3. Thrush tongue
4. Peacock comb
5. Nightingale tongue

8 Things Rupert Murdoch Owns
1. *The N.Y. Post*
2. *The Times* (London)
3. *The Australian* (Sydney)
4. *TV Guide*
5. Twentieth-Century Fox
6. Madison Square Garden
7. Fox News Channel
8. L.A. Dodgers

4 Jell-O Flavor Flops
1. Cola
2. Coffee
3. Apple
4. Celery

5 Greatest American Generals (Gallup Poll, 2000)
1. George Patton
2. Dwight Eisenhower
3. Douglas MacArthur
4. Colin Powell
5. George Washington

5 States with the Most Nuclear Waste Sites
1. Illinois—10
2. California—9
3. New York—9
4. Michigan—6
5. Pennsylvania—6

4 Most Expensive Ad Spots on a Race Car
1. Hood
2. Lower rear quarter panel
3. Behind rear window
4. Behind driver's window

10 Animals That Have Been in Space
1. Dog
2. Chimp
3. Bullfrog 4. Cat
5. Tortoise
6. Bee 7. Cricket
8. Spider 9. Fish
10. Worm

4 Most Copied Hollywood Noses (Beverly Hills plastic surgeons)
1. Heather Locklear
2. Nicole Kidman
3. Marisa Tomei
4. Catherine Zeta-Jones

7 Actors in *The Magnificent Seven*
1. Robert Vaughn
2. Steve McQueen
3. Brad Dexter
4. James Coburn
5. Horst Bucholz
6. Yul Brynner
7. Charles Bronson

A variety of mimosa is called the "sensitive plant" because it wilts when touched.

LAND OF THE GIANTS

*Back in the early 1960s, little Uncle John saw a giant statue of Paul
Bunyan at Freedomland USA, an amusement park outside New
York City. Freedomland closed in 1964, but the Paul Bunyan statue
is still around—standing behind a gas station in nearby Elmsford,
New York. And it turns out there are a lot more Paul Bunyans
around the country...if you know where to find them.*

WHO'S THAT MAN?
If you've taken a lot of car trips you've seen them—
18- to 25-foot figures of dark-haired, square-jawed
men, dressed in a short-sleeved shirt and work pants. Their arms
are extended at the elbow, with the right hand facing up and the
left hand facing down, often holding something, like a muffler or a
roll of carpet.

What you might not know is that there are more than 150 of
these gigantic fiberglass figures dotting America's highways, advertising everything from tires to burger joints to amusement parks.
Almost all of them were made by one man.

BIRTH OF THE BIG BOYS
It all started in 1962, when the Paul Bunyan Cafe on Route 66 in
Flagstaff, Arizona, wanted a statue of their namesake to stand by
the highway and attract hungry motorists. Prewitt Fiberglass in
Venice, California, was happy to supply a figure of the giant lum-
berjack and created a molded Paul Bunyan character wearing a
green cap, a dark beard, a red shirt, and jeans, and holding an axe.

That was it as far as Prewitt Fiberglass was concerned—one
customer, one Paul Bunyan. But then owner Bob Prewitt decided
to sell his business to a fiberglass boat builder named Steve
Dashew. Dashew renamed the company International Fiberglass
and, wanting to make a success of his new venture, started looking
for business opportunities.

The leftover Paul Bunyan mold caught his eye. It was such an
odd asset, he thought it might have value. Dashew began calling
retail businesses around the country and asking them if they could
use a giant advertising figure. A few said they could. When a story

about one of Dashew's customers appeared in a retail trade magazine, stating that sales had doubled after the Paul Bunyan went up, business in the giant fiberglass figures began to boom.

PAUL BUNYAN'S FRIENDS

Dashew started to aggressively market the big statues across the country, and sold them by the score. At first they were all Paul Bunyans, but Dashew soon discovered he could modify the basic mold slightly to create other figures.

• He turned them into cowboys, Indians, and astronauts. All of the figures had the same arm configuration as the first Paul Bunyan, so they were almost always holding something, like a plate or some tires.

• International Fiberglass made other figures, too—such as giant chickens, dinosaurs, and tigers—selling each for $1,800 to $2,800.

• They made 300 "Big Friends" for Texaco, figures of smiling Texaco service attendants in green uniforms with green caps.

• They built Yogi Bear figures for Yogi Bear's Honey Fried Chicken restaurants in North and South Carolina.

• To advertise Uniroyal Tires, they made a series of hulking women who looked a lot like Jackie Kennedy, holding a tire in one of her upraised hands. These women were issued with a dress, which could be removed to reveal a bikini.

But the figures made from the original Paul Bunyan mold proved to be the most popular, not to mention the most cost-effective for Dashew, who used the same mold over and over again. By the mid-1960s, the figures had made their way into hundreds of towns across the United States and were great attention-getters for retail stores and restaurants of all kinds.

BYE-BYE, BUNYAN

But by the 1970s, the big figures that had seemed so impressive years earlier were getting dingy, weather-beaten, and silly looking to the next generation of consumers. As sales of the statues slowed, Dashew concentrated his energies on other business ventures. In 1976 he sold the business and the Paul Bunyan mold was destroyed.

Today, most of the fiberglass colossi are also gone, having been destroyed, removed, or beaten down by the elements. But they haven't all disappeared. In fact, almost every state in the Union has at least one. With businesses changing hands, the figures have been modified over the years:

• One Bunyan in Malibu, California, used to hold an immense hamburger. When a Mexican food joint bought out the burger place, he was given a sombrero and a serape, and his hamburger was replaced with a taco.

• A Bunyan at Lynch's Super Station in Havre de Grace, Maryland, was dressed in desert fatigues in 1991 to show support for the Gulf War.

• One former Uniroyal Gal stands in front of Martha's Cafe in Blackfoot, Idaho, holding a sandwich platter.

• Another Uniroyal Gal, in Rocky Mount, North Carolina, has been dressed in a pair of Daisy Duke shorts, given a beach ball to hold, fitted with a queen-size stainless-steel belly button ring, and placed in front of the Men's Night Out "private club."

BIG MEN IN THE MEDIA

If you can't get to see one of the giant statues in person, you can look for them in movies and on TV:

• A Paul Bunyan was featured in the 1969 movie *Easy Rider*.

• A modified Bunyan is pictured in the opening credits of the TV show *The Sopranos*. The figure, which holds a giant roll of carpet to advertise Wilson's Carpet in Jersey City, New Jersey, is now a stop on the New Jersey Sopranos bus tour.

• Bunyans have also made appearances in the TV show *The A-Team*, in the 2000 John Travolta flick *Battlefield Earth*, and in commercials for Saturn cars and Kleenex Tissues.

*   *   *

PATRIOTIC PAUL

In the small town of Cheshire, Connecticut, a Paul Bunyan statue ignited controversy because zoning laws declared him too tall for any purpose other than holding a flag. The statue now functions as a flagpole.

In Greek mythology, Nike is the goddess of victory.

DUBIOUS ACHIEVERS

Here are some of the most bizarre world records we could find. How bizarre? One of the record holders is a bacterium.

I'M SENSING...SURGERY. Since 1979, Fulvia Celica Siguas Sandoval, a transsexual TV clairvoyant from Peru, has had plastic surgery 64 times. More than 25 of the operations have been to her face.

LIKE A ROCK. St. Simeon the Younger lived from 521 to 597 AD in Antioch, Syria. He spent his last 45 years sitting on top of a stone pillar.

CONAN THE BACTERIUM. *Deinococcus radiodurans* can withstand 10,000 times the radiation it would take to kill a human, earning it the title of "World's Toughest Bacterium." It was discovered living in swollen tins of irradiated meat in Oregon in the 1950s.

SOCK IT TO ME! Britain's Kirsten O'Brien managed to wear 41 socks at once...all on one foot. She performed the "feet" on the BBC's *Big Toe Radio Show* on May 20, 2003.

THE HOLE-IEST OF RECORDS. Having 600 body piercings is pretty impressive in itself, but in 2002, 28-year-old Kam Ma of Whitburn, England, got 600 piercings in 8 hours and 32 minutes.

CRIME AGAINST HUMANITY? On June 1, 2000, 566 accordian players gathered at the International Folklore Festival in the Netherlands. For 22 minutes they played folk songs in unison—becoming history's largest accordian ensemble ever (hopefully).

PANTS ON FIRE. John Graham (if that *is* his real name) holds the title "World's Biggest Liar." He earned it by telling the most tall tales at the Annual Lying Competition held in Cumbria, England. He's won the contest five times (or so he says).

MOOO: Most cows give more milk when they listen to music.

SORRY ABOUT THAT

There are a few lessons we all learned when we were kids—be curteous to others, share your toys, and when you screw up, say you're sorry. Some people got it…and apparently some didn't.

HO! HO! HO!
Incident: In December 2002, Reverend Lee Rayfield of Maidenhead, England, had to send out letters of apology to his parishioners. Reverend Rayfield had held a special Christmas service just for children. A horrified shock went through the room when Rayfield delivered an unexpected message: Santa Claus, he told the the kids, is *dead*. In order to deliver presents to all the children in the world, he explained, the reindeer would have to travel 3,000 times the speed of sound—which would make them all burn up in less than a second. The audience included "a lot of young children who still believe in Santa Claus," said one angry parent, "or did until last night."
Apology: "I guess I made a serious misjudgment," said Rayfield.

HOT WATER
Incident: After American-turned-Taliban John Walker Lindh was captured in Afganistan in November 2002, the press reported that he was from Marin County, California. That prompted former President Bush to describe Lindh as "some misguided Marin County hot-tubber." Jackie Kerwin, editor of the *Marin Independent Journal*, took exception to the insult and urged readers to write letters about it. And they did. Letters poured in, prompting newspapers, radio, and TV news programs to spread the story across the country.
Apology: "Dear Ms. Kerwin," Bush wrote to her, "Call off the dogs, please. I surrender. I will never use 'hot tub' and 'Marin County' in the same sentence again." He even made a personal phone call. "He gets on the phone and says 'Hot tubs for sale,'" Kerwin said, "and that pretty much set the tone for the rest of the conversation. But I think he was genuinely sorry."

HERE'S MUD (SLINGING) IN YOUR EYE
Incident: In the 2000 media guide for their men's basketball team, Ohio State University displayed photographs of some distinguished

---

Why do we all know Ann Turner Cook? Her face is on Gerber baby food jars.

alumni, including comedian Richard Lewis, who had graduated in 1969. But it turned out to be a dubious honor: the caption below his name said, "Actor, Writer, Comedian, Drunk." This was particularly insulting because Lewis is a recovering alcoholic. "I was really depressed that I would be so defamed," he said.

Apology: Red-faced officials apologized profusely...and then fired the editor, Gary Emig, who had put in "drunk" as a joke in an early draft, but forgot to take it out.

AN INFIELD HIT

Incident: Between innings at a June 2003 baseball game, the Milwaukee Brewers were staging one of their fans' favorite events: the Sausage Race. Dressed up as a bratwurst, a hot dog, an Italian sausage, and a Polish sausage, four Brewer employees raced around the infield. But as they passed the opposing team's dugout, Pittsburgh Pirate first baseman Randall Simon reached out and playfully whacked one of the runners with his bat. The employee fell to the ground, causing another runner to fall, too. The costumes were padded, so the victims received only minor knee scrapes, but Simon was taken from the park in handcuffs, charged with disorderly conduct, and fined $438.

Apology: An embarrassed Simon later called the injured sausages—Mandy Block and Veronica Piech—to personally apologize. Block, the Italian sausage that took the hit, accepted the apology and asked for an autographed bat from Simon—the one that he used to hit her. (She got it.)

I APOLOGIZE IN YOUR GENERAL DIRECTION

Incident: In an exhibit called "The Roman Experience," the Deva Museum in Chester, England, invited visitors to stroll through streets constructed to look as they did during Roman times. Hoping to provide an authentic experience, staff added an odor to the Roman latrines. They got one called "Flatulence" from Dale Air, a company that makes aromas for several museums. Unfortunately, it was too authentic: several schoolchildren immediately vomited.

Apology: Museum supervisor Christine Turner publicly apologized, saying, "It really was disgusting." But Dale Air director Frank Knight was somewhat less contrite. "We feel sorry for the kids," he said, "but it is nice to see that the smell is so realistic."

COMIC RELIEF, TOO

More funny lines from funny people.

"I don't see the point of testing cosmetics on rabbits, because they're already cute."
—**Rich Hall**

"My wife's an earth sign. I'm a water sign. Together we make mud."
—**Henny Youngman**

"When authorities warn you of the sinfulness of sex, there is an important lesson to be learned: Do not have sex with the authorities."
—**Matt Groening**

"How come if you mix flour and water together you get glue? And when you add eggs and sugar, you get a cake? Where does the glue go?"
—**Rita Rudner**

"Contraceptives should be used on every conceivable occasion."
—**Spike Milligan**

"My wife asked for plastic surgery; I cut up her credit cards."
—**Rodney Dangerfield**

"Never moon a werewolf."
—**Mike Binder**

"Mario Andretti has retired from racecar driving. He's getting old. He ran his entire last race with his left blinker on."
—**Jon Stewart**

"I buy books on suicide at bookstores. You can't get them at the library, because people don't return them."
—**Kevin Nealon**

"My mother breast-fed me with powdered milk. It was my first do-it-yourself project."
—**Buzz Nutley**

"I like to leave a message before the beep."
—**Steven Wright**

"Of course we need firearms. You never know when some nut is going to come up to you and say something like, 'You're fired.' You gotta be ready."
—**Dave Attell**

"I wonder if the Buddha was married...his wife would say, 'Are you just going to sit around like that all day?'"
—**Garry Shandling**

MANAGEMENT EXPECTS...

*JoAnn Padgett of the Bathroom Readers' Hysterical Society
sent us this page from an old almanac with a note: "And
you guys think you've got it bad." (No, we don't.)*

**In 1870, after the government passed new, "liberal" labor laws,
one business released the following manifesto to its employees.**

N O T I C E

1. Staff members must be present between the hours of 7:00 a.m.
and 6:00 p.m. on weekdays and only until noon on Saturday.

2. Daily prayers will be held each morning in the main office
with the clerical staff in attendance.

3. The staff will not disport themselves in raiment of bright colors, nor will they wear hose "unless in good repair."

4. A stove is provided for the clerical staff. Coal and wood must
be kept in the locker. Each member of the staff should bring four
pounds of coal each day during cold weather.

5. No member of the staff may leave the room without permission. Calls of nature are permitted and the staff may use the garden below the second gate. This area must be kept in good order.

6. Now that business hours have been reduced drastically, the
partaking of food is allowed between 11:30 and noon, but work
will not, on any account, cease.

7. A new pencil sharpener is available on application to Mr.
Rogers.

8. Trainees will report 40 minutes before prayer and will report
to Mr. Rogers after closing hours to clean private offices with
brushes, brooms, and scrubbers provided by the management.

9. Management recognizes the generosity of the new labor laws,
but will expect a much greater work output to compensate for
these near utopian conditions.

THE DOO-DOO MAN

In our opinion, the ability to take a negative experience and turn it into something positive is a real gift. But what inspired this man could appeal only to bathroom readers.

TRAIL HAZARD

In 1985 Dr. A. Bern Hoff stepped in something unpleasant while hiking in Norway's Jotunheim Mountains. The unpleasant "something" had been deposited right in the middle of the hiking trail and, judging from appearances, only minutes before. Maybe it was his keen eyesight, maybe it was his degree in parasitic pathology, but somehow Dr. Hoff knew right away what he'd stepped in: "people droppings," as he delicately puts it.

It wasn't the first time Hoff had trod on people droppings, either: an avid hiker, he'd had similar experiences atop Africa's Mount Kilimanjaro, Hawaii's Haleakala Crater, and the Grand Canyon in Arizona. He stepped into people's "business" so often that it seemed like every hiking trip was turning into a business trip. As a former official with the Centers for Disease Control, he understood that the problem wasn't just disgusting, it was a serious health hazard. Hoff decided it was time for action.

"I got tired of seeing and smelling this stuff on the trail," he says. "Nobody wanted to deal with it, so I said, 'Hey, I'll do it.' This has got to stop." He formed H.A.D.D.—Hikers Against Doo-Doo.

THE NUMBER TWO PROBLEM

Hoff had stumbled—literally—onto a problem that started growing rapidly in the 1980s and continues today: Record numbers of people are hiking and camping out in the wild. And since most first-timers have never been taught how to properly "do their business" in the backcountry, in many popular outdoor destinations around the country, the results are plain to see, smell...and step in.

To counter this disturbing trend, H.A.D.D. offers a number of different "business plans." It teaches new campers tried-and-true waste-disposal techniques, and serves as an international clearinghouse for new waste-disposal ideas.

Nothing to sneeze at: The common flu kills 20,000 people a year.

THE CAN

H.A.D.D. has also designed a cheap, sturdy portable privy called "The Can" that can be made from two ordinary 55-gallon drums. At last count, H.A.D.D. members have set up more than 280 Cans in wilderness areas around the world. The organization hopes to one day mount an expedition to bring The Can to the top of Mount Aconcagua, long known as Argentina's "tallest and most defiled peak," and is raising funds to improve the facilities on Russia's Mount Elbrus, which *Outside* magazine dubbed "the world's nastiest outhouse."

When Hoff founded H.A.D.D. in 1990, it consisted of only himself and his soiled hiking boots. Today the organization boasts more than 10,000 members, with chapters all over the world. "We're tongue-in-cheek, of course, but we are serious about trying to clean up the environment," Hoff says.

BUSINESS SCHOOL

Some tips on how to mind your own business in the wild:

• Pack out what you pack in. Bring several square pieces of paper, a paper bag full of kitty litter, and several zipper-type plastic bags or bags with twist-ties. Do your business onto the paper, then put the paper and your business into one of the plastic bags. Pour in some kitty litter, and seal the bag tightly. Dispose of it properly when you get back to civilization.

• If you do have to bury your business, be sure to do it: 1) at least 200 feet away from the nearest water source, trail, or campsite; 2) in organic soil, not sandy soil; and 3) in a "cat hole" dug at least six inches across and six inches deep. (*Hint:* Bring a small shovel.)

• Don't bury your business under a rock: business needs heat and moisture to decompose properly, and the rock will inhibit both.

• Don't bury it in the snow, either: snow melts...but your business doesn't. When spring comes it will reappear.

• Use toilet paper sparingly if at all; if you do use it, *don't* burn it and *don't* bury it with your business. Keep it in a plastic bag and dispose of it properly at the end of your trip.

• Pee at least 200 feet from the nearest water source, and *don't* pee on green plants—otherwise, when your pee dries, animals will be attracted to the salt.

Q: How many bedrooms are there on the board game Clue? A: None.

URBAN LEGENDS

Hey—did you hear about the guy who invented a car that can run for months on a single tank of gas? We've looked into some urban legends to see if there's any truth to them.

LEGEND: If you eat a lot of cup-of-soups, you *must* remove the noodles from the Styrofoam cup and put them in a bowl before you add boiling water. Why? There's a layer of wax lining the cup that will liquefy when you pour in hot water. The wax can accumulate in your system, causing a deadly "waxy buildup."

HOW IT SPREAD: Via word of mouth, for more than 20 years. The latest version is an e-mail that describes how a college student lived on the stuff for months to save money, only to die when so much wax built up in his stomach that surgeons were unable to remove it.

THE TRUTH: Cup-A-Noodle cups and those of similar soups don't have a wax lining—they're just ordinary Styrofoam cups. And even if the cups *did* contain wax, wax is so easy to digest that it's a fairly common ingredient in candy and other foods.

LEGEND: On the day he retires, a longtime General Motors employee is invited down to the factory lot to pick out any car he wants as a retirement gift. He picks a Chevy Caprice. But after weeks of long drives in the country he finds he still hasn't used up the first tank of gas. When he calls GM to praise the car's performance, they react suspiciously…and the very next morning he looks out into his driveway and sees two mysterious men in white lab coats working under the hood of his car. The retiree chases the men away, but from then on his car gets only normal gas mileage.

It turns out that the car he picked was actually a 200+ mpg prototype that GM is hiding from consumers, so that they have to buy more gas than is really necessary. When GM realized the Caprice had gotten out of the factory, they dispatched two company engineers to "fix" it.

HOW IT SPREAD: The story has been floating around since the 1920s, spreading first by word of mouth, then by photocopies

Exhibitionists: Houseflies prefer to breed in the middle of a room.

posted on bulletin boards and lately by e-mail. The tale resurfaces every few years with fresh new details—new auto companies and updated makes of car—that keep it believable.

THE TRUTH: This story fails the common sense test: why would any auto company suppress technology that would give it such a huge advantage over its competitors? If GM could make a 200+ mpg car using patented technology that its competitors didn't have, it would dominate the industry.

This legend has been kept alive by generations of con artists who claim to have invented 200+ mpg carburetors or magic pills that can turn tap water into auto fuel. When frustrated investors demand to see proof that the "inventions" really do work, the con artists frequently claim that the invention has been stolen by mysterious men in black suits or that it's been suppressed by the auto industry. Rather than admit they've been conned, gullible investors sometimes pass these claims along as true.

(Similar urban legends haunt the tire industry, which is supposedly suppressing tires that will last for a million miles, and the drug industry, which is accused of buying up the patents to electric headache cures so that the public has to keep buying aspirin.)

LEGEND: The screams of a UCLA coed being sexually assaulted are ignored because the assault takes place during a midnight "scream session," when students scream out their dorm windows to relieve the stress of final exams. The attack forced a change in university policy: "To this day, anyone screaming unnecessarily during finals week at UCLA is subject to expulsion."

HOW IT SPREAD: Originally by word of mouth, then by e-mail, from one college student to another.

THE TRUTH: No such attack ever happened—and UCLA doesn't expel students for screaming during finals. This legend, which has been attributed to many different universities around the country, is kept alive by the insecurities of incoming freshmen, nervous about living away from home for the first time.

LEGEND: On October 2, 1994, Lauren Archer let her three-year-old son Kevin play in the "ball pit" of a McDonald's play area. Afterward Kevin started whimpering, telling his mommy, "It hurts." That night when Archer bathed her son, she noticed an odd welt

---

Lost in translation: A French kiss is known as an English kiss in France.

on his butt. It looked like he had a large splinter. She immediately made an appointment with the doctor to have it removed the next day, but when Kevin became violently ill later that evening—she rushed him to the emergency room.

Too late. Kevin died from what an autopsy revealed to be a heroin overdose…and the "splinter" in his rear end turned out to be the broken-off needle of a drug-filled syringe. How did it get there? Police investigators emptied out the McDonald's ball pit and found, according to one version of the story, "Rotten food, several hypodermic needles, knives, half-eaten candy, diapers, feces, and the stench of urine."

HOW IT SPREAD: First by e-mail beginning in the mid-1990s, then by word of mouth from one frightened parent to another. The story's credibility is supported by the fact that the original e-mail gives specific names and dates, and even cites a newspaper article that supposedly appeared in the October 10, 1994 issue of the *Houston Chronicle*.

THE TRUTH: It's a hoax. No such incident ever happened and no such article ever appeared in the *Houston Chronicle*. Don't take our word for it—after years of denying the rumors, the *Chronicle* finally printed an official denial in February 2000. A similar story about rattlesnakes in a ball pit—at Burger King—is also false.

*   *   *

CELEBRITY EXCUSES

"Crack is cheap. I make too much money to use crack."
> —Whitney Houston, *on why crack wasn't on the long list of drugs she admitted to having used*

"I was told that I should shoplift. My director said I should try it out."
> —Wynona Ryder, *to the security guard who busted her at Saks Fifth Avenue*

"I've killed enough of the world's trees."
> —Stephen King, *on why he's quitting writing*

HOAXMEISTER

Think everything you read in the newspaper or see on the news has been checked for accuracy? Think again. Sometimes the media will repeat whatever they're told...and this guy set out to prove it.

MONKEY SEE, MONKEY SAY

Joey Skaggs's career as a hoax artist began in the mid-1960s when he first combined his art training with sociopolitical activism. He wanted to show that instead of being guardians of the truth, the media machine often runs stories without verifying the facts. And in proving his point, he perpetrated some pretty clever hoaxes.

HOAX #1: A Cathouse for Dogs
In 1976 Skaggs ran an ad in the *Village Voice* for a dog bordello. For $50 Skaggs promised satisfaction for any sexually deprived Fido. Then he hosted a special "night in the cathouse for dogs" just for the media. A beautiful woman and her Saluki, both clad in tight red sweaters and bows, paraded up and down in front of the panting "clientele" (male dogs belonging to Skaggs's friends). The ASPCA lodged a slew of protests and had Skaggs arrested (and indicted) for cruelty to animals. The event was even featured on an Emmy-nominated WABC News documentary. But the joke was on them—the "dog bordello" never existed.

HOAX #2: Save the Geoduck!
It's pronounced "gooey-duck" and it's a long-necked clam native to Puget Sound, Washington, with a digging muscle that bears a striking resemblance to the male reproductive organ of a horse. In 1987 Skaggs posed as a doctor (Dr. Long) and staged a protest rally in front of the Japan Society. Why? Because according to "Dr. Long," the geoduck was considered to be an aphrodisiac in Asia, and people were eating the mollusk into extinction. Although neither claim had the slightest basis in fact, Skaggs's "Clamscam" was good enough to sucker WNBC, UPI, the German news magazine *Der Spiegel*, and a number of Japanese papers into reporting the story as fact.

All toads are frogs, but not all frogs are toads.

HOAX #3: Miracle Roach Hormone Cure

Skaggs pretended to be an entomologist from Colombia named Dr. Josef Gregor in 1981. In an interview with WNBC-TV's *Live at Five*, "Dr. Gregor" claimed to have graduated from the University of Bogota, and said his "Miracle Roach Hormone Cure" cured the common cold, acne, and menstrual cramps. An amazed Skaggs remarked later, "Nobody ever checked my credentials." The interviewers didn't realize they were being had until Dr. Gregor played his theme song—*La Cucaracha*.

HOAX #4: Sergeant Bones and the Fat Squad

In 1986 Skaggs appeared on *Good Morning, America* as a former Marine Corps drill sergeant named Joe Bones, who was determined to stamp out obesity in the United States. Flanked by a squad of tough-looking commandos, Sergeant Bones announced that for "$300 a day plus expenses," his "Fat Squad" would infiltrate an overweight client's home and physically stop them from snacking. "You can hire us but you can't fire us," he deadpanned, staring into the camera. "Our commandos take no bribes." Reporters from the *Philadelphia Enquirer, Washington Post, Miami Herald,* and the *New York Daily News* all believed—and ran with—the story.

HOAX #5: Maqdananda, the Psychic Attorney

On April 1, 1994, Skaggs struck again with a 30-second TV spot in which he dressed like a swami. Seated on a pile of cushions, Maqdananda asked viewers, "Why deal with the legal system without knowing the outcome beforehand?" Along with normal third dimension legal issues—divorce, accidental injury, wills, trusts— Maqdananda claimed he could help renegotiate contracts made in past lives, sue for psychic surgery malpractice, and help rectify psychic injustices. "There is no statute of limitations in the psychic realm," he said. Viewers just had to call the number at the bottom of their screen: 1-808-UCA-DADA. In Hawaii, *CNN Headline News* ran the spot 40 times during the week. When people called the number (and dozens did), they were greeted by the swami's voice on an answering machine, saying, "I knew you'd call." Skaggs later revealed that the swami—and his political statement about the proliferation of New Age gurus and ambulance-chasing attorneys—was all a hoax.

THE BIGGER THEY ARE...

*Sometimes making big business decisions means
making big blunders, as these folks found out.*

BAD APPLE

In 1988 Apple Computers hired a small computer company
from Virginia called Quantum Computer Services to develop an online service for their customers. It was to be called
AppleLink Personal Edition and was set to come out in 1989. But
before Quantum could launch the service, Apple changed their
minds and terminated their contract. Bad idea. Quantum had
negotiated in their contract that if Apple let them go, they got
to keep the technology. They launched the service themselves in
late 1989, with a new name...America Online.

STAR WARS: THE PUBLISHER'S MENACE
British book publisher Dorling Kindersley saw sales of its *Star
Wars* books rise dramatically after the release of the movie *The
Phantom Menace* in 1999. Elated company execs quickly ordered a
huge printing for the Christmas sales season—and sold a whopping 3 million copies. The only problem—they had printed 13
million copies. Loss: $22.4 million. In January 2000, the already
debt-plagued company admitted the mistake and CEO James Middlehurst resigned. In March, the once-prosperous worldwide publisher was sold to media giant Pearson. (*Note:* Ten million books
would make a stack more than 150 miles high.)

A TOBACCO COMPANY TELLS THE TRUTH!
In 2001 tobacco giant Philip Morris did a study of the effects of cigarette smoking for the leaders of the Czech Republic. The report
they issued touted the "positive effects" that smoking has for government. It shortens people's lives, they said, which means lower
costs for pensions, housing, and health care for the elderly. The
details of the report were supposed to be private, but somehow the
press got hold of them and made them public. Result: A major public relations blow to a company that had just spent $100 million to
boost its image. Philip Morris issued an apology to the Czech people

Scaredy cat? Charles Lindbergh carried a Felix the Cat doll with him on his famous flight.

and then canceled plans to make similar reports in four other nations.

A FINE ROMANCE (OR TWO)
In 1991 Random House editor Joni Evans thought she could cash in on the fame of TV's *Dynasty* star Joan Collins and offered her a $4 million contract—with a $1.3 million advance—to write two romance novels. (Collins's sister, Jackie, is a bestselling novelist.) Collins turned in manuscripts for *The Ruling Passion* and *Hell Hath No Fury*, but Evans thought they were terrible and wouldn't publish them. Random House sued Collins but couldn't get the advance money back. As if giving a huge advance to an unproven writer wasn't a big enough blunder, Evans missed a clause put in the contract stipulating that Collins would be paid whether or not her manuscripts were published. Result: Collins ended up with $2.6 million of Random House's cash for two books that never went to press.

IT'S NOT OK
Before she joined Random House (see item above), Evans was a senior editor at the publishing house William Morrow, where she committed another blunder in an otherwise successful career. When Morrow was approached about the paperback rights of a certain new author, she advised her boss against it, sure that the book would never sell. The price for the rights at the time was $10,000...three months later, the rights went for $675,000. The book was the groundbreaking self-help title *I'm OK, You're OK*. It went to #4 on the *New York Times* Best Seller list in 1970 and has sold over 15 million copies since...most of them paperbacks.

LISTEN CAREFULLY
In November 2001, the privately owned Japanese company Dentsu, the world's fourth largest advertising agency, decided to go public. They had the Wall Street firm UBS Warburg handle their initial public offering, and instructed the brokers to sell 16 shares at 610,000 yen ($4,925) each. But the brokers mistakenly listed 610,000 shares at 16 yen (about 13¢) each. Before they discovered the error, 65,000 of the shares had been sold. Warburg had to buy them all back on the open market. The exact amount of Warburg's loss was undisclosed, but it was estimated to be as high as $100 million.

WORD PLAY

What do these familiar phrases really mean? Etymologists have researched them and come up with these explanations.

FLY OFF THE HANDLE
Meaning: Get very angry, very quickly.
Background: Refers to axe heads, which, in the days before mass merchandising, were sometimes fastened poorly to their handles. If one flew off while being used, it was a dangerous situation... with unpredictable results.

HIGH ON THE HOG
Meaning: Luxurious, prosperous.
Background: The tastiest parts of a hog are its upper parts. If you're living high on the hog, you've got the best it has to offer.

PULL THE WOOL OVER SOMEONE'S EYES
Meaning: Fool someone.
Background: "Goes back to the days when all gentlemen wore powdered wigs like the ones still worn by the judges in British courts. The word wool was then a popular, joking term for hair....The expression 'pull the wool over his eyes' came from the practice of tilting a man's wig over his eyes, so he couldn't see what was going on."

HOOKER
Meaning: Prostitute.
Background: Although occasionally used before the Civil War, its widespread popularity can probably be traced to General Joseph Hooker, a Union soldier who was well-known for the liquor and whores in his camp. He was ultimately demoted, and Washington prostitutes were jokingly referred to as "Hooker's Division."

LET THE CAT OUT OF THE BAG
Meaning: Reveal the truth.
Background: Refers to a con game practiced at country fairs in old England. A trickster tried to sell a cat in a burlap bag to an unwary bumpkin, saying it was a pig. If the victim figured out the trick and insisted on seeing the animal, the cat had to be let out of the bag.

The largest painting on earth is a 72,437-square-foot smiley face.

BATHROOM LORE

*It seems appropriate to begin this volume with a little background
on the room you're probably sitting in right now.*

THE FIRST BATHROOM

The idea of a separate room for the disposal of bodily waste goes back at least 10,000 years (to 8000 B.C.). On Orkney, an island off the coast of Scotland, the inhabitants, who lived in stone huts, created a drainage system that carried the waste directly into a nearby stream.

THE FIRST SOPHISTICATED PLUMBING

• Bathtubs dating back to 2000 B.C. have been found on the island of Crete (where there's also evidence of the first flush toilet). Considering that they were built almost 4,000 years ago, the similarity to modern baths is startling.
• Around 1500 B.C., elite Egyptians had hot and cold running water; it came into homes through a system of copper tubing or pipes.

THE FIRST SOCIAL BATHING

The ancient Romans took their bathing seriously, building public facilities wherever they settled—including London. The more elaborate of these included massage salons, food and wine, gardens, exercise rooms, and in at least one case, a public library. Coed bathing was not uncommon, nor frowned upon.

A STEP BACKWARD

• As Christianity became increasingly powerful, techniques of plumbing and waste disposal—and cleanliness in general—were forgotten; only in monasteries was this knowledge preserved.
• For hundreds of years, people in Europe basically stopped washing their bodies, in large part because nudity—even for reasons of health or hygiene—was regarded as sinful by the Church.
• In some cases, a reverence for dirt arose in its place. St. Francis of Assisi, for example, believed "dirtiness was an insignia of holiness."
• Upper-class citizens tried to cover up the inevitable body odors

---

First American to have plumbing installed in his home: Henry Wadsworth Longfellow, 1840.

with clothes and perfume, but the rest of the population suffered with the rank smells of filth.

CHAMBER POTS AND STREET ETIQUETTE

• Until the early 1800s, Europeans relieved themselves in chamber pots, outhouses, streets, alleys, and anywhere else they happened to feel like it.

• It was so common to relieve oneself in public that people were concerned about how to behave if they noticed acquaintances "urinating or defecating" on the street. Proper etiquette: Act like you don't see them.

• Chamber pots were used at night, or when it was too cold to go outside. Their contents were supposed to be picked up once a day by a "waste man," who carted the community's leavings to a public cesspool.

• But frequently, the chamber pot was surreptitiously dumped at night, which made it dangerous to go strolling in the evening.

DISEASE AND CHANGE

The lack of bathing took an enormous toll on the European in the Middle Ages, as epidemics caused by unsanitary living conditions became rampant. But in the 1830s, a London outbreak of cholera —a disease the English believed could only be contracted by inferior races—finally convinced the government to put its power behind public sanitation. Over the next 50 years, the British built new public facilities that set the pace for the rest of the world.

THE MODERN FLUSH TOILET

The modern flush toilet was invented by an Englishman named Alexander Cumming in 1775. Cumming's toilet emptied directly into a pipe, which then carried the undesirable matter to a cesspool. Other toilets had done this, too, but Cumming's major improvement was the addition of a "stink trap" that kept water in the pipe and thus blocked odor.

Note: It is widely believed that an Englishman named Thomas Crapper invented the toilet. That's probably a myth.

HEAD FOR THE JOHN

• In the mid-1500s in England, a chamber pot was referred to as a "Jake." A hundred years later, it became a "John," or "Cousin John." In the mid-1800s, it was also dubbed a "Joe."

The first known contraceptive was crocodile dung, used by Egyptians in 2000 B.C.

• That still may not be the source of the term "John" for the bathroom—it may date to the 1920s, when Men's and Ladies' rooms became common in public places. They were also referred to as "Johns" and "Janes"—presumably after John and Jane Doe.

• The term *potty* comes from the pint-sized chamber pot built for kids.

BATHROOMS

• The bathroom we know—with a combination toilet and bath—didn't exist until the 1850s. And then only for the rich.

• Until then, the term *bathroom*—which came into use in the 1820s or 1830s—meant, literally, a room with a bathtub in it.

A FEW AMERICAN FIRSTS

• First American hotel with indoor modern bathrooms: The Tremont House in Boston, 1880s.

• First toilet in the White House: 1825, installed for John Quincy Adams (leading to a new slang term for toilet—a *quincy*).

• First city with modern waterworks: Philadelphia, 1820.

• First city with a modern sewage system: Boston, 1823.

THE FIRST TOILET PAPER

• In ancient times, there was no T.P. Well-to-do Romans used sponges, wool, and rosewater. Everyone else used whatever was at hand, including sticks, stones, leaves, or dry bones. In the Middle Ages, nobles preferred silk or goose feathers (still attached to the pliable neck).

• Toilet paper was introduced in America in 1857, as a package of loose sheets. But it was too much like the paper Americans already used—the Sears catalog. It flopped.

• In 1879, an Englishman named Walter Alcock created the first perforated rolls of toilet paper. A year later, Philadelphia's Scott Brothers saw the potential in the U.S. for a product that would constantly have to be replaced. They introduced Waldorf Tissue (later Scott Tissue), which was discreetly sold in plain brown wrappers. The timing was right—by then there were enough bathrooms in America to make "toilet tissue" a success.

Starfish have eight eyes—one at the end of each leg.

HAPPY BIRTHDAY!

It may come as a surprise, but the fact is that celebrating birthdays is a relatively new tradition for anyone but kings and queens.

BIRTHDAY CELEBRATIONS.
The first people known to celebrate birthdays were the ancient Egyptians—starting around 3000 B.C. But only the queen and male members of the royal family were honored. No one even bothered recording anyone else's birth dates.
• The ancient Greeks expanded the concept a little: they celebrated the birthdays of all adult males...and kept on celebrating, even after a man had died. Women's and children's birthdays were considered too unimportant to observe.
• The Greeks also introduced birthday cakes (which they got from the Persians) and birthday candles (which may have honored Artemis, goddess of the moon, because they symbolized moonlight).
• It wasn't until the Middle Ages that German peasants became the first to celebrate the birthdays of everyone in the family. Children's birthday celebrations were especially important. Called *Kinderfestes*, they were the forerunner to our toddler birthday parties.

THE BIRTHDAY SONG. Mildred and Patty Smith Hill, two sisters from Louisville, Kentucky, published a song called "Good Morning to All" in a kindergarten songbook in 1893. They wrote it as a "welcoming" song, to be sung to young students at the beginning of each school day
In 1924, a songbook editor changed the lyrics to "Happy Birthday to You" and published it without the Hill sisters' permission. The new lyrics made it a popular tune, but the Hill family took no action...until the song appeared in a Broadway play in 1933. Then Jessica Hill (a third sister) sued for copyright infringement. She won, but most singers stopped using the song rather than pay the royalty fee. In one play called *Happy Birthday*, for example, actress Helen Hayes *spoke* the words to avoid paying it.
Today, whenever "Happy Birthday" is sung commercially, a royalty still must be paid to the Hills.

The U.S. government spent $277,000 on "pickle research" in 1993.

STRANGE LAWSUITS

*These days, it seems people will sue each other over practically anything.
Here are a few bizarre real-life court cases, taken from news reports.*

THE PLAINTIFF: Randall Dale Adams
THE DEFENDANT: Filmmaker Errol Morris
THE LAWSUIT: Adams was convicted of murder in
1977. Ten years later, Morris made a film about the Adams case
and became convinced he was innocent. The movie, *The Thin Blue
Line*, presented the case for Adams's innocence so effectively that
he was released from prison. Morris's reward? When Adams got out
of jail, he sued the filmmaker for $60,000 for using his story.
THE VERDICT: Settled out of court. Adams dropped the suit,
and Morris agreed that Adams should receive full rights to any further commercial uses—notably films or books—of his life.

THE PLAINTIFF: 32-year-old Mary Sue Stowe
THE DEFENDANT: Junior Davis, her ex-husband
THE LAWSUIT: An unusual custody case: When they split up,
Mary wanted custody of seven frozen embryos that had been ferti-
lized by Junior's sperm. Junior wanted them brought back to room
temperature.
THE VERDICT: The case went all the way to the U.S. Supreme
Court—which sided with Junior. Mary Sue's lawyers said she was
"devastated" by the ruling—but nevertheless would try to "talk
one-on-one with her ex-husband" to get him to change his mind.

THE PLAINTIFF: J. R. Costigan
THE DEFENDANT: Bobby Mackey's Music World, a country
music bar in Wilder, Kentucky
THE LAWSUIT: Costigan claimed a ghost "punched and kicked
him" while he was using the bar's restroom one night in 1993. He
sued the bar, asking for $1,000 in damages and demanding that a
sign be put up in the restroom warning of the ghost's presence.
The club's lawyer filed a motion to dismiss the case, citing the difficulty of getting the ghost into court to testify for the defense.
THE VERDICT: Case dismissed.

The average adult male shaves off a pound of beard growth every 10 years.

THE PLAINTIFFS: The Cherry Sisters, an Iowa singing group
THE DEFENDANT: The Des Moines *Register*
THE LAWSUIT: A landmark libel case. At the turn of the century, the Register ran a scathing review of the Cherry Sisters' act. Their reporter wrote that "Their long, skinny arms, equipped with talons at the extremities...waved frantically at the suffering audience. The mouths of their rancid features opened like caverns, and sounds like the wailings of damned souls issued therefrom." Outraged and humiliated, the singers sued for libel.
THE VERDICT: The judge asked the sisters to perform their act for him in court...and then ruled in favor of the newspaper.

THE PLAINTIFF: Andrea Pizzo, a 23-year-old former University of Maine student
THE DEFENDANT: The University of Maine
THE LAWSUIT: Apparently, Pizzo was taking a class in live-stock management one afternoon in 1991, when a cow butted her. She sued, claiming the school "should have known that the heifer had a personality problem."
THE VERDICT: Verdict unknown. (Does any reader know? Write and tell us.)

THE PLAINTIFF: Robert Kropinski, a 36-year-old Philadelphia real estate manager
THE DEFENDANT: The Transcendental Meditation Society and the guru Maharishi Mahesh Yogi
THE LAWSUIT: Kropinski worked with TM groups for 11 years, but he finally sued them because "he was never able to achieve the 'perfect state of life' they promised, and suffered psychological disorders as a result. One broken agreement: he had been told he would be taught to 'fly' through self-levitation, but he learned only to 'hop with the legs folded in the lotus position.'"
THE VERDICT: A U.S. district court jury in Washington, D.C., awarded him nearly $138,000 in damages.

Musical note: A "Big Band" is any band with 10 or more musicians.

THE BIRTH OF KLEENEX

*Feel a sneeze coming on? If you're like most Americans,
you reach for a Kleenex, without even thinking about it.
But that wasn't always true. In fact, not so long ago there
was no such thing. Here's how they were invented.*

MILITARY SUPPLIES

The Kimberly-Clark Corporation originally designed the product that evolved into Kleenex tissues for *military* use.
• It started in 1914—World War I was being fought in Europe, and the cotton soldiers needed for bandages was starting to run out.
• So Kimberly-Clark devised a product called Cellucotton—an absorbent, soft paper that could be used to dress wounds.
• It was so effective that the army looked for other uses. And they found one: They used it as an air filter for soldiers' gas masks.

PEACETIME PROBLEM

Kimberly-Clark got too enthusiastic about their new material and overproduced it. After the war, they had so much Cellucotton left over that they *had* to find a new way to sell the stuff.
• Their clever solution: They marketed it as a modern women's tool for cleaning off makeup and a "sanitary cold cream remover."
• Calling it Kleenex Kerchiefs, they hired movie stars to endorse it as a secret path to glamour. It was a big success.

SURPRISE SOLUTION

But Americans found another use for the product. Kimberly-Clark was inundated with letters that informed them the Kleenex Kerchiefs were great for nose-blowing.
• Men, in particular, wanted to know why Kleenex had to be a woman's product. And women griped that men were stealing their Kleenex to sneeze into.
• During the 1920s, Kimberly-Clark introduced a pop-up box that always left one tissue sticking out of the box, waiting to be used.
• But the question remained—were people buying Kleenex as a cold cream remover, or a nose-blower? A survey showed that 60 percent of the people used it as the latter. So that's what K-C emphasized, and that's how we think of it today.

THE ORIGIN OF SHERLOCK HOLMES

Sherlock Holmes is one of the most widely recognized characters in all of English literature. He isn't just a person, he's a cultural icon. His adventures are also some of our favorite bathroom reading. In his honor, we've done a little detective work and uncovered these facts.

THE DOCTOR IS IN

The year was 1877. Dr. Joseph Bell, a brilliant surgeon and lecturer at Scotland's prestigious Edinburgh University Medical School, was standing next to one of the hospital's patients. His students—including an 18-year-old named Arthur Conan Doyle—stood around him as he motioned to the patient and systematically ticked off his first observations about the case. "You'll notice, gentlemen," Dr. Bell began, "that the man is clearly a left-handed cobbler."

How could Dr. Bell tell a man's occupation—and the fact that he was left-handed—from a single glance at someone he had never met before? Doyle and the rest of the students were amazed. And this wasn't the first time, either. Bell made these amazing deductions every time he examined patients in front of the class.

Dr. Bell continued with his observations, this time pointing to the man's pants. "Notice the worn places in the corduroy breeches, where a cobbler rests his lapstone."

It was the pants! Dr. Bell read the man's life story from a patch of worn corduroy. It was amazing, and Arthur Conan Doyle would never forget it.

FROM BAD TO VERSE

Nine years later, in 1886, *Doctor* Arthur Conan Doyle—who had put himself through medical school largely through the sale of short stories—turned again to writing to try to save his failing medical practice. He decided to write a detective story using Dr. Bell as a model. "I thought of my old teacher," Doyle later recalled, "and his eerie tricks of spotting details. If he were a detective, he would surely reduce this fascinating but unorganized

Humans are the only primates that don't have pigment in the palms of their hands.

business to something nearer to an exact science. It was surely possible in real life, so why should I not make it plausible in fiction? It is all very well to say that a man is clever, but the reader wants to see examples of it——such examples as Bell gave us every day in the (hospital) wards. The idea amused me."

The Name Game

Originally, Doyle named his detective Sherrinford Holmes, after Oliver Wendell Holmes—and named Holmes's sidekick Ormand Sacker. But during the three weeks it took to write the story, Doyle renamed the characters: Sherlock Holmes, after a cricket player he had once played against, and Thomas Watson, after Patrick Watson, a colleague of Dr. Bell's.

Doyle sent the manuscript for *A Study in Scarlet* to a publisher ...but it was returned unread. So he sent it to a second, a third, a fourth, and a fifth...and was rejected each time. Finally, Ward, Lock & Company agreed to publish it in a magazine called *Beeton's Christmas Annual,* where it was read by the English public and quickly forgotten.

BORN IN THE USA

Fortunately for Doyle, a pirated version of the story was printed in *Lippencott* magazine. "The wife of the editor of *Lippincott* liked *Study in Scarlet,*" says Sherlock Holmes expert Ely Liebow, "and her husband arranged to dine with Doyle and a writer named Oscar Wilde" when he was visiting England. It was one of the most productive business meetings in the history of English literature, Liebow recounts. "At the end of the meal, the editor had commitments from Doyle for his second Holmes novel, *The Sign of the Four*, and from Wilde for *The Picture of Dorian Gray*,"

But it wasn't until 1890 that Doyle made enough money from his writing to enable him to shut down his medical practice, and it wasn't until the story *Scandal in Bohemia* was published in Strand magazine in 1891 that he really made it big. "That story established his reputation," Liebow says. "Sherlock Holmes became very popular, and the money started pouring in."

THE PERFECT CRIME

Just as actors resent being typecast, so too did Doyle come to resent Sherlock Holmes. His interests turned to more "serious" works... but the public continued to clamor for Holmes tales. In 1893, Doyle decided to kill Holmes off. He sent him over Switzerland's Reichenbach Falls wrestling with arch-villain Professor Moriarity. Called *The Final Problem*, the story killed both characters. The public was outraged—more than 20,000 people cancelled their subscriptions to the *Strand*—but Doyle still hoped it would be the end of Sherlock. "I am weary of his name," he sighed to a friend.

Beyond and Back

It wasn't the end. Public demand for Sherlock Holmes stories continued unabated. Doyle succumbed to the pressure in 1902 and published *The Hound of the Baskervilles*, in which Watson discovers a manuscript describing a previously unknown Holmes case. But even this partial resurrection wasn't enough for Holmes fans, so in 1903 Doyle gave in and brought Holmes back to life in *The Adventure of the Empty House*. Why the change of heart? An American magazine offered him $5,000 per story, and a British publisher offered him almost $3,000 per story for the British rights, unheard-of sums in those days.

CASE CLOSED

Sir Arthur Conan Doyle would write a total 56 short stories and 4 novels featuring Sherlock Holmes, and, just as he feared, the general public came to associate him exclusively with that body of work. Still, his fate wasn't that terrible—his 1902 historical study of *The Great Boer War* won him great praise from historians and earned him a knighthood, and his 6-volume history of World War I is considered a masterpiece, even though it never won him the fame his novels did. Doyle became a very rich man—by the 1920s he was the highest-paid writer on Earth, and he left an estate so huge that his heirs were still suing each other over it well into the 1990s.

Note: How good a real-life sleuth was Dr. Joseph Bell? So good— at least according to legend—that he correctly identified "Jack the Ripper." "The story," says Dr. Ely Liebow, "is that Bell and his friend analyzed the Ripper killings and put the name of the killer in an envelope. They gave the envelope to the Edinburgh police, who sent it to London, where the crimes occurred. The contents of the envelope were never divulged, but there were no more murders after they named the killer."

Ten percent of the Russian government's income comes from the sale of vodka.

HOW FAMOUS CAN YOU GET?

The people listed on this page are so famous that they only need one name for us to recognize them. Can you fit all 39 of them into their proper places in the grid, crossword-style?

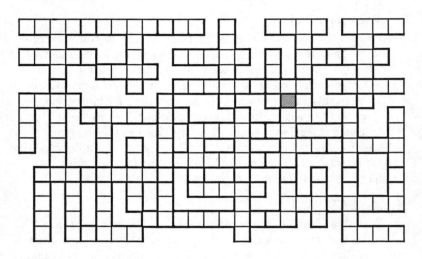

4-letter words
Bach
Bono
Cato
Cher
Enya
Iman
Nero
Ovid

5-letter words
Aesop
Bjork
Charo

Elvis
Evita
Medea
Midas
Nehru
Oprah
Plato
Sting

6-letter words
Castro
Chanel
Merlin

7-letter words
Cochise
Galileo
Picasso
Saladin

8-letter words
Einstein
Hannibal
Mohammed

9-letter words
Aeschylus
Anastasia

Aristotle
Beethoven
Fernandel
Nefertiti
Sacajawea

10-letter word
Blackbeard

11-letter word
Charlemagne

12-letter word
Michelangelo

ANSWER, PAGE 369

FAMOUS LAST WORDS

When you gotta go, you gotta go. Here are some final quotes from people who really knew how to make an exit.

"I'll be in hell before you've finished breakfast, boys...let her rip!"
—**"Black Jack" Ketchum,** *murderer, before being hanged*

"The Countess Rouen sends her compliments but begs to be excused. She is engaged in dying."
—**The Countess Rouen,** *in a letter read by her attendant to her guests*

"Go away...I'm all right."
—**H. G. Wells,** *writer*

"God bless...God damn..."
—**James Thurber,** *writer*

"If this is dying, I don't think much of it."
—**Lytton Strachey,** *writer*

"Four o'clock. How strange. So that is the time. Strange. Enough."
—**Sir Henry Stanley,** *explorer*

"You sons of bitches. Give my love to mother."
—**"Two Gun" Crowley,** *sitting on the electric chair*

"Now comes the mystery." —
Henry Ward Beecher, *preacher*

"Oh God, here I go."
—**Max Baer,** *boxer*

"Friends applaud, the Comedy is over."
—**Ludwig von Beethoven**

"All my possessions for a moment of time."
—**Elizabeth I,** *queen of England*

"And now, in keeping with Channel 40's policy of always bringing you the latest in blood and guts, in living color, you're about to see another first—an attempted suicide."
—**Chris Hubbock,** *newscaster who shot herself during broadcast*

"Drink to me."
—**Pablo Picasso**

"Why yes—a bullet-proof vest."
—**James Rodgers,** *murderer, before the firing squad, when asked if he had a final request*

A FOOD IS BORN

These foods are common, but you probably don't know where they come from. If you want that info, keep reading.

KETCHUP. The Chinese invented *ke-tsiap*—a concoction of pickled fish and spices (but no tomatoes)—in the 1690s. By the early 1700s, its popularity had spread to Malaysia, where British explorers first encountered it...and by 1740 the sauce— renamed *ketchup*—was an English staple. However, it wasn't until the 1790s that New England colonists first mixed *tomatoes* into the sauce. The reason: Until then, it was widely believed that tomatoes (a close relative of the toxic belladonna and nightshade plants) were poisonous.

Making tomato ketchup at home is a tedious all-day project, and American housewives hated the process. So when Henry J. Heinz introduced bottled ketchup in 1875, he promoted it as a labor-saving device. His first slogan was: "Blessed relief for Mother and the other women of the household." By the 1980s, Heinz ketchup was in one of every two households in the U.S.

WHEATIES. Invented in 1921 by a Minneapolis health spa owner who fed his patients homemade bran gruel to keep them regular and help them lose weight. One day he spilled some on the stove, and it hardened into a crust. He was going to throw it out, but tasted it first. To his surprise, the flakes he scraped off the stove were better than the stuff in the pot. He made more and showed them to a friend at the Washburn Crosby Company (predecessor of General Mills). People at the company liked the flakes, too, but didn't like the way they crumbled. So they came up with a better flake—using wheat. Then they held a company-wide contest to name the product. Jane Bausman, the wife of a company executive, suggested *Wheaties*.

BUBBLE GUM. The first bubble gum was invented by Frank Fleer in 1906—but never made it to market. It was so sticky that the only way to remove it from skin was with vigorous scrubbing and turpentine. It took Fleer more than 20 years to fix the recipe. In 1928, the "new, improved" gum was introduced as Dubble Bubble gum. Fleer made it pink because pink happened to be the only food coloring on the shelf the day the first commercial batch of Dubble Bubble was made. When his gum became the largest selling penny candy on the market, other manufacturers copied it... including the color. Now pink is the standard color for bubble gum.

GIRL SCOUT COOKIES. The Girl Scouts were founded in 1912. For 20 years they raised money by selling knitted clothes, baked goods, and chickens. Then, in 1934, a Philadelphia Girl Scout leader (who was also a press agent) came up with the idea of selling a vanilla cookie in the shape of the Girl Scout seal. She contracted with a local bakery to make them.

One day she heard that reporters would be interviewing actresses at a local flower show. Figuring her Girl Scout troop would get free publicity if they showed up selling cookies, she sent *a* contingent to the show. They were astounded by the response. The troop got so much publicity and sold so many cookies that Girl Scout troops all over the country began emulating them. Within three years, more than a hundred local councils were selling the same professionally baked cookies. It was the beginning of an American institution. In 1990 the Girl Scouts sold 130 million boxes of cookies— the equivalent of 13 cookies for every person in the United States.

PEPPERIDGE FARM PRODUCTS. One of Margaret Rudkin's sons suffered from severe asthma, a condition that became worse when he ate processed food. She couldn't find any bread that didn't make him ill, so in 1935 she started baking him stone-ground, whole-wheat bread. One day she brought a loaf to the boy's doctor; he liked it so much, he began recommending it to other patients. After building up a small mail-order business to local asthmatics and allergy-sufferers, she expanded her customer base to include people who weren't sick—and named her company after the family's 125-acre farm in Connecticut, *Pepperidge Farm*.

LIFESAVERS. In 1912, a Cleveland candy-maker named Clarence Crane decided to make a mint to sell in the summer. Until then, most mints were imported from Europe; Crane figured he could cut the price by making them in the U.S. He had the candy manufactured by a pill-maker—who discovered that his machinery would only work if it punched a hole in the middle of each candy. So Crane called the mints *Lifesavers*.

U.S. hens lay enough eggs in a year to circle the equator 100 times.

MYTH AMERICA

You've believed these stories since you were a kid. Most Americans have, because they were taught to us as sacred truths. Well, sorry. Here's another look.

SAVAGES

The Myth: Scalping was a brutal tactic invented by the Indians to terrorize the settlers.

The Truth: Scalping was actually an old European tradition dating back hundreds of years. Dutch and English colonists were paid a "scalp bounty" by their leaders as a means of keeping the Indians scared and out of the way. Finally the Indians caught on and adopted the practice themselves. The settlers apparently forgot its origins and another falsehood about Indian cruelty was born.

MOTHER OF THE FLAG

The Myth: Betsy Ross, a Philidelphia seamstress, designed and sewed the first American flag at the behest of the Founding Fathers.

Background: This story first surfaced in 1870 when Betsy Ross's grandson told a meeting of the Pennsylvania Historical Society that his grandmother had been asked to make a flag for the new nation. The tale must have touched a nerve, because it quickly spread and soon was regarded as the truth.

The Truth: While Betsy Ross did in fact sew flags for the Pennsylvania Navy, there is no proof to back up her grandson's tale. Ironically, no one is sure who designed the flag. The best guess is that the flag's design is derived from a military banner carried during the American Revolution.

MIDNIGHT RAMBLER

The Myth: Paul Revere made a solitary, dramatic midnight ride to warn patriots in Lexington and Concord that the British were coming.

Background: Revere's effort was first glorified in Henry Wadsworth Longfellow's poem, "The Midnight Ride of Paul Revere." Longfellow may have written the ode out of guilt—his grandfather had tried to court-martial Revere during the Revolutionary War.

Study results: Termites eat wood twice as fast when lisening to heavy metal music.

The charge: "Unsoldierly behavior tending toward cowardice." (Revere was not convicted.)

The Truth: Paul Revere was actually one of two men who attempted the famous ride...and it was the other one, William Dawes, who made it to Concord. Revere didn't make it—he was stopped by British troops. As for Revere's patriotic motives: According to Patricia Lee Holt, in *George Washington Had No Middle Name*, "Paul Revere billed the Massachusetts State House 10 pounds 4 shillings to cover his expenses for his ride."

AMERICUS THE BEAUTIFUL

The Myth: Amerigo Vespucci, a Florentine navigator, made four trips to the New World from 1497 to 1502. The newly discovered land was named in his honor.

Background: Vespucci wrote an account of his four voyages. An Italian mapmaker was so impressed by it that he put "Americus's" name on the first known map of the New World.

The Truth: America is named after a probable fraud. Scholars doubt Vespucci made those trips at all.

THANKSGIVING

The Myth: The Pilgrims ate a Thanksgiving feast of turkey and pumpkin pie after their first year in the New World, and we've been doing it ever since.

The Truth: Thanksgiving didn't become a national holiday until Abraham Lincoln declared it in 1863, and the Pilgrims ate neither the bird we call turkey, nor pumpkin pie.

TAKING A STAND

The Myth: General George Armstrong Custer's "Last Stand" at Little Bighorn was a heroic effort by a great soldier.

The Truth: It wasn't heroism, it was stupidity. Custer had unwarranted contempt for the American Indians' fighting ability. His division was supposed to be a small part of a major attack, led by General Alfred Terry—who was planning to meet Custer in two days with his troops. Custer was instructed to wait for Terry. Instead, he led his 266 men into battle. They were all slaughtered.

THE BIRDS

Some inside dope on one of Alfred Hitchcock's spookiest films.

A lfred Hitchcock's 1963 film The Birds was a milestone: no one had ever tried to work with so many animals at once; and no one has ever used live animals so effectively in a suspense film.

Much of the credit goes to Hollywood's #1 bird expert, Ray Berwick. He was familiar with the Daphne DuMaurier short story on which *The Birds* was based, but never imagined anyone would try to film it. Then, one morning at 6:30, he got a call telling him to be at Hitchcock's office in an hour. He walked in on a Birds production meeting, where he was told that $250,000 had already been spent on mechanical birds that didn't work. Could they use live birds? Not even Berwick was sure. But he agreed to try.

BERWICK'S APPROACH

• Although thousands of untrained birds—sparrows, finches, buntings, seagulls, and ravens—were ultimately used, Berwick only trained about 125 ravens, blackbirds, and seagulls for the film.

• Of the trained birds, only 25 to 30 were well trained; that's all they needed. Birds, says Berwick, have a tendency to follow leaders, so the well-trained birds led the others wherever the director wanted them to go.

• The small birds weren't trained—and they didn't have to be. In one convincing scene, for example, they were just "dumped down a chimney."

• According to Berwick: Once the wild birds were tamed, they lost their fear of humans and actually became "the birds," attacking members of the cast and crew.

• Hitchcock wanted to include an owl among his feathered fiends, but had to cut the owl's scene because it looked comical.

BEHIND THE SCENES

Years after the film was released, Berwick revealed the secret of making seagulls look as though they were attacking humans:

• He taught the birds to land on people's heads whenever people were standing still. And each time they performed that stunt successfully, they were fed.

• In the film, the audience sees what looks like people running down a street being chased by seagulls; in reality, the seagulls were flying along with the people, waiting for the people to stop moving so the birds could perform their trick.

• As soon as the director yelled "Cut!" the actors stopped running and the birds landed on their heads—and received their food rewards.

Postscript: After the film was completed, the seagulls that had been used were taken to the Pacific shore and set free. According to Berwick, trained seagulls will forget what they've been taught in about a week, if no one's working with them. But for the first week after the birds were released, there were strange reports of seagulls landing on people's heads at the beach. No one believed the reports, of course—except the people who'd worked on *The Birds*. And they weren't about to explain it to anyone.

ADVENTURES IN CINEMAGIC

In one carefully crafted scene, co-star Tippi Hedren was rowing across a lake when a seagull seemed to swipe her across the head— leaving her bloodied. Here's how Hitchcock's crew did it:

• They ran two tubes up Hedren's dress: one, which went to her forehead, spurted "blood"; the other, which went to the top of her head, was attached to an air compressor.

• Then they released the gull, which was one of the birds trained to land on people's heads.

• The gull started to land on Hedren's head. But at the moment it touched her, the air compressor was turned on. The burst of air scared the bird into flying away.

• At the same moment, the "blood" squirted through the other tube, making it seem as though the bird had attacked. A complicated stunt, but clever and effective.

AFTERMATH

Hitchcock and Berwick made a lot of enemies in pet shops with *The Birds*. After the film was released, sales of pet birds plummeted.

• Turnabout: Years later, Berwick was also responsible for a bird "boom" when he brought Fred the cockatoo to the screen in the TV show "Baretta."

Technically, snow is considered a mineral.

THE 7 "OFFICIAL" ATTRIBUTES OF THE PILLSBURY DOUGHBOY

In *Uncle John's Bathroom Reader Puzzle Book #1*, we encrypted such trivial information as crimes punishable by death according to the Code of Hammurabi. But this time, let's get serious—let's talk about little blobs of dough that wear pastry hats and giggle on TV. To that end, we've taken the seven official attributes that make the Pillsbury Doughboy who he is, and we've encrypted them using a simple letter-substitution code.

In this particular puzzle, **the letter substitution remains constant throughout the whole list.**

1. PVG GXVU SJGI BYYX BVXC LYJOP: "YDD-FPVIC, GSYYIP, RJI UYI OBYGGM"

2. GBVOPIBM BJSVUYJG, RJI UY GPCCU

3. UY XUCCG, CBRYFG, FAVGIG, DVUOCAG, CQAG, YA QUXBCG

4. ACQA KVCFG LY UYI VUTBJLC "RJUG"

5. FQBXG FVIP Q "GFQOOCA"

6. GIYSQTP VG ZAYZYAIVYUQB IY IPC ACGI YD PVG RYLM

7. PC VG UYI ZYAIBM   **ANSWER, PAGE 372**

* * * * *

LOST IN TRANSLATION

What James Bond film was was originally translated as
We Don't Want a Doctor in Japan?

ANSWER, PAGE 372

MYTH AMERICA

Here are a few more patriotic stories we all learned when we were young…all of which are 100% baloney.

THE MYTH: Nathan Hale, an American soldier during the Revolutionary War, was captured by the British and sentenced to hang. When the Redcoats asked if he had any last words, he replied defiantly: "I regret that I have but one life to lose for my country."

THE TRUTH: He never said that—or anything close to it. According to the diary of a British soldier who was there, Captain Frederick MacKenzie, Hale's last words were brave, but not very inspiring. They were: "It is the duty of every good officer to obey the orders given him by his commander-in-chief."

THE MYTH: Abraham Lincoln hurriedly composed his most famous speech—the Gettysburg Address—on the back of an nvelope while riding on a train from Washington, D.C., to the site of the speech in Gettysburg.

BACKGROUND: The story apparently originated with Lincoln's son, Robert, who first created it in a letter he wrote after his father was assassinated.

THE TRUTH: Lincoln actually started writing the speech two weeks before the event, and wrote at least five drafts before even leaving Washington for Gettysburg. He wasn't particularly keen on speaking spontaneously—in fact, he refused to say anything to the crowd that met him at the Gettysburg train station because he was afraid he might say something foolish.

THE MYTH: The Liberty Bell was rung on July 4, 1776, to commemorate the colonists' declaration of independence.

BACKGROUND: This tale was invented by writer George Lip-pard in his 1847 book, *Legends of the American Revolution*.

THE TRUTH: The Liberty Bell was installed in Philadelphia in 1753—23 years before the colonists rebelled—and it has nothing whatever to do with the Revolution. Its nickname, "Liberty Bell," was coined by abolitionists in 1839. They were referring to the end of slavery in America, not to freedom from England.

More than 2.2 million Americans play the accordion.

FINAL THOUGHTS

*When you gotta go, you gotta go. Here are some "last words," from
some people who really knew how to make an exit.*

"No. I came here to die. Not
make a speech."
—**Cherokee Bill,** *outlaw,*
when asked "if he had
anything to say"

"So little done, so much to do."
—**Alexander Graham Bell**

"I hope that the edge of your
guillotine is sharper than your
scissors."
—**Jean-Francois Ducos,**
to the executioner,
who was cutting off his hair

"Ah...you might make that a
double."
—**Neville Heath,** *murderer,*
asking for a last whiskey

"It is a reproach to the faculty
that they cannot cure the
hiccup."
—**James Hogg,** *poet, ...who*
died from hiccups

"I've never felt better."
—**Douglas Fairbanks, Sr.**

"I have only two regrets—that
I have not shot Henry Clay or
hanged John C. Calhoun."
—**President Andrew Jackson**

"Are you sure it's safe?"
—**William Palmer,** *murderer,*
stepping onto the gallows

"Go on, get out! Last words are for
fools who haven't said enough."
—**Karl Marx, communist**

"I am dying like a poisoned rat
in a hole. I am what I am! I am
what I am!
—**Jonathan Swift**

"I shall hear in heaven!"
—**Ludwig van Beethoven**

"At least one knows that death
will be easy. A slight knock at
the window pane, then..."
—**Bertolt Brecht,** *playwright*

"Get my swan costume ready."
—**Anna Pavlova,**
Russian ballerina

THIS BECKS FOR YOU

*A mega-rich, perfectly coiffed, trend-setting superstar. Friend
to the stars and one half of Britain's most (sort of) glamorous
couple. But did you know that David Beckham also played football?
But never mind about that. The boy done so good that he became his
own brand. Wanna piece?*

It wasn't long into David Beckham's career with Manchester
United that people simply forgot he played football. By the
time Labour won their second term in government in 2001,
you could be forgiven for thinking that the Prime Minister was
the Rt. Hon. D. Beckham M.P. Two years later, a study by War-
wick University claimed that he was probably the 'most influential' figure in the UK for everyone aged between 5 and 60.

WORKING-CLASS HERO

The clues to his iconic status, if there are any, are certainly not to
be found in his upbringing. David Robert Joseph Beckham was
born 2 May, 1975 in Leytonstone, East London. He showed early
talent as a footballer and was snapped up as a kid by Manchester
United. By the time he left that club in 2003, few argued that he
was not only a world-class footballer, but an icon for all sport in
the UK. It still didn't explain why even those who had never
watched a football game in their life knew him and loved him.

PERFECT PITCH

Perhaps he scored so well with the public because of his reputation for being a nice, ordinary family man in an age when foot-
ballers were seen as drunken, violent, sex-crazed yobs (which they
are). Being married to Victoria Adams, the Poshest of the Spice
Girls, helped raise his profile, as did his chiselled, blond good
looks. Their 1999 wedding was the event of the year. Her dress
cost £60,000 and the reception itself came in at £500,000 – well,
437 staff and matching his'n'hers thrones don't come cheap. The
couple were as much ridiculed as they were admired, both for
those expensive tastes and their supposed lack of brain power.

I SAY, I SAY

The Beckham joke quickly supplanted Essex girl gags as a main-stay of pub humour ('What's the difference between Airfix and David Beckham? One is a glueless kit and the other's... a clueless git'). But he never seemed to be riled by the sniping. It was said that he wore Posh Spice's knickers, and he was photographed in a sarong. His daring outfits were topped off by an increasingly wild selection of haircuts. The man's got style!

Openly admitting to being in touch with his feminine side, a rare thing for a footballer, he appeared delighted to learn he was a gay icon. 'The face of an angel', sighed gay style magazine *Attitude*, 'and the bum of a Greek god'. At the same time, *Hello!* magazine proclaimed that the Beckhams were ideal representatives of family values. *Hello!* was right in that everyone could see the parents were devoted to their divine offspring: Romeo, born on 1 September, 2002, a brother for the Beckhams' other son, Brooklyn.

GOODBYE THE REDS

Beckham's world became a more troubled one in 2002. His boss at United, Sir Alex Ferguson, was said to be fed up with his star player's increasing fame and dropped him from key matches. At the same time, the Beckhams were caught up in a bizarre kidnap plot against them involving Albanian gangsters. Not surprisingly, it was later revealed to be a fabrication. By the end of 2002 Beckham was the world's most searched-for sportsman on the Internet, inspiring fanatical devotion across Europe and into China, Japan, and southeast Asia. Where will it all end? Watch this space...

Here are some interesting facts and figures about our Dave:

• A 2003 study found a third of Britons wanted David Beckham's picture to replace Charles Dickens on the £10 note.

• One survey showed that 8 out of 10 Japanese would buy products if he endorsed them

• Despite his world fame, Beckham has yet to crack the USA: in May 2003 *USA Today* called him 'The most famous man Americans don't know'.

Your brain uses 40 percent of the oxygen that enters your bloodstream.

GOING DOWN
THE TUBE

How did the world's first underground railway come to be. More importantly, will they ever get it to work properly? They've only had 100 years to fix it. Mind the gap!

Travelling on London's tube network is something that once experienced is not lightly forgotten. It is noisy, confusing, dirty, a bit scary, and subject to its own skewed laws of time, space and speed. Love it or hate it (or should that be hate it or *really* hate it) it's a fascinating subterranean world with a more than interesting history.

ALL BLOCKED UP

In the mid-1800s traffic was threatening to choke London to a standstill (no change there then). And this was even before the car was invented! Victorian gentlemen would quietly steam under their top hats as they sat for hours in horse-drawn-carriage-jams. Something had to be done to relieve the pressure on the capital's roads – and reduce the mountainous piles of horse dung that were being deposited on them. The recently-opened overground railways had been a hit, allowing people to move out to the new suburbs. So, some asked, why not build railways in the city?

As Londoners did not want a railway running *through* their city, it was decided to build one *under* it, between Farringdon Street in the City and the mainline station of Paddington. The driving force behind the scheme was Charles Pearson, Solicitor to the City of London. He help to set up the Metropolitan Railway Company in 1854, and did much to raise the £1 million needed to build the first underground railway line.

GOING UNDERGROUND

The idea was frighteningly new and radical – would people be frightened by the dark, or asphyxiated by the fumes? Until electric trains were introduced in 1890 (with the opening of the City & South London Railway), underground steam trains diverted smoke

---

Camels are born without their humps.

to their own water tanks. When they reached specially-built ventilation shafts that led from the tunnel to the world above, they would pump out the remainder. There's still a ventilation shaft at Great Portland Street station near Euston.

To lay the track, streets were dug up and either re-covered later or left open – as at Farringdon Road station, which is still open to the elements to this day. The first train ran on what was called the Metropolitan Line on 10 January, 1863, along the 6 km of track from Farringdon Street to Paddington Station. It was an instant success, the trains carrying 40,000 passengers on the first day alone. The one sad element was that Charles Pearson was not there to enjoy it – he died four months before the grand opening.

THE NEXT TRAIN DEPARTS IN 100 YEARS
The opening of the Metropolitan Line was the start of a massive programme of building by a number of companies. It took 150 years to complete the entire tube network we have today, but all the main lines were in place by the start of the 20th century. In 1890, the City & South London Railway (now part of the Northern line) was the first in the world to be electrically operated, although its trains were at first supposed to be hauled along the tracks by cables, like the cable cars of San Francisco.

One odd fact about the first tube trains was that they didn't have any windows: the railway companies thought there was no need for them, as a guard was employed to yell out the name of each station as the train pulled in. However, the fact that the guards couldn't be heard over the noise the trains created soon caused the train companies to change their minds.

PICK OF THE BUNCH
The tube network was brought together when the London Passenger Transport Board was formed in 1933. The new authority ensured a uniform corporate style, with bright, modern stations featuring good lighting and handy ticket machines. An official named Frank Pick, in charge of planning and improving routes, made a highly visible contribution through his design and PR work. The Underground had found someone passionate about style, who even believed it had a civilizing effect. The look and feel of the Underground, even today, is largely Pick's work.

Even the network's map became a design icon. Harry Beck, a 29-year-old electrical draughtsman, produced a simple representation of the tube network based on circuit diagrams. Until his masterstroke, tubs maps showed every complicated twist and turn that the tubes took. Beck simplified the map down to its bare essentials. His first design was rejected as being too revolutionary, but in 1933 his next effort was accepted and is still in use today.

GIMME SHELTER

During World War II London's tube stations were pressed into action for a dramatic new use – as bomb shelters in which Londoners could hide during the Blitz. At the height of the bombing campaign, 177,000 citizens were sleeping in tube stations every night. The war left the Underground largely intact and fully operational, but in urgent need of new signals, escalators and rolling stock. Yet 1930s vintage trains were still running well into the early 1980s. It said much for their original build and design that they ran millions of miles virtually non-stop for 50 years.

TRAVELLING IN STYLE?

The latest addition to the tube network is the Jubilee Line, which was completed in 2000, just in time for the opening of the Millennium Dome (the Jubilee Line station of North Greenwich stops just outside the Dome).

But in contrast to the shiny, new Jubilee line, much of the rest of the network has suffered years of neglect, lack of investment and falling staff levels. A journey on a rush hour tube is akin to a journey to hell and back: the tubes are massively overcrowded, and boiling hot in the summer and freezing cold in winter. Delays and random track closures only add to passenger stress levels. A tube train at 8.30 a.m on a weekday morning is not a place where you will see Lononders at their best.

But as pioneers of the underground railway, Londoners can be proud of a system that has been emulated around the world, from Moscow to New York, and from Tokyo to Berlin. Despite competition from buses and cars and the introduction of new and often wacky alternative forms of transport – from rickshaws to rollerskates – the Tube is still the quickest (if not the most comfortable) way to get around the capital.

Scotland was once part of a continent called Laurentia, which included North America.

TUNNEL VISION

So, when you're next stuck on the tube, waiting patiently for the train to crawl into the next station, impress your fellow passengers with some of these Underground statistics:

• Ongar on the Central Line is the start point for measuring the network. Every 200 metres there is a reference marker for engineers and other workers.

• The 27 km of the Northern Line makes it the longest continuous tunnel in the UK (for many years it was the longest tunnel in the world).

• Epping to West Ruislip on the Central Line is the longest continuous journey—4 km. It takes about 90 minutes to get from one end to the other—on a good day!

• Gillespie Road was the only station to be renamed after a football club. Since 1932 it's been called Arsenal.

• There are 475 km of Underground routes, of which 235 km are in the open, 150 km in tunnels and just 32 km in cut-and-cover tunnels.

• There are 2.8 million trips taken on the tube each day. Some 866 million journeys were made in the last two years of the 1990s.

• Hampstead is the deepest station in the tube network, being 58 metres under ground. Its escalators are also the longest in the system, at 55 metres.

• At night, a Tunnel Cleaning Train runs through the tube network, sucking up tonnes of dust a debris from the track. Experts estimate that due to the build-up of dust in tunnels and stations, for the average passenger a 20 minute tube journey is the equivalent to smoking a cigarette.

• Julian Lloyd Webber was the first licensed busker allowed to perform on the Underground.

WIGS IN THE DOCK

Silence in court! Stop that sniggering! No, it's not a dead ferret on the judge's head! Of all the odd rituals in English law is anything odder than making judges and barristers wear wigs in court?

Surely that's not the judge's real hair, making him look like a superannuated sheep. Of course not, it's a wig – and a ruddy stupid one at that. No court is complete without a full complement of be-wigged advocates, swapping legal arguments whilst dressed as Regency pantomine villains. But why? Well, it turns out the history of legal wigs is long and as dignified as it's possible for anything made out of horsehair to be.

LOOK SMART
The courtroom falls silent as the judge rises to pass sentence. But first he zips up his tracksuit top and adjusts his backwards-facing baseball cap to a jauntier angle and… It's not a very likely scenario, is it? The legal system needs to look as authoritative as it sounds, and it's hard to picture that courtroom scene without a stern-faced judge in formal attire topped off by a wig.

HAIR TODAY
The wig, that most solemn piece of head furniture, dates back to ancient times. Some have been found buried with the remains of Egyptian mummies. By contrast, its legal role came relatively recently, in 1680. There had long been some kind of official headgear used in court until then – in early Tudor times it was the flat, black cap. In 17th century fashion, wigs or periwigs (the word comes from the French *perruque*) were a part of everyday culture and a natural badge of authority for the legal authorities. Their formal black dress worn in court dated from a little later, 1714, originally donned as a sign of mourning for Queen Anne.

WIGGED OUT
Times change and those white wigs the judges still wear would look distinctly odd in any other workplace – even bishops no longer sport wigs and they can hardly be accused of living on the

edge of fashion. Only judges and barristers are be-wigged in the 21st century. As a sign of modernity, wigs are not worn during cases involving children.

It's not even as if wearing a wig is comfortable. True, they can cover a multitude of sins for some of the more follically-challenged members of the legal community, but that's not a great excuse for continuing to wear them in this day and age. It seems that the reason judges and barristers still wear them is that great old British stand-by: tradition.

HAIR TODAY

All the finest wigs are made by hand and start at around £300-£350 for the basic barrister style (which can last for an entire career), worn on the back of the head with a ponytail hanging down. The best part of £1,500 goes on those full shoulder-length ones used for ceremonial purposes (from which we get the term 'big wig' for someone who fancies themselves as a major player). Modern wigs are made of horsehair, although they were originally made from human hair.

The owner will keep a wig in good shape by taking it to a professional cleaner, although there is a bonus to be had in them looking a little shabby, as it conveys a sense of age and, hopefully, wisdom. For junior barristers, that authority is much needed and for the same reason it's a source of annoyance for solicitors that they are not allowed to wear wigs in court (apart from solicitor Q.C.s). Judges have another use for the wig – as a disguise, figuring that, once they've taken it off after work, it's far less likely they might be recognized on the street and have an awkward discussion with someone they once put away for a long stretch.

TO WIG OR NOT TO WIG

These days, experts are divided over whether to keep wigs in court. Scottish lawyers came out broadly for wigs when surveyed in late 2002. The next year, another survey found that only 30 per cent of the public favoured wig wearing, in line with what senior legal types think (the junior members are still quite taken with the idea). It remains to be seen whether or not this outmoded yet oddly timeless accessory will survive another 300 years.

THE SKIFFLE KING

Without Lonnie Donegan the 'British invasion' of rock 'n' roll might never have happened. Donegan was the creator of skiffle, a mix of American blues, jazz, gospel and folk music that caught the imagination of young British musicians like John Lennon, Paul McCartney, Pete Townshend and Elton John. Donegan racked up three number ones and numerous top 10 hits in the UK and U.S. in the 1950s and 1960s.

It took a British musician to meld uniquely American styles of music – jazz, folk, blues and gospel – into a brand new sound that swept a nation and changed the direction of music forever. Lonnie Donegan reportedly just wanted to play banjo in a jazz band. He wound up creating influential music that reverberates even in today's songs. He became one of the most respected and loved musicians in the UK with tunes that climbed up the music charts in leaps and bounds.

He was an enthusiastic performer, infusing his songs with such joy that young people were inspired to pick up guitars, banjos, basses and drums and form their own skiffle bands. Donegan reportedly picked up the word 'skiffle', an American slang term meaning 'party', from a record album. The party was still going on in 2002, when Donegan died of a heart attack in the middle of a tour, aged 71.

MUSICAL ROYALTY IS BORN

Lonnie Donegan was born Anthony James Donegan in April 1931, in Glasgow. His father was an amateur concert violinist. The boy's parents divorced when he was very young and he moved to London's East End with his mother when he was two.

The reports of how Donegan got his stage name conflict. According to one source, an over-excited master of ceremonies mixed Donegan's name up with that of blues guitarist and banjoist Lonnie Johnson, but most reports claim that Donegan took Lonnie Johnson's first name as a tribute to the musician, whom he greatly admired.

Leaf-cutter ants can build anthills 5 metres deep and 2 hectares square.

ALL THAT JAZZ

Donegan bought his first guitar at 14 and was inspired by the American blues and jazz he heard on the BBC. In an interview with writer Lee Raymond, he said his interest took off when he was 16 and saw a jazz band perform.

> 'I'd never heard jazz out loud – it was so dynamic!' he said. 'That's really, I suppose, what gave me the impetus. These days, for instance, if you had not heard rock 'n' roll and you walked in and heard Chuck Berry, you'd go: "Wow! What the blazes is this!"'

Donegan assembled his own band, the Tony Donegan Jazz Band, and wound up playing in London jazz clubs. One of the most exciting performances of his life was when his band was asked to open for Lonnie Johnson, his hero. He also began playing in other bands, most notably with singer/trombonist Chris Barber, with whom he began recording.

THE KING THROWS A ROCK

Jazz was exciting, but it wasn't the only music that interested Donegan. He got the chance to perform blues and folk tunes in Chris Barber's band, but it was a recording of Leadbelly's 'Rock Island Line' by Donegan in 1956 that set the UK – and the world – aflame.

The song rocketed up the British and American music charts and sold three million copies. Other popular tunes include 'Does Your Chewing Gum Lose its Flavour on the Bedpost Overnight?', 'Cumberland Gap', 'My Old Man's a Dustman' and 'Puttin' on the Style', a song he learned when he first started to play the guitar.

Donegan, who had left Barber's band, was quickly sent to America to perform his hit single, and wound up on the *Perry Como Show*, alongside other guests including Ronald Reagan and a budding comedian named Woody Allen.

INFLUENCING A GENERATION

'Rock Island Line' is credited by many as the song that inspired young British musicians like John Lennon and George Harrison, who formed their own skiffle group called The Quarrymen. They later joined with another skiffle musician, Paul McCartney, and along the way, The Beatles were born. McCartney is said to have remarked:

> When we were kids in Liverpool, the man who really started the craze for guitars was Lonnie Donegan. We studied his records avidly. We all bought guitars to be in a skiffle group. He was the man.

Guitarist Pete Townshend started a skiffle group with singer Roger Daltrey called The Detours, which later became The Who, and singer Van Morrison played in an Irish skiffle band called The Sputniks. Elton John recalled: 'He was the first person I ever saw on British television who played something different. It was fantastic to see someone change music that much.'

Across the pond, Elvis Presley recorded one of Donegan's songs, 'I'm Never Gonna Fall in Love Again', as did Tom Jones.

THE MUSICIANS REMEMBER

When the British rock industry took off Donegan's music became less popular, but he continued to perform and tour all over the world on the cabaret circuit. He also appeared as the lead in the musical *Mr. Cinders* in London's West End in the 1980s, and in the early 1990s, he was still busy performing in his band.

The musicians Donegan influenced never forgot him. Paul McCartney organized a 1978 tribute album to the master called *Puttin' on the Style*, featuring other admirers such as Elton John, Ringo Starr, blues guitarist Albert Lee and Queen guitarist Brian May. Donegan also entered into a close relationship with Van Morrison, who collaborated with him on 1998's *Muleskinner's Blues*. Morrison also recorded *The Skiffle Sessions – Live in Belfast*, in 1998, a tribute that also featured Chris Barber.

THE END AT THE BEGINNING

Donegan was made an OBE in 2000. That year he was honoured by Martin Guitars, which created two 'Signature Editions' in Donegan's name. When Donegan died in November 2002, he was halfway through a tour of British theatres. The Skiffle King's last show was in Nottingham, the first city he performed in when he became a star in 1957.

THE TIME IT TAKES

Everything takes time. For instance, it takes .06 seconds for an automobile's airbag to fully inflate, and it took 69 years for the Soviet Union to rise and fall. Here are 10 time-takers; can you put them in order from the least to the most amount of time they take?

_____ The time it takes for a human hair to grow half an inch

_____ The time it takes for a hummingbird's wings to beat 70 times

_____ The time it takes for a newborn baby to wet or soil 80 diapers

_____ The time it takes for a U.S. Marine to go through boot camp

_____ The time it takes for Easter to recur on the same date

_____ The time it takes for Los Angeles to move two inches close to San Francisco (due to the shifting of tectonic plates)

_____ The time it takes for plutonium-239 to become harmless

_____ The time it takes for the elevator in Toronto's CN Tower to reach the top (1,518 feet)

_____ The time it took for the *Titanic* to sink after it struck the iceberg

_____ The time that the average American spends asleep in a lifetime

ANSWER, PAGE 372

HELLO? DOLLY?

Small crostic puzzles are solved just like the big ones (directions on page 13) but the first letter of the fill-in words **do not** spell out a hidden message.

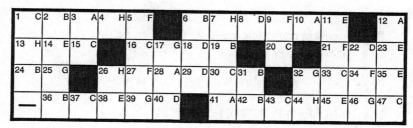

A. Hue

$\overline{41}\ \overline{10}\ \overline{3}\ \overline{12}\ \overline{28}$

B. Best Picture of 1986

$\overline{6}\ \overline{24}\ \overline{36}\ \overline{19}\ \overline{2}\ \overline{42}\ \overline{31}$

C. One of the Teenage Mutant Ninja Turtles

$\overline{1}\ \overline{30}\ \overline{43}\ \overline{20}\ \overline{47}\ \overline{15}\ \overline{37}\ \overline{16}\ \overline{33}$

D. Mall tenant

$\overline{18}\ \overline{29}\ \overline{22}\ \overline{8}\ \overline{40}$

E. Jukebox fee, at least when they were invented

$\overline{11}\ \overline{38}\ \overline{14}\ \overline{35}\ \overline{45}\ \overline{23}$

F. NBC morning news stalwart

$\overline{9}\ \overline{34}\ \overline{21}\ \overline{27}\ \overline{5}$

G. The suns, in sunnyside-ups

$\overline{25}\ \overline{17}\ \overline{32}\ \overline{39}\ \overline{46}$

H. Factory

$\overline{26}\ \overline{4}\ \overline{7}\ \overline{13}\ \overline{44}$

ANSWER, PAGE 373

SHELL-SHOCKED

'Humpty Dumpty' must be one of the best-loved of all nursery rhymes, sung by children the world over. But few people know the true origins of the tale about the downfall of the talking egg.

There are many different theories about the rhyme's origins. Some believe Humpty was the name given to a huge cannon; others that it referred to Richard III (who supposedly had the Princes in the Tower, his nephews, murdered).

HARD-BOILED ROUNDHEADS
The best explanation comes from the period of the English Civil War (1642–1649) when Charles I besieged the Parliamentarian stronghold of Knaresborough in Yorkshire. The Royalist army had laid siege to the town for nearly three months, but could not breach the Roundhead army's defences. Charles ordered a great siege engine to be built to help his men storm the battlements.

Watching this terrible weapon of war being built, the children of the town became very afraid and the adults came up with the name 'Humpty Dumpty' as a way to ridicule the engine and stop the children becoming too alarmed.

The resourceful defenders of the town decided to dig under the ground, to weaken the area where Humpty would sit, and they also soaked the ground around the battlements at night.

EGG ON ROYALIST FACES
When the time came for the big attack, Humpty was wheeled into place against the battlements ('sat on the wall') but because of its weight and the weakened ground, the earth beneath it collapsed and it fell over ('had a great fall'). Despite the troops' best efforts to pull it out of the quagmire, it was too damaged to repair. ('All the king's horses and all the king's men couldn't put Humpty together again.') At this point Charles abandoned the siege, and a war that had been going in his favour began to turn against him. The rest, as they say, is history.

If you visit, bring suntan lotion: Neptune's summer is 40 years long.

IN THE NAVY

Britannia may no longer rule the waves, but did you know that many of the sayings we still use every day actually originated in the lingo of Admiral Nelson's navy?

In the 18th and 19th centuries the navy was a harsh employer. For example, boys as young as 10 were used to carry cannonballs from the ship's armoury to the gun placements. The poor lads were known as 'powder monkeys' and the wood and metal stand they placed the cannonballs on was called the 'brass monkey'. In extreme cold weather, the wood and metal of its rails expanded, causing the balls to roll off on to the deck. Hence the term: 'It's cold enough to freeze the balls off a brass monkey.'

SWINGING THE LEAD
This phrase is still frequently used to imply someone who's lazy or workshy. It comes from the method that ships used to measure their speed through the water. A long piece of hemp rope was tied with knots at equal distances along its length and a lead weight was tied to the end to help it sink. The rope was then thrown out to sea and pulled in after a set time; the amount of knots that disappeared underwater showed the speed at which the ship was travelling. 'Knots' remain the official measure of speed for all sailing vessels.

An unfortunate deckhand (usually someone on a punishment) performed this backbreaking task, and had to swing the leaded rope around his head to create enough momentum to get it over the wake of the ship. If he wanted to avoid the really hard work of dragging the sodden rope back in, he'd keep swinging the rope around his head, until a whip from the Bosun's cat-o'-nine-tails made him stop 'swinging the lead'.

A CAT WITH TOO MANY TAILS
The British Navy was the most highly disciplined navy in the world and punishment for even minor crimes was swift and brutal. The most feared punishment of all was a series of lashes from the cat-o'-nine-tails, a whip made from nine lengths of leather with

knots along each length. The damaged wreaked on the back of the unhappy recipient often led to death. But this not-so-charming instrument of torture is also the source of many phrases we use today. For example:

'To let the cat out of the bag': the whip had to be kept moist in a wet leather carrying bag.

'No room to swing a cat': punishment often took place in a small area of the deck, making the man doing the lashing complain he didn't have enough space to do it properly.

'A cat has nine lives': a well-trained whip man could make each of the nine tails of the cat land separately, causing increased damage to the recipient's back.

'You scratch my back and I'll scratch yours': it was such a punishment-based society on board ship, the person being whipped knew that one day he might be the one dishing out logging to the man now punishing him. He wanted to encourage his tormentor to go lightly on him.

* * *

THINGS ONLY A SAILOR WOULD KNOW

RUN THE GAUNTLET: An old naval punishment for men convicted of theft was to make the offender walk between two rows of men each equipped with rope ends with which to strike him. The offender could not pass through too quickly because the Master-At-Arms held a sword against his chest to slow the miscreant down.

SON OF A GUN: Wives of Royal Navy crewmen were allowed to accompany their men on some long voyages. If any of the women became pregnant while at sea, the safest place for them to give birth was in a shelter behind the canons on the gun decks. If a male child was born, he was called a Son of a Gun. The term was also used to imply that the identity of the father might be in question. Today the term is not used to cast aspersions on a person's parentage and is generally used to mean a 'good fellow'.

No wonder they're gone: in ancient Egypt, pillows were made of stones.

IT'S YOUR ROUND

Come the end of a Saturday night in your local, it's a safe bet that most regulars will be barely capable of coherent speech. So it may surprise you to know how many pub-based phrases there are.

There is no more important institution in the whole of British society than the good old pub. It's the hub of many of our social lives, where we meet friends, have a chat, share a joke – and get plain, old-fashioned, falling-down drunk. Here are some well-known sayings that originated in pubs

A BIT OF ORDER PLEASE, GENTLEMEN
In the last century, beer was served in two measures, Pints and Quarts. When things got a bit rowdy toward closing time, as they usually did, here was a good chance that most of the beer mugs would get smashed or damaged. So, whenever a fight broke out, the landlord would cry out 'Mind your Pints and Quarts, folks'. Which is why we still ask people to 'mind your P's and Q's'.

MAKE MINE A PINT
The pint measure comes from the attempt by government to regulate standard measurements, with the Weights and Measures Act of 1824. All beer mugs had a mark painted on them to show the measure the customer could expect. This was known as the 'paint mark'. Over time, probably with a bit of help from one too many beers, 'paint' was garbled into 'pint' and the name stuck.

THE LONG STRETCH
There is a rather grisly origin for two well known drinking phrases. In the 18th century, executions in London were carried out at Tyburn (now Marble Arch).The condemned were brought along what is now Oxford St., which in those days was little more than a country road. Prisoners would be allowed to stop off in a pub at the beginning of Oxford St., where they would be offered their last drink, or 'one for the road'. After drinking their final ever draught of the good stuff, they went outside and climbed 'back on the wagon' to be taken off to execution.

What a horrible thought. It's enough to drive you to drink!

HOW SCROOGE INVENTED CHRISTMAS

Christmas was being Scrooged out of existence until a ghost story came along to make it popular all over again.

Everyone knows about Ebenezer Scrooge—that coldhearted miser who won't help his underpaid but jolly employee, Bob Cratchit, to celebrate Christmas. Fortunately, on Christmas Eve, the Ghosts of Christmas Past, Present and Future give Scrooge such a fright that he reforms and changes his money-grubbing ways. But did you know that the tale of Scrooge not only changed how we celebrate Christmas; it probably saved it from extinction, too?

On 19 December, 1843 a slim, gilt-edged book, *A Christmas Carol*, by Charles Dickens, appeared in London bookshops. In that same year, no one wished each other a Merry Christmas. They'd probably never even heard the phrase. And Christmas itself was on the wane. In the 17th century, Oliver Cromwell and his Puritans came to power and abolished the holiday. Even after the monarchy was restored, Christmas traditions never really recovered.

By winter 1843, the industrial revolution was hammering the final nails in the Christmas coffin. Many people had migrated from the countryside to cities. The old country Christmas that had been celebrated for twelve festive (and boozy!) days was already gone. Most urban employers, like old Scrooge, weren't about to give workers even one day off just to have a party with their families. The dying traditions of Christmas, it seemed, would soon be a quaint part of England's history – if they were remembered at all.

CHARLES 'SCROOGE' DICKENS

When Dickens wrote *A Christmas Carol*, he was making a plea for the renewal of the customs his own father had known – mulled wine, roasted goose and the warmth of yule logs on a snowy Christmas night. But like Scrooge, what he really hoped for was profit, namely 'a thousand clear' from his holiday tale.

In his push to make *A Christmas Carol* a best-seller, Dickens gave readings of his little book, sometimes for charity, often for a fee. Dickens was a wonderful storyteller and his readings achieved as much for Christmas as they did for his bank balance. 'I feel,' an American factory owner said, 'that after listening to Mr. Dickens' reading of *A Christmas Carol* tonight, I should break the custom we have hitherto observed of opening the works on Christmas Day.'

NOT SO HAPPY FAMILIES

Dickens' own parents had never been as warm and loving as the Cratchits. At 12, his careless father went to debtors' prison and Dickens laboured in a rat-infested boot-blacking factory. The dark memory made the author into a passionate reformer of workhouses and child labour laws. It also helped him value family celebrations like the one he created in *A Christmas Carol*. And, of course, it made him desperate to be as rich as Scrooge.

MERRY CHRISTMAS

As *A Christmas Carol* became beloved throughout the English-speaking world, Dickens' idea of how to celebrate Christmas caught on. People couldn't spend twelve days at it, but, like Bob Cratchit, they could wish each other Merry Christmas. They could spend Christmas Eve and Christmas Day with their families. They could strive for good times and goodwill.

In 1870, so the story goes, a young Cockney girl heard that Dickens was dead. She gasped: 'Dickens dead? Then will Father Christmas die too?' The reformed Scrooge would have been happy to tell her that Father Christmas would remain alive and well.

* * *

DICKENS TRIVIA

Q: What character was inspired by Dickens' own father?
A: The character of Wilkins Micawber in *David Copperfield* (said to be Dickens' favourite work) was based on Dickens' father, a navy clerk who seldom had the wherewithal to support his large family, but who remained endlessly optimistic.

Q: What was Dickens' job at Warren's Blacking Factory?
A: He pasted labels on shoe polish bottles.

A hibernating bear can go as long as six months without a toilet break.

TWO-FINGERED SALUTE

We've all given someone the 'two-fingered salute' at some point. Many people believe this very British gesture dates back to the 15th century.

During the Hundred Years War, Henry V was en route to Calais in France to meet reinforcements. His army decimated by disease and hunger, he had a mere 6,000 or so weary troops left. But his enemy Charles d'Albret, Constable of France, still had 25,000 well-rested, well-armed troops at his command. The scene was set for the Battle of Agincourt.

VIVE L'ARROGANCE

The French were hugely dismissive of the English, because the French forces consisted of men from noble families and their retainers, while the English army was a ragtag bunch of lesser nobility and rough peasant stock. The French were also contemptuous of the English archers (mainly, in fact, from Wales), even though they were considered to be the best in the world and their arrows could pierce armour at many paces. So sure of victory were the French that they issued a warning – once they had defeated the English, they would cut of the first and middle fingers of any archer left alive, so he would never be able to draw a bow again.

FRENCH TOASTED

History reports the disaster that befell the French from the very beginning of the encounter. Their horses, laden down with knights in heavy armour, became bogged down in mud in front of the
English lines, where they were torn to shreds by the arrows of the Archers. The battle was over in a matter of hours, with horrendous losses to the French.

The French had no choice but to surrender. Later that day, when their surviving troops and leaders were paraded in front of their victors, the English archers raced to the front and waved their two fingers in front of the faces of the shamed French, in a final act of triumphant defiance. Five hundred years later, we still use this gesture to succinctly demonstrate our contempt.

Uncle John's PRESENTS®

DUBIOUS DECOR AWARD

S ince September 11, 2001, airports everywhere
have been answering the call for better security
by adding new scanning measures for luggage,
being more vigilant about the identities of passengers,
and buying fake plants.

What? You're not exactly sure how the purchase of
fake plants aids in the global struggle against terrorism?
Well then clearly you're not a member of the Airport
Authority of India (AAI), which in May 2003 allocat-
ed roughly $2.7 million to replace the live plants at
India's many airports with more than 22,000 fake ones.

The thinking was that live plants need to be
watered, which means extra staff trolling about the airport—extra staff that could be infiltrated by terrorists.
Eliminate the live plants and you eliminate gardeners
wandering around, and that's one less possible point of
entry for the terrorists. But you have to have *some* sort of
greenery—otherwise the airports would just look industrial and creepy. Fake plastic trees solve the problem.

Voodoo Economics
The thing is, the Airport Authority of India didn't
have $2.7 million just lying around to buy fake plants.
(Who does?) So its members came up with some real
out-of-the-box thinking: why not take the money that
had been allocated for boundary walls and fire safety
and buy fake plants with that? Because, you know, the
terrorists wouldn't just try to sneak into the airport
over the fences. That'd be too obvious. And once

you've eliminated the "terrorist gardener" scenario, you've also apparently eliminated much of your need for fire safety.

The AAI's potted-plant decision was such creative thinking that when the *Indian Express* newspaper asked India's federal civil aviation minister Syed Shahnawaz Hussain about it, he was taken entirely by surprise. Hussain promised to investigate immediately. In the meantime, enjoy your flight to the subcontinent! And especially enjoy those fake plants.

Source: Ananova

* * *

WHERE WAS SMOKEY THE BEAR WHEN WE NEEDED HIM?

Cigarettes start forest fires, and of all people, we expect a fireman to know that. So it's with some measure of disappointment that we note that a fire in British Columbia was caused by a fireman improperly flicking his cigarette while installing a satellite dish in his backyard. To the fireman's credit, as soon as he realized what he'd done, he ran to his neighbors' to warn them of the approaching wall of flame. But when you've started a large fire that causes 8,500 people to flee from their homes and destroys 65 homes, owning up to it is still a little weak. In the aftermath, the fireman wasn't sure if he should go back to the fire station: "I'm not sure if they want me to work there anymore."

Source: Canadian Press

A CHEESY AIRPORT SECURITY STORY

Okay, these days it's not a bad idea for the security guys at the airport to be a little paranoid about everything. Why? Well, as just one example, as we were getting ready to write up this particular piece for the book, CNN was blaring out a story of a nine-year-old's teddy bear that went through an airport scanner with a loaded pistol tucked inside its adorably cuddly belly. The kid said he had no idea how that gun got into the teddy bear; it'd been a gift from a girl he met at the hotel where his family had been vacationing. The point is paranoid airport security people have reason to be paranoid. That's okay by us.

Still, let's also admit there's a difference between nabbing a pistol-packin' plush toy and what happened to Norwegian-born Tore Fauske as he got ready to board a plane in Brussels for a trip back to England, where he resides.

What a Cheesy Gift!

While in Brussels for a business trip Fauske was presented with the Norwegian delicacy *geitost* (it's pronounced "yay-toast")—a type of goat cheese that the Web site Cheese.com assures us has a "sweet, fishy, caramel flavor that is really irresistible." (We're pretty sure that any food that is described as tasting both of fish and of caramel is something we could resist, yeah, with a vengeance, even.)

Clearly Fauske did not have the same problem; he

happily received the cheese and stuffed it into his carry-on bag, which apparently didn't have anything in it that would suffer from smelling like fishy cheesy caramel after a long flight. Off he went to the security gates. As his carry-on went through the security checkpoint, a funny thing happened: Fauske was stopped and everyone behind him in line was shooed off to other checkpoints. Then security people asked Fauske to open his bag. "The guards visibly took a step backward when I unzipped it," he told the *Stavanger Aftenblad* newspaper.

An Unexplosive Situation

There sat the geitost, brown and hard and, clearly, suspected of being some sort of explosive device. (Which it might very well be if you're lactose intolerant.) Fauske tried to explain to the security guards what the substance was, but as you might imagine, anything smelling both of fish and caramel might not strike the uninitiated as edible. Eventually Fauske had to eat some in front of the guards. "It wasn't until I demonstrated that it clearly was something edible that they relaxed," he said.

The moral of the story: If the airport security guards are worried you might explode, don't be afraid to cut the cheese.

Sources: *Stavanger Aftenblad, Aftenposten* English Web Desk, Cheese.Com

THAT'S SOME BANK ERROR

I t all began when "Francesca" went to the Estado de Santa Catarina bank in Santa Catarina, Brazil. Francesca was getting money from her husband Alonzo's pension and as his wife, she didn't expect there would be any problem withdrawing the cash.

So, of course, there was a problem: the people at the bank told Francesca that she wasn't Alonzo's wife. And they knew that because Alonzo had a bank account with an entirely different woman, and *she* was his wife. They even showed Francesca the account on the computer screen with the name of her husband . . . and some other woman.

But, Honey . . .

Francesca marched home and confronted Alonzo about the bank account and the other woman. Alonzo naturally protested and told her that there was no "other woman," and that this was some weird error. But Francesca had seen the bank records, and to her, it probably seemed like the old Richard Pryor joke about a man getting caught with another woman and saying, "Who are you going to believe? Me or your own lying eyes?" In this case, Francesca believed her own eyes and divorced her still-protesting husband.

Don't "Honey" Me!

You'd think the moral of the story here is that if you're going to cheat on your wife, don't be so dumb as to put your mistress on your bank account. But you're wrong.

Because Alonzo *wasn't* cheating on his wife—it was the bank that had made the error. After five years fighting the case in the courts, Alonzo was finally able to get the bank to admit the error. As a consequence, the court had the bank pay Alonzo and Francesca about $16,500 in damages. So the moral actually is: when your husband pleads with you not to divorce him because the bank made a computer error, maybe you should entertain the notion that he might be telling the truth.

Does this mean Alonzo and Francesca are going to patch things up? Not necessarily; Francesca told the *Jornal Nacional* that she wasn't sure she wanted to get back together with her now-proven-innocent-but-still-ex ex-husband. As for Alonzo, he was philosophical: "The money is good, but it doesn't make up for a failed marriage, does it?"

Sources: *Jornal Nacional*, Ananova

* * *

"People are stupid; given proper motivation, almost anyone will believe almost anything. Because people are stupid, they will believe a lie because they want it to be true, or because they are afraid it might be true. People's heads are full of knowledge, facts, and beliefs, and most of it is false, yet they think it all true. People are stupid; they can only rarely tell the difference between a lie and the truth, and yet they are confident they can, and so are all the easier to fool."

—Terry Goodkind

MON *DIEU!* STOP THE MUSIC!

Valerie Faure was both a French lawyer and an avid player of the accordion—two facts that, when combined, would make one suspect it would be impossible for her to find a spouse. Nevertheless, she was married to a man who played the violin. For fun and relaxation, the two liked to hang out on the street corners of their hometown of Bergerac and play their instruments for the amusement of passersby, who may or may not drop coins into their open music cases.

One day, two of those passersby happened to be French lawyers—French lawyers who became incensed that one of their own would be doing such a horrible, awful thing. Successfully defending potential criminals is one thing, but playing an accordion on the street, well, that was just très *sick.* French lawyers have a reputation to protect, and they're not above disbarring a lawyer when her conduct is unbecoming and unprofessional. Indeed, there's a rich tradition of French lawyers getting the boot for extracurricular activity. As far back as 1826, a French lawyer was disbarred for performing in the theater, because you can't have a lawyer as an actor. Actors are professional liars! And that's not like a lawyer at all.

And so Mme. Faure was hauled up in front of her local bar association, which suspended her from practicing law because of her penchant for playing the accordion on the street. But Faure—who was a lawyer, after all—filed an appeal and her perseverance paid off; her bar association's decision was overturned.

Interestingly, the decision noted that Faure couldn't have demeaned the profession of lawyer by her accordion playing because she wasn't wearing her lawyer's robes while she was performing. So all you French lawyers who like to perform in the street, just make sure you do it in casual attire. Also, based on this line of reasoning, the lawyer in the 1826 case has excellent grounds for appeal. Free the French lawyers!

Source: Agence France-Presse

* * *

MISSING THE POINT

A Russian tightrope walker was told to wear a hard hat while performing his act in Britain—this despite the fact that the man does his act without a net. Goussein Khamdoulaev, a performer with the Moscow State Circus, traded in his usual Cossack hat when the circus was told by insurers that it had to comply with new workplace rules put in place by the European Union. What value the hard hat would have if Khamdoulaev fell from the traditional tightrope height of 50 feet is unclear.

Source: London *Times*

BABY, YOU CAN DRIVE
MY CAR—IN SEVEN YEARS

When reading this story, give "Otto," our hero, this much credit: he knew he was too drunk to drive. When it came time to go, Otto took a moment of (relatively) sober reflection and realized that more people than just himself would be at risk if he got behind the wheel. So let it be noted that Otto chose not to drive drunk. In the moment of truth, he took his keys and handed them to his friend "Susie" and told her to drive.

Too bad she was nine years old.

While Susie was behind the wheel, Otto's car veered off the road and hit a tent at a campground in Moses Lake, Washington. Unfortunately, there were people in the tent at the time; two were injured but fortunately were expected to make a full recovery.

Meanwhile, Otto is in trouble with the Grant County sheriff's office. True enough, he didn't drink and drive. But handing the keys to someone whose entire driving experience up to that point may have consisted of pushing along her Malibu Barbie Corvette really isn't any better. Friends don't let friends drive drunk—or prepubescently.

Source: Associated Press

* * *

"The older I grow, the more I distrust the familiar doctrine that age brings wisdom."

—H. L. Mencken

DUMB MUNICIPAL CODES IN ACTION

Some people can't handle alcohol very well, and not because they've had some sort of industrial accident that has left them without the opposable thumbs needed for truly competent handling of beer steins. We mean that they're alcoholics, burdened with a disease that makes them especially susceptible to the addictive nature of drink. Alas, the way most people find out they are alcoholics is by drinking themselves into trouble. It's sort of a catch-22 that way.

A Pack of Kools and Some Kool-Aid

"Catch-22" is also the way to describe the situation faced by the owner of the Keep It Simple club in Edmonton, Canada, in August of 2003. Keep It Simple was a "bar" for recovering alcoholics, in that it provided all the ambiance of a bar (bars being a second home for many alcoholics, for obvious reasons) but without all that troublesome alcohol. Part of the ambiance, along with the pretzel bowls and pool tables, is the haze of cigarette smoke: Recovering alcoholics are notorious smokers. Sure, it's trading one addiction for another, but on the other hand, smoking two packs of cigarettes won't cause you to wrap your car around a tree like a case of cheap beer will. In the short-term, it's an understandable trade.

But Edmonton has smoking laws, and the Keep it Simple bar had a problem: The only bars you can smoke in are the ones that serve alcohol. So, in order to allow smoking on the premises, the bar had to apply for a liquor license.

A.K.A. the Quibbling Commission

Fine, said Tom Charbonneau, the co-owner of Keep it Simple; he went to get the liquor license, but didn't plan to actually use it. When the Alberta Gaming and Liquor Commission heard about that, however, they refused to give over the license. "They weren't looking for a liquor license, they were looking for a smoking license," said Alberta Gaming spokeswoman Marilyn Carlyle-Helms. Not that they give out smoking licenses. That'd just be silly.

Thus the catch-22: Recovering alcoholics smoke. A non-alcoholic bar wants them to be able to smoke, in part so they won't head over to bars that serve alcohol. But in order to allow these patrons to smoke, this non-alcoholic bar has to sell booze. Which, in the case of recovering alcoholics, is defeating the whole purpose of giving them a booze-free bar environment.

Smoking Allowed

"If they say I have to serve a 12-pack, I will buy a 12-pack of beer, sell it for $5 a can, call all the media, stand in front of our sober club and pour it all out on the ground, just to show them how ridiculous it is," Charbonneau said. We say, you go, Charbonneau. Normally we're not much for folks charring their lungs, even folks who benefit from universal health care, but given the choice between recovering alcoholics charring their lungs someplace where no one's drinking, or charring their lungs where everyone's abusing their liver, well, one's the smart(er) choice. Or at the very least, one makes the roads safer after the bars close.

Source: *Edmonton Journal*

ANATOMY OF A DUMB EXCUSE: THE NEKKID PILOTS

Welcome to Anatomy of a Dumb Excuse, in which we show how someone perpetrating a really stupid maneuver just makes it worse by offering up an even stupider excuse.

Our Contestants: Two pilots, working for a national airline. Let's call them "Bob" and "Fred."

The Dumb Move: While piloting their 757, Bob and Fred are discovered by a flight attendant to have removed most or indeed all of their clothing (reports are sketchy on this point). They were subsequently dismissed by the airline due to "inappropriate conduct."

The Even Dumber Excuse: Bob and Fred contend that they removed their clothing because coffee spilled on one of them.

Why This Is a Dumb Excuse: "Coffee spilled on one of them." This is a fine excuse for the one who actually had the spill—Fred. Hot coffee equals third-degree burns, which equals painful gyrations, which could mean accidentally bumping into the flight yoke and plunging an airliner 4,000 feet in three seconds and plastering all the passengers onto the cabin roof. No one wants that. So, all right, fine, Fred's off the hook. *He's* got an excuse for taking off at least one article of clothing.

But then there's Bob. Bob had no free-flying

caffeinated beverage issues. He had no reason for taking off his tie, shirt, pants, and shoes, except possibly that he was performing a sympathy strip for Fred, so Fred wouldn't feel uncomfortable being naked in the cockpit. This impulse, while considerate, has its own psychological pathology that one hopes doesn't exist in the people who control a metal tube filled with other people, hurtling through the air at several hundred miles an hour, and at an altitude of 28,000 feet.

The Truth, As Far As We Can Tell

All told, it's better to think this was just a couple of guys, who happened to be pilots, doing something stupid. Really, who's gonna know they're naked and flying a plane? Perhaps *all* pilots do it when they think no one is looking. We don't know. And now that they've installed those secure cockpit doors, we may never be able to find out.

The airline itself seems to have given more credence to the "guys doing dumb things" idea—*USA Today*, which reported on the story, noted that the company was treating the incident as a "prank that went too far." Not too mention too high up in the air.

Sources: *USA Today*, CNN/Money.com

* * *

"One must be a little foolish, if one does not want to be even more stupid."

—**Michel de Montaigne**

THE RUNNING
OF THE MORONS

Running with the bulls in Pamplona: dumb. The bulls are run down the street to a bull ring, in which they will all soon be killed. No matter what, those bulls are doomed. Inasmuch as this is the case, these animals are entirely within their rights to take out as many humans as possible before they get to their destination, as a way to even out the karmic scales.

What sort of person would place himself in front of a ton of angry, confused animals just for the fun of it? Running in front of a rampaging bull to save a child? Fine—admirable, even. Running in front of a rampaging bull to save a kitten? That's fine, too. Running in front of a rampaging bull for your own amusement? You're a damned fool.

A Lot of Bulls

Just about the only thing the running of the bulls has going for it is tradition: they've been doing it for centuries, and you know how they are about tradition in Europe. If they've been doing it since forever, then that's a good enough reason to keep doing it. The major drawback is that Pamplona is in Spain, which as we all know is far away from North America, where a remarkable number of dumb guys would happily taunt a bull.

Now there is good news for dumb North Americans: you don't have to go to Spain to be trampled by bulls. In Strathmore, Alberta, Canada, there's a new attraction for the Town's Heritage Days: the Heritage Days Stampede. In the stampede, up to 30 bulls chase a couple hundred Canadians and Americans who have paid $100 Canadian for the privilege. Should they survive (the runners, not the bulls), they get a T-shirt and a bandanna. "It's guaranteed adrenaline," organizer Jim Cammeart told the *Ottawa Citizen* newspaper.

This Idea Is Bull***!

And now, a comment from the loyal opposition: Dr. Louis Francescutti, director of the Edmonton-based Alberta Centre for Injury and Control Research. "I think this would rank up there as the most idiotic idea I have heard in my life," the doctor told the *Citizen*. "These people really need to get their heads checked."

We're with the good doctor on this one, although we'd like to point out that this won't stop a bunch of sensation junkies from seeing if they can outrace steers. We just hope they'll remember when they get a hoof through the spleen that they don't even have the excuse that this is something people having been doing since the Middle Ages. This is all-new stupidity.

Enjoy it, guys.

Source: *Ottawa Citizen*

* * *

"The easiest person to deceive is oneself.
—**Edward Bulwer Lytton**

NOTE TO SELF: 911 DOESN'T TAKE REQUESTS

Maybe "Hal" was drinking and driving. Or maybe he just liked swerving down the road at high speeds. For whatever reason, our man Hal was rocketing down the road in Oklahoma and Texas, sometimes reaching speeds of more than 100 mph, trailing cop cars behind him like a string of Christmas lights tied to his bumper. All those cop cars on his tailpipe were getting on Hal's nerves.

So Hal decided to do something about it. He called 911. When the line for emergency services was picked up, Hal asked the dispatcher to call off the cop chase. Then he hung up and did it again. "I think he would just hit 9-1-1 and talk to whoever came on," said Oak Ridge police chief Clint Powell.

And it worked, sort of: the cops did stop chasing Hal. Not because he asked them to, but because they laid down road spikes outside of Powell, Oklahoma, which popped Hal's tires and made him stop. Hal was tossed into the clink on various vehicular charges and held on a $33,000 bond.

Let's hope his one phone call from jail was to another number.

Source: Associated Press

Good Moms
Movie Festival

It's the maternal instinct—at 24 frames a second!
Herewith a sampling of films featuring some of
the best moms the cinema has to offer.

Aliens—Wait a minute, you say? Sigourney Weaver's Ellen Ripley may be a xenomorph-killin' action heroine in this classic 1986 sci-fi film and she even saves a little girl, but she's not a *mother*. Ah, just go to your local video store and rent the director's-cut version on DVD and you'll discover that Ripley is indeed a mother, who learns to her grief that she was 57 years late to her daughter's 11th birthday party because she was floating in space for all those years. This maternal grief and guilt provides an extra dimension of depth to her subsequent bonding with preteen alien-attack survivor Newt (Carrie Henn) and illuminates the lengths she'll go to in order to protect her, including fighting hand to hand (well, claw to mechanical claw) with the 20-foot-high queen alien in the film's climactic scenes. It's a "good mom/bad mom" kind of thing. Shame that *Alien 3* came along and ruined everything. But forget about that and just enjoy Ripley's fierce maternal instinct, backed up by guns. Lots and lots of guns.

Bambi—The world's most selfless mother. First she raises the child of the ruler of the forest as a single mother, with no help at all from the dad. She teaches her child the ways of the forest, explains about evil ("Man was in the forest"), and then, when that evil threatens her child, sacrifices herself so her child can live. Only then does Dad show up (yeah, nice absentee parenting there, *pops*). Bambi's mom is so selfless that she doesn't even *get her own name*. Go on, see if you can think of it. The death of Bambi's mother famously traumatized generations of tiny filmgoers into an aversion to killing deer so pronounced that it actually has a term in wildlife management circles: "the Bambi effect."

Dolores Claiborne—In a slightly different take on the definition of "good mom," Kathy Bates plays a hardscrabble Yankee suspected of murdering the woman for whom she works. As the film goes on, we find out that this isn't the first time she's been suspected of killing someone—and that the previous suspected murder has to do with Dolores's now-estranged daughter, played by Jennifer Jason Leigh. The movie is based on the Stephen King novel of the same name, but the film both elaborates and centers on the contentious relationship between mother and daughter and just how far a mother will go to protect the innocent child in her care. Not cheerful, but certainly gripping.

Stella Dallas—The world's most selfless mother, human division. Ironically the film shares some plot points with *Bambi*. There's a mom raising the child of a powerful man as a single mother, teaching the kid the ways of the world, and then sacrificing herself for the good of her offspring. In this case, however, mom doesn't take a bullet, she just sends her kid to go live with the rich and powerful dad. The story is not unfairly described as a politically incorrect melodrama by critics, who are legion, but as film historian scholar Leslie Halliwell noted: "Audiences came to sneer and stayed to weep." If you're interested, this film comes in three flavors: the hard-to-find 1925 silent version; the classic 1937 *Stella Dallas*, which features Barbara Stanwyck as the selfless mom in question, and the more recent 1990 version *Stella*, which features Bette Midler. Whichever one you choose, keep the tissue box nearby.

Almost Famous—Frances McDormand plays a mother who lets her 15-year-old son, a budding journalist, tour with a rock band in the hedonistic days of the early 1970s. Normally this would probably qualify someone as a *bad* mom. But McDormand's character is neither stupid nor clueless, and shows how a good mom is not only the mother to a child, but the midwife to the man that the boy will become. She understands and trusts her son enough to let him have the adventure—one which does ultimately open his eyes to the world. Which is not to say mom passively waves good-bye to her kid as he goes on the road. One of the film's best scenes has one of the rockers picking up the phone to charm McDormand and getting slapped down by her no-nonsense awareness of what's really going on out there on tour. Anyone who can humble a rock star deserves your respect.

"You have this myth you're sharing the birth experience. Unless you're passing a bowling ball, I don't think so."
—Robin Williams

Your Mother
Should Know...

Music to Moms' Ears

Mom, Mama, Momma, Mother . . . the lovely words for the maternal have worked their way into a lot of songs. Think you can match the mama-lyric with the title and artist?

____ 1. Oh, Mama, can this really be the end?

____ 2. And no one's gettin' fat, except Mama Cass.

____ 3. Your momma's waiting for you
      Wearing her high-heeled shoes and
      her low-necked sweater

____ 4. Cause your mama told you that love ain't right
      But don't you know good lovin' is the spice of life

____ 5. "Kids are different today," I hear ev'ry mother say
      Mother needs something today to calm her down

____ 6. My daddy was the family bassman,
      My momma was an engineer

____ 7. Don't let 'em pick guitars and drive them old trucks
      Make 'em be doctors and lawyers and such

____ 8. I love you, Mamaaaaaa
      More than golf with Arnold Palmmmaaaa

____ 9. I come home in the morning light
      My mother says "When you gonna live your life right?"

____ 10. I said, "Mom, what are you doing, you're ruining my rep"
      She said, "You're only sixteen, you don't have a rep yet"

____ 11. When I was just a baby, My mama told me, "Son
      Always be a good boy, Don't ever play with guns"

____ 12. Mama, life had just begun
But now I've gone and thrown it all away
____ 13. Hey, Hey, Mama the way you move
Gonna make you sweat, gonna make you groove
____ 14. You say your mother told you all that I could give you
was a reputation
Awww, she never cared for me, but did she ever say a
prayer for me?
____ 15. Oh, Mama, I'm in fear for my life from the long arm
of the law
Lawman has put an end to my running and I'm so far
from my home

A. "Mama, Don't Let Your Babies Grow Up to Be Cowboys,"
Willie Nelson
B. "Parents Just Don't Understand," DJ Jazzy Jeff and the
Fresh Prince
C. "Stuck Inside of Mobile with the Memphis Blues Again,"
Bob Dylan
D. "Renegade," Styx
E. "Mother's Little Helper," The Rolling Stones
F. "Mother's Day Song," Adam Sandler
G. "Only the Good Die Young," Billy Joel
H. "Black Dog," Led Zeppelin
I. "Bohemian Rhapsody," Queen
J. "Creeque Alley," The Mamas and the Papas
K. "Folsom Prison Blues," Johnny Cash
L. "Girls Just Wanna Have Fun," Cyndi Lauper
M. "Get Back," The Beatles
N. "Baby Driver," Simon and Garfunkel
O. "Mama's Pearl," The Jackson Five

Snugl Up!

Ann Moore made the world better for babies
with a lesson she learned from African mothers.

In the 1960s, newlyweds Ann and Mike Moore went to Togo in West Africa as Peace Corps volunteers. Ann was a pediatric nurse who had taught at Columbia University and worked with refugees in East Germany and earthquake victims in Morocco. Well-educated and experienced, she was eager to share her information and expertise with mothers from a developing, poverty-stricken nation.

OUT OF AFRICA

While Ann fulfilled her assignment teaching nutrition classes in Togo, she was surprised to find that Africans could teach the industrialized world a thing or two when it came to raising children. African children and their mothers had a closer bond than most mothers and children did back in America.

Ann knew that back in the States when a sick child had to go to the hospital, mother and child were separated and the medical staff took over, leaving the traumatized child alone with strangers. In Africa, mothers stayed at the hospital to be with their sick babies. Ann saw how comforting it was for suffering children to be able to rely on the presence of their mothers. She saw that the closeness between mother and baby was of benefit to both.

Outside the hospital Ann saw more of African mothers and babies practicing togetherness. What most impressed

Ann was the African mothers' custom of carrying their babies in fabric slings tied to their backs. Togo babies rarely cried and seemed remarkably contented compared to Western infants. Moore came to the conclusion that the babies were calm because being so close to their mothers made them feel secure.

OOPS, IT'S NOT AS EASY AS IT LOOKS

Soon after their Peace Corps assignment was over and Ann and Mike returned to the United States, their daughter was born. Wanting the very best for little Mande (Mande's full name is Mandela, after South African freedom fighter Nelson Mandela) and remembering those contented Togo babies, Ann decided to carry her own daughter in a fabric sling. Unfortunately it wasn't as easy as African mothers make it look. Mande kept slipping out of the sling.

Luckily, Ann's own mom was an excellent seamstress. She sewed a sling for her granddaughter according to Ann's design. With Mande safely swaddled on her back, Ann (or Mike) could clean, cook, run errands, or enjoy a walk or bike ride while keeping Mande close, comfortable, and secure. The Moores' baby carrier may have been based on ancient ideas, but it was totally new to Americans, and the soft carrier turned heads wherever they went.

Some observers warned the Moores that they were spoiling their daughter by allowing her to be constantly close to them. Mike and Ann explained that making infants feel secure and loved helped create self-confident and independent children. Many loved the whole concept and wanted to know how to get a backpack of their own or for a gift. As they began to produce more and more baby carriers for envious mothers, Mike and Ann began to feel they had a mission and a business.

AMERICA STARTS SNUGLING

Soon Mande's grandma was hiring friends to help her keep up with orders. Ann worked to improve the carrier with adjustable straps and a pouch to hold up the baby's head. Many moms wanted to be able to carry their babies on their chests, so Ann adapted the carrier for "front loading." By 1969 Ann had a patent on the Snugli carriers and by 1984 the company had sales of more than $6 million.

Ann's successful innovation and enterprise has brought her recognition—the *Wall Street Journal* named her one of the most influential inventors of the millennium. But Ann has been quick to stress that she adapted a centuries-old technique developed by African mothers. "There have been so many times that I've been thankful in my prayers to the African mothers," Ann has said. "They were really our inspiration and it is so wonderful to think that we in America can have the same closeness with our babies."

The Moores sold their company in 1985, but in the late 1990s, when their grandchildren were born, Ann went back to the drawing table and devised another soft carrier called the Weego. Once again the Moores were in a booming baby business, but this time they had the help of their three grown daughters: Mande in charge of marketing, Hopi in charge of sales, and Nicole running purchasing. The Moores may also have a ready-made market, since many new moms and dads were, themselves, once contentedly viewing the world from inside a soft Snugli.

Ante Up, Mom!

We're not bluffing. Be sure to bet on this poker-playing mama.

In the never-ending quest of working moms to find the best way to raise a family and earn a living, moms have moved into such traditionally male-dominated careers as steel workers, firefighters, and investment bankers. But card sharks?

You can bet on it. Today's working mother can just as easily be a professional gambler who ambles up to a green-felt poker table as an office worker who spends the day with a computer in a cubicle. Just ask Annie Duke, a working mother of four and one of the top-rated poker players in the world.

The Bellagio, a luxury hotel in Las Vegas, Nevada, features an 8.5-acre lake and more than a thousand fountains; it houses luxury stores, art masterpieces, botanical gardens . . . and, oh yes, slot machines and poker tables. Thirty to forty hours a week, Annie Duke takes leave of her husband, Ben, and her kids, Maud, Leo, Lucy, and Nelly. Then, often clad comfortably in jeans and a T-shirt, she heads off to the cushy casino, where she is one of but a handful of women who are serious contenders in the world of high-stakes poker.

A MAN'S GAME?

The origin of the game of poker is somewhat in doubt. Some say it began in China, some say Persia, others Egypt or even India. The version played in the United States probably came from a "bluffing and betting" card game called "poque," which French settlers brought to New Orleans. Poque was likely the origin of the game that card sharks used to fleece travelers on the steamboats of the Mississippi River. By the time of the Civil War, poker and draw poker were popular pastimes—for men.

Today the World Poker Tour and the World Series of Poker fascinate both tournament crowds and TV fans at home. If the popularity of poker hasn't faltered since the Civil War, neither has its reputation as a man's game. So in 2000 it was quite an event when a thirtysomething soccer mom who was over eight months pregnant came in tenth place in the World Series of Poker. No small accomplishment. For Annie, it was just evidence that the high-stakes world of poker could be a great career choice for a mother.

THE DUKES OF VEGAS

Big money, job flexibility, time for her kids . . . it's all a dream come true for Duke, who came to her unusual profession in the usual way. She had to juggle marriage and kids and she badly needed money. But some say that gaming is in the lady's genes.

Born into the Lederer family, Annie grew up on the grounds of a preppy boarding school in New Hampshire where her father taught English. Card games and chess were family obsessions, and poker playing seems to run in the family. Annie's older brother, Howard, dropped out of college to play chess, but he eventually moved into the world of professional gambling. Now he is also one of the world's poker greats.

Annie stayed in school and attended Columbia University, where she was a member of its first coed class, and then went on to graduate school to study cognitive psychology at the University of Pennsylvania. She was finishing up her dissertation for her PhD when she realized that she didn't really want to spend the rest of her life in academia. With a boldness that would eventually serve her well at the poker tables, Annie proposed to her boyfriend, who said yes. The two married and went to live in Montana.

A scarcity of jobs and a need to help keep the roof over her family's head inspired Annie to call her brother Howard and ask him to teach her to play poker. She did so well that the Duke family eventually moved to Las Vegas. Her husband, Ben, who ran his own investment business from home, agreed to take on the child-care chores when she was away at the casino . . . and the rest, as they say, is poker history.

STRAIGHT FLUSHES, STRAIGHT PRIORITIES

For Annie, her "beautiful family" remains her first priority. This responsibility to her family may help keep her ego in check and make risk management a lot easier. It may be that self-control that has contributed to her great success. Very few players can win as consistently as Annie Duke does—or cope with losses as well. But win or lose, Annie considers poker the perfect job. That's because she's an involved, hands-on mom with a simple strategy. "If I have a sick child or a soccer game, I don't have to play." Sounds like the perfect work schedule for any parent!

She was even a no-show at a game where she could have taken home a six-figure pot. Why? She had decided it was more important to be at her daughter's sixth birthday party. "I didn't care what kind of money was at stake . . . I'm not missing that party," she said. "You know what?

When she's 25 and in therapy, she's going to be talking about how I missed her sixth birthday party."

PLAYING IS WORK

So play is actually work for Ms. Duke, but rest assured it's no easy gig. She relies on skill, not luck, to make her living. She has to memorize cards and calculate the odds in order to bust some bluffs and second-guess her opponents' moves. She considers her gender an asset, as it rattles some men who are a little touchy about losing to a woman. When they're rattled, they lose more.

She treats the game as strictly business, managing her money carefully. Annie has a separate cash stash specifically set aside for her playing stake. She never gambles her winnings on other games, unlike some poker players who will immediately gamble their winnings at the craps or roulette tables. Annie doesn't take her work home, either. Her kids have no playing cards. Guess gambling isn't a family affair.

"My mother used to say, 'He who angers you, conquers you!' But my mother was a saint."—Elizabeth Kenny

The True Story Behind Mother's Day

A daughter's answer to her mother's prayer creates Mother's Day. Trouble is, the success of the holiday made her want to quash it.

The American Mother's Day had its origins after the Civil War, when Ann Maria Jarvis worked hard with other mothers to start Mother's Friendship Day in an effort to bring together a community divided by the Civil War. Inspired by her mother's work and words, Anna Jarvis lobbied for Mother's Day to become a national holiday.

MOTHER'S FRIENDSHIP DAY, THE ORIGINS

The daughter of a minister, Ann Maria (1832–1905) gave birth to twelve children, but, sadly, only four survived to adulthood. She lived in West Virginia and was very active in her church. There she formed the Mother's Day Work Clubs, where local moms could raise money for the poor.

In 1861, Ann Maria and the Mother's Day Work Clubs faced a terrible challenge. When the Civil War began, the inhabitants of West Virginia were deeply divided. Some West Virginians served the Confederacy while others stayed true to the Union. Determined that the political division wouldn't end the Mother's Day Work Clubs, Ann Maria and the other mothers declared themselves neutral, serving both Rebels and Yankees. Blue and Gray mothers worked together to nurse, clothe, and feed all the sick solders.

When the war was over, Ann Maria set out to heal the civil wounds by initiating a Mother's Friendship Day in the summer of 1865 for all the mothers and their families living in Taylor County, West Virginia. The occasion marked the reunion between Blue and Gray, and the event was an amazing success, as humble mothers and house-wives were able to bring once-bitter enemies together. For several years after, Mother's Friendship Day was an annual celebration. Ann Maria's unexpected success inspired Julia Ward Howe and then her own daughter, Anna, to propose special mother's days of their own.

MOTHER'S DAY, THE BEGINNING

It started innocently enough. Ann Maria's daughter, Anna Jarvis (1864–1948) centered much of her life on the church where Ann Maria taught. The legend goes that Ann Maria gave a stirring talk on the mothers of the Bible and concluded with a prayer that someone would establish a day to commemorate mothers and their service to humanity. Twelve-year-old Anna committed that prayer to memory and silently vowed to fulfill it.

After her mother died on May 9, 1905, Anna began seri-ous work to answer Ann Maria's prayer. Being the daughter of a dedicated activist, she knew how to get things done. By the second anniversary of her mother's death Anna had convinced the minister of Andrews Methodist Church in Grafton, West Virginia, to hold a Mother's Day memorial service. Anna passed out white carnations, her mother's favorite flower—an act that would later come back to haunt her. Eventually those whose mothers had died wore white carnations, while those whose mothers were living wore pink or red carnations.

MOTHER'S DAY, THE HOLIDAY

Anna kept on fighting to make Mother's Day an official holiday. With the help of some wealthy supporters, her efforts began to pay off by the third anniversary of her mother's death. By May 10, 1908, the Mother's Day Sunday service in Philadelphia brought out a crowd of more than 15,000! The idea really took off in the following year, and by 1909 forty-five states, plus the territories, Canada, and Mexico, observed the holiday.

Congress finally woke up and smelled the flowers. They voted in 1913 to have government officials from the president on down wear carnations on Mother's Day. By 1914, Woodrow Wilson proclaimed it an official holiday.

MOTHER'S DAY GOES COMMERCIAL

Anna wanted Mother's Day "to brighten the lives of good mothers. To have them know we (their children) appreciate them, though we do not show it as often as we ought." What Anna didn't appreciate were the commercial interests that looked at moms and began to see dollar signs. She opposed the sale of Mother's Day cards, "A printed card . . . means nothing except you're too lazy to write." She opposed candy sales too, since she thought that adult children brought a box of candy to mother, then ate most of it themselves! But it was the florists who made her blood boil. They had turned Mother's Day into a day to purchase flowers. "I wanted it to be a day of sentiment, not profit," Anna said.

She tried urging practical gifts like new eyeglasses or comfortable shoes. When that failed, she worked to get rid of the darned day altogether. But this time, letters and lobbying didn't work. In 1923, her lawsuits to stop Mother's Day celebrations in New York failed and her protests even landed her in jail. In the 1930s, perhaps a little unbalanced from the long battle, Anna was removed by police after she disrupted a sale of carnations . . . by the American War Mothers.

MOTHER'S DAY, THE LEGACY

Despite Anna's best efforts, she could not undo her work, nor the work of greeting card manufacturers. Mother's Day lived on and thrived. Nations across the globe now formally honor mothers with their own special day. But we wonder, in answering her mother's prayer, did Anna create a monster? We don't think so. Even though commercialism can run amok, the sentiment of the holiday does shine through. Grateful women fondly remembered Anna as the mother of Mother's Day and sent her cards for years. Oh, the irony.

"Mother's Day is in honor of the best Mother who ever lived—the Mother of your heart."
—Anna Jarvis

"Time is the only comforter for the loss of a mother."
—Jane Welsh Carlyle

Great Mama Ape!

Binti Jua shows some maternal moxie!

Mom saves a little boy from ferocious gorillas! Showing a calm intelligence when everyone around her had panicked, a brave mother (with her own baby still clinging to her) saved a three-year-old toddler who'd fallen approximately 20 feet to the floor of the gorilla enclosure at Illinois's Brookfield Zoo. The catch? The heroic mom was one of the gorillas.

SAVED BY THE MOM

On August 16, 1996, at the Brookfield Zoo's Primate World exhibit, a rambunctious toddler climbed the stone-and-bamboo barrier and then fell to the floor of the gorilla compound. The horrified crowd panicked and the boy's mother screamed, "The gorilla's got my baby!" A female gorilla, Binti-Jua (whose name means "Daughter of Sunshine" in Swahili) was the first to act. Carrying her own baby, Koola, on her back, she approached the unconscious boy and picked him up.

Gorillas are five and a half feet tall when they stand straight up on their hind legs and can weigh from 200 to 600 pounds. Their fierce reputation is undeserved, but even the zookeepers who were familiar with the gentleness of giant apes were worried. The helpless child was suddenly under the control of a wild animal.

Binti-Jua cradled the child in her arms and rocked him gently. She seemed to hesitate as to where best to take the little boy; then, keeping other gorillas away, she crossed the compound and placed him near the door where the zookeepers usually entered. She placed the child gently down in a place where waiting staff and paramedics could easily take over. Then, as a stunned crowd watched, the rescuer casually returned to her comfortable spot and began to groom her own baby. The little boy spent a few days in the hospital and was released as good as new.

MOTHER OF ALL CONTROVERSY

Binti-Jua's actions hit the headlines. Celebrated for her amazing rescue, she also became the focus of controversy. Dr. Morris Goodman, a molecular phylogeneticist and the man who discovered the small genetic differences in the coding between human and gorilla DNA, believed that Binti-Jua had some sort of thought process similar to a human's regarding the safety of the child. She had recognized the toddler as vulnerable and displayed intelligent behavior by moving him to safety. Others praised her ability to cope intelligently in a new and unexpected situation.

Skeptics argued that Binti-Jua was only trying to win the approval of her keepers and avoid punishment by retrieving something for them. They pointed out that Binti had been reared by humans, and when she became pregnant, the zoo staff gave her mothering lessons. This led some researchers to argue that Binti-Jua acted more like a human mom because she'd been raised and learned parenting skills from human keepers.

Witnesses, however, claimed that regardless of what did or did not go on in her brain, Binti treated the boy with as much gentleness and care as if she'd been his own mother. And as the rescued toddler recovered from his injuries, Binti was praised as a genuine heroine. Letters and gifts (including pounds of bananas) poured in from all over the world. The heroine received a medal from the American Legion, an honorary membership in a Downey, California, PTA, and a spot as one of the 25 most intriguing "people" in *People* magazine.

Did You Know?

Largest Dog Litter: 23 Puppies
The record is held by three different dogs: an American Foxhound in 1944, a Saint Bernard in 1975, and a Great Dane in 1987. All had 23-puppy pregnancies.

Largest Rabbit Litter: 24 Baby Bunnies
Two separate New Zealand rabbits mums each gave birth to a litter of 24 kits: one mama in 1978 and the other in 1999.

Largest Bird Egg: 5 pounds, 2 ounces
In June of 1997, a big mama ostrich laid a very big egg in Datong, Shanxi, China.

Uncle John's BATHROOM READER. PLUNGES INTO

7 WONDERS OF THE ANCIENT WORLD

We were wondering what was so wonderful about the ancient wonders of the world, so we did a little excavating. Here are the wonders, presented in order of appearance.

1. THE GREAT PYRAMID AT GIZA
Where: The greater metropolitan area of Cairo, Egypt
Who Built It and Why: Pharaoh Khufu built it for his tomb.
When: Around 2500 B.C.
Particulars: The oldest of the seven ancient wonders and the only one still standing. Each of the pyramid's four sides is perfectly oriented to north, south, east, and west. Its base covers 13 acres. The Great Pyramid was the tallest structure on earth for more than 4,000 years, topped by the Cologne Cathedral in 1880 (515 feet), the Washington Monument in 1884 (550 feet) and then the Eiffel Tower in 1889 (986 feet).
What's Left: Originally 481 feet high, time and nature have worn the pyramid down to about 450 feet. It's still one of the most popular tourist attractions in the world.

2. THE HANGING GARDENS OF BABYLON
Where: Ancient Babylon, near present-day Baghdad, Iraq
Who Built It and Why: Babylon was very flat, so King Nebuchadnezzar built it for his wife, Amyitis, who was homesick for the mountains of her native land.
When: About 600 B.C.
Particulars: Picture a terraced garden, built on higher and higher levels, covered with trees, flowers, fountains, and waterfalls. Estimates say it probably covered 100 by 150 feet. Now picture the whole thing supported by columns 75 feet high. Reports say that slaves worked around the clock to irrigate the garden with water from the nearby Euphrates River.
What happened: While there is no concrete proof of their existence, if they were real, time eroded them.
What's Left: Virtually nothing, but stay tuned; archaeologists are still digging.

Lady Nancy Astor, the first woman in the British House of Commons, was born in Virginia.

3. THE TEMPLE OF ARTEMIS AT EPHESUS
Where: The ancient city of Ephesus, near modern Selcuk, Turkey
Who Built It and Why: King Croesus, the man from whom we get the term "rich as Croesus," was the heaviest contributor to the shrine to Artemis, the Greek goddess of the hunt and wild nature.
When: About 550 B.C.
Particulars: Except for the roof, the temple was made entirely of marble. Writers called it the most beautiful structure on earth, with pillars of gold, glorious frescoes on the walls, and its most famous feature: four bronze statues of Amazons, the women warriors who were Artemis's most faithful followers. The temple was a bustling tourist center, where everyone was expected to leave gifts for the goddess. Outside the temple, souvenir stands sold little statues of her. In one of her forms, Artemis was the goddess of the moon. Her father, Zeus, and her brother, the sun god, Helios, were honored with wonders of their own (read on).
What Happened: A fire set by a pre-Christian publicity seeker destroyed the temple in 356 B.C. It was rebuilt, then burned down by invading Goths. Early Christians demolished what remained.
What's Left: Excavations have uncovered the foundation and one column. You can see other columns that were excavated and shipped to the British Museum in London.

4. THE STATUE OF ZEUS
Where: Olympia, Greece, the site of the ancient Olympic Games
Who Built It and Why: The Greeks wanted visitors to the ancient Olympics to be impressed, so what was originally a simple temple to Zeus was turned into the home of an enormous statue of Greece's most powerful god.
When: Around 450 B.C.
Particulars: The 40-foot-high statue of Zeus sitting on a throne made the temple look like a playhouse. Zeus's head was just below the ceiling, giving the impression that if he stood up, he'd go right through the roof. His body was made of ivory, and his beard, robe, and sandals were made of gold. His throne, also made of gold, was encrusted with precious stones.
What happened: A fire in A.D. 462
What's Left: Nothing is left of the statue. The temple is one of those picturesque ruins you can visit on vacation.

The castle of Bavaria's King Ludwig II was the model for Cinderella's castle at Disney World.

5. THE MAUSOLEUM AT HALICARNASSUS
Where: Southwestern Turkey
Who Built It and Why: Queen Artemisia built it as a tribute to her husband, King Mausolus.
When: About 353 B.C.
Particulars: Except for the fact that Artemisia was King Mausolus's sister as well as his wife, the only interesting thing about him was his death: The word for a large above-ground tomb, "mausoleum," comes from his name.
What's Left: Some of the foundation. Once again, the British Museum scores big, with statues taken from the tomb.

6. THE COLOSSUS OF RHODES
Where: Overlooking the harbor of Rhodes, a Greek island in the Aegean Sea
Who Built It and Why: The people of Rhodes built it in honor of Helios, the sun god, to celebrate a military victory.
When: 282 B.C.
Particulars: The Colossus was a colossal statue of Artemis's brother, Helios. No one knows exactly what it looked like, but most artists' reconstructions show him naked, or at least scantily clad, which must have been quite a sight at 120 feet high from his toes to his sunburst-shaped crown. In fact, Frenchman Fréderic Bartholdi used the statue for inspiration when he designed the "New Colossus," America's Statue of Liberty, who wears the same pointy headdress.
What Happened: An earthquake hit around 226 B.C. and the statue broke off at its weakest point—the knee.
What's Left: Nothing.

7. THE LIGHTHOUSE OF ALEXANDRIA
Where: The ancient island of Pharos, in Alexandria harbor, Egypt
Who Built It and Why: Finally, a wonder that actually served a purpose. Designed to guide ships into the harbor, it was completed during the reign of King Ptolemy II.
When: About 270 B.C.
Particulars: This wasn't some puny little wooden lighthouse. We're talking magnificence: Covered in marble and close to 400 feet high (the height of a 40-story skyscraper), the lighthouse was

famous enough to be pictured on Roman coins minted in Alexandria in the second century A.D. During the day, an enormous mirror reflected the sun; at night, a fire at the top did the job. It was apparently also a tourist attraction, selling food on the first level, with a balcony above for climbers who wanted the scenic view. After 1,500 years as a working lighthouse, it became the last of the six lost wonders to disappear.

What Happened: Another earthquake, this one in the 14th century A.D.

What's Left: Deep-sea divers may have found the ruins in 1996. There are plans to turn it into a tourist attraction again, though visitors may have to snorkel to see the best stuff.

AND THE WINNERS ARE:

We were so impressed with the people who built the wonders that we held an awards dinner—hosted by Mother Nature and Father Time. A round of applause for:

Best Builders: Egyptians
Most Ostentatious Display of God-Worshipping: Greeks
Most Romantic: Babylonians
Most Far-Sighted Accumulators of Other People's Ruins: British
Best Adapters (Copiers) of the Ancient Style: French

* * * *

OTHER WONDERS

The U.N. World Heritage has compiled a list of the natural wonders of the world. They include: Angel Falls in Venezuela; the Bay of Fundy in Nova Scotia; the Grand Canyon in Arizona; the Great Barrier Reef in Australia; Iguassu Falls in Brazil/Argentina; Krakatoa Island in Indonesia; Mount Everest in Nepal; Mount Fuji in Japan; Mount Kilimanjaro in Tanzania; Niagara Falls in Ontario and New York; Paricutin Volcano in Mexico; and Victoria Falls in Zambia/Zimbabwe. Yes, there are 12! No one could agree on just seven when faced with the glory of Mother Nature.

When the Civil War started, Robert E. Lee owned no slaves, but Ulysses S. Grant did.

THE STICKY HISTORIAN

Psst! How would you like to watch acts of sex and violence from over 25 million years ago? All you need is a special specimen of fossilized tree sap—better known as amber. The catch is that the ancients who were caught in the act are…well…bugs.

Millions of years ago, while eating, hunting, killing their prey, and even while having sex, insects were trapped in the sticky resin of trees. Over centuries this resin hardened into honey-colored, translucent stones called amber. And when amber contains what the scientists call "inclusions" of anything from flies and mosquitoes to flowers and frogs, it becomes a picture of prehistoric life, frozen in time.

TINY BUBBLES
Amber traps air bubbles, too, and scientists think they might hold a clue to the mystery of what killed off the dinosaurs. The bubbles tell us that 67 million years ago, Earth's air contained 35 percent oxygen to today's 21 percent. Was that 35 percent oxygen level crucial to dinosaur life? Evidence in amber shows that the oxygen in the atmosphere began to fall significantly at the end of the Cretaceous period—the era when the dinosaurs disappeared from the earth.

AMBER GOES HOLLYWOOD
In the movie *Jurassic Park*, scientists extracted dinosaur blood from the stomach of a mosquito that had been encased in amber. The DNA from that blood was used to clone packs of dinosaurs that roamed the park and terrified everybody, on-screen and in the audience. It should come as no surprise that the science in the movie wasn't completely accurate. The *Jurassic Park* amber was discovered at a fictional amber mine in the Dominican Republic. But amber from the Dominican Republic was formed 30 to 50 million years ago, when dinosaurs had already been extinct for more than 15 million years.

WHAT'S OLD IN NEW JERSEY
But amber that was formed in the age of the dinosaurs does exist. Scientists at New York City's American Museum of Natural

History have collected 93-million-year-old amber fossils at a secret site in New Jersey.

PREHISTORIC CLONES?

Scientists don't know if reality will ever catch up to the movies. A couple of examples: In 1995, researchers at California Polytechnic State University revived *Bacillus* bacteria spores from the stomach of a bee encased in amber. The bee's estimated age was somewhere between 25 to 30 million years. If prehistoric bacteria can live again after millions of years, what other ancient creatures might someday revisit Earth? On the other hand, the British Museum of Natural History reports that the DNA stored in amber fossils is too corrupted to use for cloning. Still more scientists disagree and continue to investigate the extraction of DNA from amber fossils and the possible re-creation of prehistoric life.

CAVEAT AMBER

The success of *Jurassic Park* inspired a new worldwide industry in fake amber fossils. Con artists have created fossils out of plastic; they look just like like amber and supposedly contain prehistoric insects, feathers, or the hair of ancient mammals. So, how can you tell if amber is real or not? One good way is to stick a heated needle into your so-called "amber fossil." If you smell burning plastic, you just bought a fake.

* * *

UNZIPPED

We thought this was a cool story, but couldn't fit it in anywhere. It has nothing to do with amber, but with something else that's sticky. Swiss mountaineer George de Mestral was out hiking with his Irish pointer on a fine summer day in 1948, when he noticed little burrs sticking to his pants and clinging to his dog's fur. The tenacious burrs inspired de Mestral to race home, neglect his burr-infested dog, and examine the burrs under a microscope. He noticed hundreds of little hooks clinging to the fabric and thought he might be on to something that would replace the zipper. The idea "stuck" in his head—he "clung" to his idea for years and finally had it patented in 1955. It took several years for the public to get "hooked," but eventually Velcro (a combination of the words "velvet" and "crochet") "caught on" and became a multi-million dollar industry.

THE RICH HISTORY OF CHOCOLATE

Among the ancients, it was revered as the "elixir of the gods."

Today, it is the one sweet temptation that most of us find impossible to resist. Yet, for most of its 3,500-year history, it was not eaten but rather consumed as a beverage—and a cold one at that. Although its form and flavor have taken many twists and turns through the millennia, its appeal, once discovered, has been universal. So, why not treat yourself to a tour of the rich history of chocolate.

THE OLD GRIND
1500 B.C.: The Olmec civilizations of Guatemala, the Chiapas and the Yucatan regions of Central America cultivate the cacao tree and make use of its product by grinding the beans and then mixing with water.

MONEY GROWS ON TREES
A.D. 200: The Olmecs have been overthrown by the Mayan civilization. The vast cacao plantations are used as a source of currency, with the little black beans being traded for goods or services. The bean is only consumed by the ruling classes. By now the process of making the drink has become more sophisticated—the beans are roasted and then ground with water before spices such as chili are added. The resulting mixture is shaken until it develops a frothy top, at which point it is ready to be enjoyed.

A HEAVENLY DRINK
A.D. 1200: The Mayans have been supplanted by the Aztecs who heartily embrace the product of the cacao tree, even incorporating it into their mythology. Their god Quetzalcoatl is said to have pilfered a cacao tree from the heavenly realms and deposited it on the Central American plains ready to be converted into a health elixir and powerful aphrodisiac. Famed Emperor Montezuma enjoys the drink so much that he reputedly downs 50 goblets full every day (the amount of time he spends on the royal lavatory as a result of such liquid overload is not recorded).

Jimmy Hoffa was last seen alive at the Machus Red Fox restaurant.

WRONG CURRENCY

1502: Christopher Columbus, on his fourth voyage to the New World, takes possession of a Mayan trading vessel containing what he takes to be almonds and which function as a means of monetary exchange for the Native Americans. He thereby becomes the first European to encounter the cacao bean, though he scarcely gives it any attention and certainly never tastes it.

JUST A SPOONFUL OF SUGAR

1519–1544: Spanish explorer Hernando Cortes leads an expedition into the heart of Mexico in search of gold and silver. He is welcomed by the Aztecs and served their greatest delicacy—a cold, bitter drink that they call "cacahuatl." Cortes introduces this strange new brew to the Spanish court. It becomes an instant hit, even more so when sweetened with sugar. The Spanish would keep the secret of chocolate to themselves for the next 75 years.

ENGLISH COOKING

1579: The English let the chocolate opportunity slip through their fingers when they seize a Spanish cargo ship on the high seas. The British Buccaneers are surprised to find that the ship holds a cargo of what they take to be sheep droppings and set it on fire. Eight years later they get a second chance when another Spanish ship carrying cacao beans is seized. Again, however, they destroy the cargo, declaring it to be useless.

GOES A COURTING

1609–1643: The secret is out. Chocolate makes its way across Europe, causing a sensation among the royal courts who are first introduced to it. France's Sun King, Louis XIV is so taken with the delicacy that he appoints a representative to manufacture and sell it. The first book entirely devoted to chocolate is printed in Mexico. Throughout the French nobility, the aphrodisiac properties of the drink are highly regarded. Both Casanova and the Marquis de Sade are said to be prolific consumers.

FAST FOOD

1662: The Church of Rome declares that the consumption of chocolate, although highly nutritious and filling, is not considered to be food and can therefore safely be taken in its liquid form during periods of religious fasting.

JUST WHAT THE DOCTOR ORDERED

1765: Chocolate, by now highly regarded as a liquid delicacy and a medicinal remedy in Europe, makes its way to the United States where Dr. James Baker of Massachusetts begins a chocolate manufacturing plant. Cacao beans are ground into chocolate liquid and pressed into cakes that can be dissolved in water or milk to make drinking chocolate. At the same time, James Watt invents the steam engine in Europe, which will soon be applied to the mechanized manufacture of chocolate.

WARRANT FOR HIS ASCENT

1824: John Cadbury opens a grocery in Birmingham, England, selling roasted cacao beans on the side. Very soon he is concentrating solely on the cacao beans and, in 1854, receives a Royal Warrant to be the sole provider of chocolate to Queen Victoria. A century later Cadbury is the largest food company in the world.

BAR KING

1847: The modern chocolate bar is born when British manufacturer Joseph Fry mixes melted cacao butter into a paste that is then pressed into a mold and sold as a solid bar. Soon the public has become educated to eat, rather than drink their chocolate.

1893: Milton Snavely Hershey enters the chocolate business. The world is introduced to the milk chocolate Hershey bar, followed by Hershey's Kisses. His operations grow at such a rate he takes over the entire town of Derry Church, Pennsylvania, renames it Hershey, and turns it into the chocolate capital of the world.

1900 to present: The creation of chocolate delicacies becomes an art form. In 1908, the Swiss Toblerone bar is offered, in 1922 the European Chocolate Kiss, chocolate-covered cherries in 1929, and that old favorite—the chunky bar filled with nuts and raisins in the mid-1930's. During World War II, chocolate bars become standard issue item for the U.S. military. When man conquers Mt. Everest in 1953 and heads into space in the 1960s, the chocolate bar goes along. By the end of the 20th century, science acknowledges what the Aztecs knew all along—that chocolate is a powerful fighter against fatigue, giving the eater added strength and energy. But, the scientists found, that energy comes at a price— a one-and-a-half-ounce chocolate bar contains 220 calories!

Sarajevo caused trouble before. The death of an archduke there started World War I.

I FOUND IT ON EBAY

A small sampling of the wacky items that have been auctioned on eBay. We've provided the opening bid; using the list at the bottom of the page, see if you can figure out what each item went for.

DESCRIPTION: "With our coworker Brady!!! He drives a Miata!!!"
OPENING BID: 50¢   **WINNING BID:** _____

ITEM: Frog purse, made from a real frog
DESCRIPTION: "Be the first person on your block to own a coin purse made out of most of a frog. Rest assured, you'll never be asked for spare change again."
OPENING BID: $1   **WINNING BID:** _____

ITEM: A picture of my butt.
DESCRIPTION: "I'm a sexy guy from Florida, you know you want this, you pay shipping if out of USA."
OPENING BID: 75¢   **WINNING BID:** _____

ITEM: One pound real Arkansas Civil War dirt
DESCRIPTION: "100% guaranteed to be from the Civil War era. Comes with certificate of authenticity if desired."
OPENING BID: $1   **WINNING BID:** _____

ITEM: Bridal wedding gown
DESCRIPTION: "Very soiled and spotted."
OPENING BID: 99¢   **WINNING BID:** _____

ITEM: Francis D. Cornworth's virginity
DESCRIPTION: "I figured with the latest eBay craze, I'd see exactly how much I could get for my virginity. I live in Miami, FL. If you live in Florida, I could probably meet you halfway up to Orlando. Otherwise you'll have to arrange to meet me."
OPENING BID: $10   **WINNING BID:** _____

ITEM: Muhammad Ali's broken-jaw X-ray
DESCRIPTION: "Used to determine the extent of his injuries following his bout with Ken Norton."
OPENING BID: $9.99   **WINNING BID:** _____

ITEM: Set of 50 "antique" eyeballs
DESCRIPTION: "Lifelike detail; the veins in the eyes are stunning!"
OPENING BID: $50   **WINNING BID:** _____

ITEM: The raft Elian Gonzales's family used to flee Cuba
DESCRIPTION: "A genuine piece of American history...sure to be a big moneymaker!"
OPENING BID: $20   **WINNING BID:** _____

ITEM: Cadaver bag
DESCRIPTION: "This bag is new, never used. I would have to be a sick freak to sell these used."
OPENING BID: $15   **WINNING BID:** _____

$1	**$5.50**	**$15**	**$255.01**	**$613**
$2.75	**$6.19**	**$15.50**	**$280**	**$10 million**

ANSWER, PAGE 373

DEADLY AS MOLASSES IN JANUARY

What was 15 feet high, moved at 35 miles per hour, and killed 21 people in 1919?

The 50-foot high tank at the Purity Distilling Company of Boston, Massachusetts, was going full-bore. Filled to near-capacity, it contained two million gallons of steam-heated molasses, soon to be gallons of rum and industrial alcohol. Little did the Purity people and the citizens of Boston know the tragic and bizarre disaster in store for them that warm January day.

THE FIRST SIGNS
Witnesses later reported hearing a banging and tapping sound coming from the tank. The sounds they heard were the rivets that held the tank together popping free. Next thing anyone knew, the tank burst, sending—did we mention two million gallons?—warm, sticky molasses into the streets of Boston, moving at 35 miles an hour. Which might have been funny if it hadn't also been carrying huge, jagged sections of the tank with it.

MOLASSES IN JANUARY
In an irony only found in truth, this event really did take place during January. Too bad it had to be an unusually warm January day, 43 degrees, well above freezing. If the weather had been more typical, it might have given the soon-to-be victims time to notice the oncoming calamity, maybe pack their things, move their belongings, and get the hell out of there, before the brown wall of molasses reached them.

THE BLOB
Moving with a dull, muffled roar, the 15-foot-high wall of brown goo surged and rumbled into Boston's North End. It crushed trolley cars, swallowed trucks, horses, and carts, and knocked buildings off their foundations.

AMAZING RESCUE
The parts of the tank propelled by molasses tore into the supports

---

Charlemagne's parents were Pepin the Short and Bertha of the Big Foot.

holding up the Atlantic Avenue elevated train. The steel trestles twisted and snapped and the track collapsed to the ground, just as a train was approaching. A quick-witted motorman reacted with enviable cool. He walked to the rear of his train and reversed the engines. The train ground to a halt, saved from the still-surging molasses below.

STICKY DOOM

The greatest number of fatalities that day was at a Public Works building, where municipal employees were just having lunch. The molasses slammed into the building, shattering it and throwing fragments 150 feet in the air. Another city building was similarly torn from its foundations; the tenement apartments on the upper floors collapsed into kindling.

MOLASSES SWALLOWS PEOPLE

It was literally a tidal wave, swallowing dozens of people, rolling and crushing them under its brown mass. Dozens were critically injured by the debris picked up and carried by the sticky mess, while others were simply crushed to death by the heavy molasses.

THE RESCUE

Finally, the molasses began to cool and congeal. The tidal wave slowed, then stopped. The first group of rescuers arrived: sailors from the harbor patrol ship *Nantucket*. They plunged into the mess and started pulling survivors out. Right behind them were the local boys in blue, followed by soldiers from a nearby army base. The Red Cross arrived next, in their crisp white uniforms, but soon you couldn't tell them apart: everyone was covered with the same brown goo.

PUMPING IRONY

The final toll was 21 people dead, 150 injured. The clean-up crew pumped sea water from the harbor via hoses. But the molasses and saltwater didn't mix, and soon the whole area was buried under brown foam. It took months before the streets of Boston were their old familiar dirty gray again. How could anything as harmless—and sweet—as molasses cause such devastation?

The mummy of Ramses II, thought to be the pharaoh in Exodus, is in the British Museum.

THE OLYMPICS
EXPOSED

If you wish we could return to the ancient Olympics when athletes played for love of the game instead of medals, when sportsmanship was king… Oh, dear. Uncle John is going to disillusion you again.

The first Olympic Games were held in 776 B.C., but their real beginnings are shrouded in myth. Legend tells us that Herakles (who later made a Roman name for himself as Hercules) won a race on the sacred Greek plain called Olympia. He decreed that the Olympian race should be re-enacted every four years.

NAKED GAMES
A big difference between the ancient Olympics and the modern games is that back then there were no commercial logos on the athlete's clothing because nobody wore clothing: the ancient games were played in the nude.

The first competitors wore shorts, until 720 B.C. Then, according to the ancient writer, Pausanias, one guy tossed his trunks so he could run faster. After the shortless guy won, clothing was abolished.

ROUGH, TOUGH, AND IN THE BUFF
Some historians think it may have been the militaristic Spartans who pushed for nudity. They trained in the nude (both men and women, the latter—naked women in public!—being very controversial). But the Spartans were top athletes, so the other city-states may have wanted to imitate them.

MORE NAKED GAMES
The first Olympic games were just races, but more sports were added as the years went by: the pentathlon, horse races, chariot races, and the pankration, which was a combination of boxing and wrestling. At one time or another, there were 23 Olympic sports events. While nudity may have helped the runners, it didn't help the Olympian jockeys much. They were bare and rode bareback—no saddles, no stirrups. Controlling the horse was a challenge!

During the 1918 U.S. flu epidemic, the death toll was so high that there was a coffin shortage.

PEACEFUL ENEMIES

There was one more very important reason for the "undress" code: without their clothes athletes couldn't hide any weapons. At the time, the Greek city-states were often at war. But during the Olympic festival, they called a truce so that everyone could travel to Olympia safely.

Hostilities, weapons, and armies were forbidden. Even the death penalty was suspended. All the same, nobody really trusted anybody else. The games had their roots in warfare and the athletes were prepared for battle as well as for sporting competitions. For the most part the Olympic truce held.

WHEN MEN WERE MEN AND WOMEN WEREN'T ALLOWED

Women weren't allowed to watch the men's games, much less compete. This supposedly had more to do with the religious aspects of serving Zeus than it did with nudity. Women had their own races anyway, at Olympia in honor of the goddess Hera (a.k.a. Mrs. Zeus), where they could be just as naked and win their own darn laurel wreaths. By the way, any woman caught watching at the male Olympics was thrown headfirst off the cliffs of Mount Typaeum.

ANCIENT MAULERS

War and women were forbidden in the ancient Olympics, but violence was allowed. Some of the early Olympic games probably made professional wrestlers look like sissies. Entrants could trip, punch, and kick their opponents, even in their, um, private parts. Pankration entrants could also break fingers for a quick win, and one pankratiast became so good at this that he was called "Finger Tips."

THOSE RICH ATHLETES

Today's millionaire pros are cousins to the ancient Olympians. We may like to think of Greek athletes as idealistic amateurs, but the word "athlete" is derived from Greek words meaning "one who competes for a prize." Aristotle, Plato, and Socrates whined about the declining morality that money brought to the Games. Galen, a Greek physician asked, "Are athletes to be worshipped like kings because they have large incomes?" Hmmm.

MORE THAN THE KEY TO THE CITY

Olympic competitors had to pay their way into the Games—and it wasn't cheap. They also expected payment for the glory they brought to their cities. In 6 B.C., Athens offered bonuses equal to around $600,000 today. Athenian champions got front row seats at the theater and free meals in the city hall for life. They even made money by doing "appearances" at other festivals.

A SHOW OF STRENGTH

Athletes trained hard. By the sixth century they were hiring coaches. There were fads involving diet and exercise just like today. Athletes from Croton in Italy believed in a meat diet, and beans were a no-no. The greatest wrestler of the ancient Olympics, Milo of Croton, supposedly ate 40 pounds of meat and bread at one meal, washing it down with eight quarts of wine. It worked: Milo won himself 32 titles in his career.

SLEAZY POLITICS

Then as now you couldn't keep politics out of the games. Politicians gave speeches between the races (but it's not known if people hung around to listen). Campaigning politicians sponsored chariots to gain popularity with the crowds. There were even violent political disputes over which city should control the Sanctuary of Zeus in Olympia where the games were staged.

THE MORE THINGS CHANGE

Despite all its problems, the Olympics did promote cherished ideals of peaceful competition and individual achievement. In A.D. 395, Emperor Theodosius I banned them during a purge of pagan festivals. But he couldn't kill the spirit of the Olympics and, in 1896 in Athens, the modern Olympics began. This time everyone wore clothes, but they still have problems that are an awful lot like the ones the ancient athletes used to face.

* * *

TELL THEM TO COME BACK LATER

The ancient Greeks gave the Olympics top priority. Even when the Persians were invading in 480 BC and the survival of the Greek city-states was endangered, thousands of spectators watched the finals of boxing bouts at the Olympian stadium.

The future Pope John XXIII was an Italian sergeant during World War I.

HOW MOSQUITOES CHANGED HISTORY

They may be small, but they're powerful. Mosquitoes have been manipulating the course of human history since its very beginnings.

1,600,000 B.C. Africa—Our ancestors take their first upright steps. Thanks to mosquitoes, they are already infected with malaria.

500 B.C. India—Brahmin priest Susruta deduces that mosquitoes are responsible for the spread of malaria. No one pays any attention for the next 2,400 years.

323 B.C. Babylon—Alexander the Great is felled by a mosquito, dying from malaria at the age of 33. His dream of a united Greek empire collapses within a few years, and widespread malarial infection contributes to the decline of Greek civilization.

A.D. 410 Rome—Marauding Visigoths finish off the Roman Empire, already undermined by a fifth column of malaria-spreading mosquitoes in the low-lying areas surrounding the capital. Shortly afterward, Alaric, leader of the vanquishers, is vanquished in his turn by a treacherous mosquito.

1593 Africa—Mosquitoes send yellow fever and malaria to their relatives in the New World via the slave trade, setting the stage for epidemics that would decimate both colonial and aboriginal populations.

1658 England—Bitten by a Royalist mosquito, Oliver Cromwell dies of malaria, paving the way for the return of the British monarchy.

1690 Barbados—Mosquitoes spread yellow fever to halt a British expedition en route to attack the French in Canada.

1802 New Orleans—Napoleon sends troops to reinforce France's claim to Louisiana and put down a slave rebellion in Haiti. Of the 33,000 soldiers, 29,000 are killed by mosquito-borne yellow fever. Louisiana becomes part of the U.S.; Haiti becomes independent.

1902 Stockholm—British army surgeon Dr. Ronald Ross receives the Nobel Prize for establishing the link between mosquito bites and malaria.

1905 Panama—Mosquitoes almost succeed in halting construction of the Panama Canal, as panicked workers flee a yellow fever epidemic.

1939 Colorado—DDT is tested and found to control mosquitoes and other insects. Mosquitoes eventually develop resistance to the chemical; humans don't.

1942 Dutch East Indies—Japanese troops seize the islands that provide most of the world's quinine, then the only reliable malaria therapy known, hoping mosquitoes will become their best allies in fending off Allied forces. Nearly half a million U.S. troops in the East are hospitalized with malaria between 1942 and 1945.

1965–1975 Vietnam—Mosquitoes infect as many as 53 U.S. soldiers per thousand with malaria every day.

1995 Geneva—The World Health Organization (WHO) declares mosquito-born dengue fever a "world epidemic," while deaths from malaria rise of 2.5–3 million a year.

* * *

Besides malaria and dengue and yellow fevers, mosquitoes have been in the news for a carrying a whole host of new and deadly blood-borne diseases.

Until 1999, West Nile virus, originating from the Nile River valley, had not previously been documented in the Western Hemisphere. The virus causes encephalitis, an inflammation of the brain, and can be transmitted by mosquitoes. West Nile was found in "overwintering" mosquitoes in the New York City area in early 2000, a sign that the virus is permanently established in the U.S. In the year 2000, 21 cases of the illness were reported, including two deaths in the New York City area.

THE REAL BRAVEHEART

*Movie fans will never forget William Wallace, the Scots rebel
leader that Mel Gibson portrayed so convincingly in
Braveheart. But was Wallace nearly forgotten
in Scotland until Hollywood rescued his legend?*

Randall Wallace, the producer of the 1995 film *Braveheart*,
was researching the production in Scotland when he visited the Wallace Memorial at Elderslie, Renfrewshire. The
producer talked to local teens sitting near the statue and asked
them what they thought about their hometown's great hero. The
kids had no idea the statue represented William Wallace; in fact
they'd never heard of him.

WILLIAM WHO?
They know who Wallace is now. And in Wallace's rising historical
fortunes, it's easy to forget the darker, bloody side of his battle to
free Scotland. Wallace was the great leader of Scotch resistance
against the English - who also wiped out villages, burned down
churches, and flayed his enemies to make battle ornaments.

DEATH, LIES AND THE MOVIES
Artistic license was taken with Wallace's family history in *Braveheart*. One brother was written out completely, and another, along
with Wallace's father, was conveniently axed early so as not to get
in the way of the action. The historic accounts of Wallace's life
were also slanted to make storytelling easier. Accounts written in
Scotland made Wallace a noble conquering giant; those written in
England called him a murderer and outlaw.

WALLACE'S STORY GETS VERSE
Braveheart is based on a view of Wallace presented in the *Scoticho-
rum* of Walter Bower. Bower wrote it in the 1440s, 135 years after
Wallace's death, and his main source was anti-English propaganda
where Wallace got excellent, but not always accurate press.
Bower's account was the source for a romantic epic poem, *The
Wallace*, by "Blind Harry." The poem became Scotland's national
myth for several hundred years. In some Scottish homes it held an
honored place near the Bible.

WILL THE REAL WILL PLEASE STAND UP?

But what's the scoop on the real, non-mythologized Wallace? Well, for one thing, remember his statue? It might be in the wrong hometown. Most of the facts about 13th century Scotland are hazy, but modern research indicates that the great man was actually born in Ellerslie, Ayrshire. The name "Wallace" means "Welsh," and he was probably a descendant of Welsh-speaking immigrants who came to live in West Scotland. William was the son of a knight and minor landowner. He was not a noble, but he was an educated member of the prosperous Scottish upper classes. In *Braveheart*, Mel Gibson could have portrayed a well-dressed, well-heeled, brilliant, 13th-century warrior (though fans would have missed all that wild hair and face paint).

A STIRLING VICTORY

Wallace was a brilliant commander. A high point of his military career was the Battle of Stirling Bridge of 1297 where the Scots were badly outnumbered. Stirling Bridge was very narrow, allowing few soldiers to cross at once. The outnumbered Wallace managed to split the English forces in two; the English who had crossed to the north side of the bridge had no room to maneuver, and they were cut off from retreat. Wallace's men slaughtered some 5,000 English that day; and the despised English treasurer's flayed skin made a belt for Wallace's sword.

WALLACE WAS NO ANGEL

Wallace led his army into the English border region of Northumberland. Here the darker side of Wallace's story emerged. The English commanders had tried to subdue Scotland by burning and pillaging it. Now, Wallace and his men sacked the English cities for food to take back to starving Scotland. They burned towns and killed the inhabitants so that the English soldiers would find no help if they returned. (And Wallace knew they would try to return). The great Wallace and his men were as merciless in Northumberland as the English had been in Scotland.

WALLACE WAS NO FOOL

In the summer of 1298, when King Edward I led a large army through the area into Scotland he rode through a barren landscape. Thanks to Wallace, who'd laid waste to Northumberland, the approaching English army was almost starved out.

A NOBLE KNIGHT BUT NOT A NOBLE

Sometime in early 1298, Wallace was knighted, most probably by Robert Bruce, Earl of Carrick, and he became sole Guardian of Scotland. In the Middle Ages it was an amazing achievement for a mere knight to become more powerful than nobles were, but Wallace was a man of amazing achievements. Still, his rapid rise as one of the most powerful men in Scotland made him enemies. Independence was restored in Scotland (thanks to Wallace), and Robert Bruce was enthroned as king.

But in 1305, Scottish noblemen who were less entrenched against the English than they were against Wallace handed him over to England and Edward I.

MARTYRDOM IN ENGLAND

The English took Wallace to London for a show trial. Maybe the worst mistake King Edward I ever made was to have his old enemy tortured, mutilated, disemboweled and hacked to pieces in public. Edward I made Wallace a martyr in Scotland, and a symbol of Scotland's quest for independence. Wallace's life (darker side and all) came to stand for bravery in the pursuit of freedom. As the 18th century Scottish poet Robert Burns said: "The story of Wallace poured a Scottish prejudice into my veins which will boil along till the floodgates of time shut in eternal rest." Wow. And Burns hadn't even seen Mel Gibson.

*   *   *

Robert the Bruce, once deemed a turncoat by the Scots, ended up a greater hero than Wallace. He repeatedly made and broke peace with the English. But in 1304, Bruce made a treaty with the church to help him gain the Scottish throne, and the support of the people. In 1305 he went to Scone to claim the throne and was crowned King Robert I of Scotland. A number of battles ensued with mixed results. After one bloody defeat, he hid in a dark cave to escape the English army. As the famous legend has it, while he sat there depressed at his failures, he saw a tiny spider trying to climb its silken thread to its web, and repeatedly tumbling back down. Yet, the spider continued its struggle. Bruce was so inspired by the spider's tenacity that he grabbed up his sword and shouted "If at first you don't succeed—try, try again!"

MIX-UP AT THE HONKY-TONK

Country music expresses universal sentiments like "You Stuck My Heart in an Old Tin Can and Shot It Off a Log." Yeah. For this quiz, we've taken 10 actual country song titles and removed two key words from each one. Can you put the 20 removed words back in their proper places? Everybody down at the honky-tonk would be mighty grateful.

1. "He's Been _____ Since His Wife's Gone _____"
2. "I Don't Know Whether to _____ Myself or Go _____"
3. "If _____ Showed Up on _____, Wonder Whose I'd Find on You"
4. "I'll _____ You Tomorrow but Let's _____ Tonite"
5. "I've Been _____ from the _____ of Your Heart"
6. "I've Got the _____ for Your Love and I'm Waiting in Your _____ Line"
7. "Mama Get the _____ (There's a _____ on Papa's Head)"
8. "_____ Me with More Than Your _____"
9. "She Made _____ Out of the _____ of My Heart"
10. "When We Get Back to the _____ (That's When We Really Go to _____)"

BATHROOM	BOWLING	DRUNK	FARM
FINGERPRINTS	FLUSHED	FLY	HAMMER
HANDS	HONEYMOON	HUNGRIES	KILL
MARRY	PUNK	SKIN	TIMBER
TOOTHPICKS	TOUCH	TOWN	WELFARE

ANSWER, PAGE 373

BASEBALL NAMES

In *Uncle John's Bathroom Reader Puzzle Book #1*, we ran a quiz called "Basketball Names"—AND THE FANS WENT WILD!!! Well, maybe not wild, but at least sort of enthusiastic. That's why we decided to replay it, this time with baseball team names. Once again, we've thrown you a few curve balls: not all the stories are true. Can you figure out which ones should be pitched?

Los Angeles Dodgers: The streets of 19th-century Brooklyn were full of trolleys—and pedestrians constantly scurrying out of their way. Hence the name of its baseball team: the Brooklyn Trolley Dodgers, later shortened to just "Dodgers." The team moved to L.A. in 1958, to Brooklyn's great chagrin.

Pittsburgh Pirates: Originally known as the Alleghenies (after the nearby Allegheny River), they earned the "Pirates" nickname in the 1890s after stealing a few players from a rival Philadelphia team.

San Francisco Giants: Logging was a big industry in New York back in the late 1800s, and the owner of the New York Gothams wanted to honor the men who provided the wood for their bats. The team almost became the New York Lumberjacks, but instead became the Giants—with Paul Bunyan as their mascot. Paul Bunyan didn't catch on, but the name did, and the team moved to San Francisco in 1958.

Cleveland Indians: The Indians were another team that tore through nicknames early in their career. The Forest Citys, the Spiders, the Blues, the Broncos, the Naps...whew. Player-manager Nap Lajoie loved cigars, and was almost never seen in the dugout without a cigar in his hand. When a lot of Nat's teammates abandoned chewing tobacco for cigars, rival teams joked that they looked like a bunch of cigar-store Indians. Cleveland decided they liked that name and kept it.

Montreal Expos: Given that the reason Montreal was awarded a baseball franchise in the first place was that the 1967 Montreal

World's Fair (otherwise known as Expo '67) was such a success, it seemed only fair to name the team in honor of the event.

Cincinnati Reds: When the team was originally formed in 1869, they were the Red Stockings. (What is the obsession baseball teams have with their socks?) That got shortened to the Reds—until the early '50s, when McCarthyism was rampant. No one wanted to be called a "Red" in those days, so the team actually made an official name change, to the Redlegs. When the patriotic panic died down, they quietly switched back to being the Reds.

New York Yankees: Originally called the Highlanders and the Hill-toppers (because their park was located at the highest point in the city), sportswriters grumped about the difficulty of squeezing the long name of the team into headlines. In 1909, a newsman arbitrarily called them Yankees—patriotic slang for "Americans." Around World War I, when jingoistic fervor was at its peak ("The Yanks are coming!"), the team officially became the Yankees.

San Diego Padres: Although they became a major league team in 1969, the Padres had been a minor league team since 1936. Their religious-sounding name was inspired by the original manager's strict rules against drinking, smoking, chewing tobacco, and entertaining ladies in hotel rooms. He quit in a huff after he discovered that every single player was breaking his rules, but there was no corresponding name change to the San Diego Sinners.

ANSWER, PAGE 372

THEM'S FIGHTIN' WORDS: IN THE TRENCHES

In World War I thousands of miles of trenches held thousands of troops in a four-year-long stalemate.

Of course, the use of trenches to conceal military forces predates 1914 by a long, long time, and in fact, they were called "trenches" from about 1500 on. But their use in World War I, where they far exceeded any prior deployment, gave our language a number of lasting terms.

in the trenches
During the war being **in the trenches** meant being in action. The same thing today is meant by the term, that is, actively working at something. Thus, "He spent years in the trenches before they made him president of the company."

digging in
After the trenches were dug, soldiers on both sides lived in them for months on end, with neither side advancing or retreating measurably. From this, **digging in** acquired the meaning of standing firm in one's position or views.

foxhole
In addition to very long trenches, soldiers occasionally used a small slit trench that housed one or a few men. Although it was used much more rarely, the name given it, **foxhole**, survived. It was to play a much larger role in subsequent wars.

trench coat
The trenches were frequently, if not always, wet. Consequently, the officers wore long waterproof coats, or **trench coats**, a noun later applied to and still used for similar civilian raincoats.

trench mouth
The long months in the trenches took a terrible toll on a soldier's health. One condition that afflicted many of them was **trench mouth** (formerly called Vincent's disease), characterized by painful, bleeding gums and bad breath. It was caused by poor oral

hygiene and nutrition, heavy smoking, and stress—all conditions endemic in the trenches. Today **trench mouth** is readily treated with dental care and antibiotics.

shell shock

In addition to physical ailments, soldiers frequently suffered from nervous conditions. One was an acute stress syndrome resulting from exposure to constant shelling by the enemy and therefore called **shell shock**. It was thought to be caused by both the noise of the artillery and the constant fear it engendered. Today this term is still loosely used to describe the after-effects of any traumatic experience, as in, "That series of lousy boyfriends gave her a bad case of shell shock."

screaming-meemies

A similar expression is **screaming meemies**, a term that was coined for German artillery shells that emitted an exceptionally high-pitched whine before exploding. The term was later used to describe a state of extreme nervousness, bordering on hysteria.

over the top

When ordered to advance, the soldiers climbed over the parapet of front-line trenches to attack the enemy's front line. The "top" referred both to the trench's top and to the open no-man's-land between them and the enemy. After the war, the term survived, assisted by Arthur Guy Empey's use of the term as the title for his popular World War I account. In civilian use it was extended to mean taking the final plunge and doing something dangerous or notable.

no-man's-land

Although **no-man's-land** dates from the 1300s, when it meant the waste ground between two kingdoms, it didn't take on its military meaning until World War I, when it was applied to the territory between the thousands of miles of Allied and German trenches. This area, a virtually stationary battle line for three years, was covered with barbed wire and pitted with shell holes made by the artillery of both sides. Since then, this term also has been used loosely to describe an indefinite situation where one is neither here nor there.

tripwire
Troops who advanced close to the German line often had to cut through a wire that had been strung to set off a trap or an alarm. The soldiers called it a **tripwire**, because it was meant literally to trip them up. Later the term was used to signify anything that might trip someone up, as in a *New York Times* headline on October 7, 1997, "Looking for Tripwires, Ickes Heads to the Witness Stand." (The term today is also employed for a small military force used as a first line of defense.)

various (now politically incorrect) names for the enemy
During this period the traditional offensive slang for a German was **kraut,** an abbreviation for what was regarded as a quintessential German food, sauerkraut. Another was **Heinie,** an abbreviation for the common German name Heinrich. A third was **Jerry,** either derived from the British nickname for chamber pots (which the German helmets resembled), or a shortening of "German." These terms survived, on a small scale, but again came into wider use during World War II, when Germany was again the enemy of the Allies.

Christine Ammer's book, *Fighting Words,* explores the linguistic legacy of armed conflicts over the centuries, from biblical times to the present.

* * *

GAS ATTACK
World War I originated more than vocabulary: gas warfare was first used in WWI with as many as 17 different kinds of gases tried out by both sides. There were three kinds of gases, of which only the lachrymator (tear gases, from the Latin *lachrima* "tear") were combatible by gas mask. The other two varieties included asphyxiant, or poisonous, gases such as chlorine, and the dreaded blistering gases, such as mustard gas which produced burns on contact.

A contemporary news report of the use of poison gas:
"[The] vapor settled to the ground like a swamp mist and drifted toward the French trenches on a brisk wind. Its effect on the French was a violent nausea and faintness, followed by an utter collapse. [The] Germans, who charged in behind the vapor, met no resistance at all...." *New York Tribune,* April 27, 1915

KITCHEN CHEMISTRY

The cavemen creep out of their cave, thanking the gods of fire for sparing them from the blaze. As they venture into the burned wasteland, Og stumbles over a burned deer carcass. Never one to miss an opportunity to eat, he rips off a hunk and stuffs it into his mouth. To his surprise, the cooked meat is much more delicious than usual. He calls out to everyone, and they enjoy an impromptu feast. The science of cooking has begun.

Could the first cavemen ever have imagined a soufflé? Or a doughnut? They had to begin somewhere, probably by dabbling with simple things like meat. So shall we.

A MEATY SUBJECT

What actually happens when meat browns? First, the heat causes the proteins and sugars in the meat to break down—to literally separate into the elements they're made up of. (Some elements, like gold, oxygen, or carbon, can't be broken down, but that's another story. Back to the kitchen.) Once the proteins and sugars have broken down, they recombine again and again while the meat cooks. As they do so, different flavors develop. That's why rare meat has a different taste than well-done meat.

Aging also produces flavors. This is because when meat is allowed to sit, it starts to break down—a slower process that gives it more time to release enzymes that attack the meat fiber, resulting in more tender meat. Of course, you wouldn't want to let it age too long, as rotting and aging are essentially the same thing.

ACCORDING TO THE EGGS-PERTS

Why do eggs turn white when you cook them? We're glad you asked. In their transparent, uncooked form, egg-white molecules are like overdone spaghetti that sticks to itself, proteins that are made up of strings of amino acids folded and jumbled together. It's these crosslinks that hold the protein together.

Heating unjoins the links (so does beating them or adding chemicals, like vinegar). Heating shakes the crosslinks apart, and the strands unravel and start forming new links with neighboring strands. As more links form they create a network, only this one is much tighter than before. The new network is tight enough to block light, which is why eggs lose their transparency and turn white as they cook. And once this network forms, it can't be undone—nothing you can do will make a cooked egg raw again. If you want to see this web, simply overcook your eggs; you'll eventually drive all the moisture out of the egg, and you'll wind up with egg lace.

FLOUR POWER

Flour is an amorphous substance, which means literally that it doesn't dissolve in water (in contrast to crystalline substances like salt and sugar). But it does thicken. And as it does so, the flour granules swell and form a network with other granules. That's why you only have to add a little flour to gravy to make it thicken. If you do the opposite—add only a bit of moisture and a lot of flour, you make the transition from cooking to baking. By definition, baking is the art of making breads and pastries. Both take place in the kitchen, and both involve a lot of the same ingredients. But cooking and baking are separate sciences. A chef is both a cook and a baker, but a baker is a baker is a baker.

BAKIN' AND EGGS

Have you ever wondered how cakes can call for both oil and water when they don't mix? Everyone knows that oil forms bubbles in water, but it doesn't actually mix, it just kind of sits there. You can beat it with a blender until the bubbles are so small you can't see them, but eventually they'll come apart.

The secret to mixing oil and water is an emulsifier—something like eggs—that allows you to thoroughly mix the unmixable. This is because the lecithin in egg whites is attracted to oil molecules at one end and water molecules at the other. Together, they form happy little chains, preventing the oil and water from unmixing. Other emulsifiers are gelatin, nonfat milk, and mustard.

YEAST IS YEAST, BUT...

You've heard that bread rises—you may have even seen it happen. But you may be surprised to learn *how* it happens.

Yeast is kneaded into the bread as it's mixed. Then the whole wad is left to sit in a warm place. While it sits, the yeast is eating the sugar in the bread. As it does so, it leaves behind certain waste products. One of the waste products is carbon dioxide. That's what forms the tiny bubbles in the bread, causing it to rise. The other waste product is sugar alcohol, which burns off when the bread cooks, but adds to the bread's flavor. If this sounds like fermentation to you, you're right. Wine is made the same way.

THE BUN ALSO RISES
Baking soda and baking powder also form bubbles of carbon dioxide, but what's the difference between the two? (Admit it—you've always wondered.) The answer is virtually no difference, since baking powder is just baking soda with a dry acid (calcium acid phosphate) mixed in. The acid produces two chemical reactions. The first one takes place when you add moisture to the mixture. The acid reacts against the baking soda, producing carbon dioxide. Once you place the batter in the oven, the gas expands, and the cake rises.

Baking soda is much stronger than baking powder because it's pure. Recipes that call for baking soda also call for some sort of acid (like lemon or milk). When you mix the two together, the baking soda starts working at once. That's why you have to put batters made with baking soda into the oven immediately, so all the gas bubbles don't escape before the cake is baked.

That's a free tip from Uncle John's kitchen.

* * * * *

Myth:
If you want to lose weight you have to change your diet.
Fact:
You can eat the same amount of the same foods and still lose weight—if you stay away from the North or South Pole and head to the equator. The centrifugal effect at the equator counteracts gravity's pull and makes everything at the equator a bit less weighty. A person who weighed 151 pounds (68 kg) at the North or South Pole is a paltry 150 pounds (68 kg) at the equator.

Lettuce is part of the sunflower family.

ACCIDENTAL DISCOVERIES

Some of the biggest scientific breakthroughs have been the result of mistakes, coincidences, accidents, and even incompetence. Here are a handful of scientific bloopers that have changed the world for the better.

CLOSE THAT WINDOW!

Dr. Alexander Fleming had spent most of 1928 working in a cramped laboratory in a London hospital. While working on the influenza virus he had filled his lab with culture dishes containing staphylococci bacteria. Exhausted from too many late nights, Fleming decided to take a holiday, giving strict instructions to his assistants on how to care for his precious specimens. On his return, however, Fleming was annoyed to find that someone had left a window open the previous night. The result? A foreign mold had flown in through the window and settled on the culture dishes. They were now useless. A devastated Fleming began collecting the dishes to dispose of when something caught his eye—while moldy patches were growing all over the plates, there were rings of clear space around these patches where there were no bacteria at all. Looking closer, Fleming saw that the bacteria closest to these clear rings were either shriveling or dissolving. The ever-astute doctor began experimenting with this strange mold that appeared to eat up bacteria. After years of research he was able to extract from it a drug—penicillin—that has gone on to save millions of lives. And it was all because someone forgot to close the window.

SNAKES ALIVE!

Nineteenth-century German chemist Friedrich Kekulé had a problem that had been nagging at him for years. He studied organic compounds (chemicals containing carbon atoms) and had found one compound—benzene—that behaved in a totally unpredictable way. Why it did this and what was the structure of its atoms consumed Kekulé's every waking hour. One evening in 1865 it also consumed his sleeping hours. Kekulé had what has been called the most important dream of all time when he saw, in his mind's eye, atoms dancing in midair. The atoms formed chains that danced around like snakes. Then one of these "snakes" formed a circle with its head chasing its tail. In the next instant Kekulé awoke. He spent the rest of that night sketching in his notebook and making calculations. What he came up with was a revolutionary new proposal to explain the nature of benzene—rather than lining up in chains like other organic compounds, the atoms in benzene joined each other in a circle, just like the snake in his dream. This started a scientific revolution in which chemists combined organic compounds in new and exciting ways, allowing them to produce new products such as durable fabrics, more efficient fuels, and a host of lifesaving medicines.

SPILLING HIS GUTS

Dr. William Beaumont was a frustrated army surgeon. Stationed on Mackinac Island in Lake Huron as part of a peacekeeping force in 1822, he felt that his surgical skills were being wasted. With nothing to interrupt the tranquility of the island, Beaumont had little call for his talents. That was until one day when a drunken man accidentally discharged his rifle into the torso of a fur trader by the name of Alexis St. Martin.

Beaumont rushed to the young man's side to find a massive hole where his belly button had been. Part of the stomach was actually spilling out. Expecting the man to die, Beaumont cleaned the wound and applied a dressing. St. Martin did not die. Instead his stomach healed in a very strange way—the stomach attached itself to the wall of his chest while the hole remained open with a loose flap of lining hanging over it like a curtain. By pushing this aside people could actually see inside the man's stomach.

Dr. Beaumont immediately recognized the opportunity this presented. He could be the first man to study and examine a living digestive system. Convincing St. Martin to cooperate, Beaumont began experimenting by tying tiny bits of food on silk threads and inserting them in St. Martin's stomach. Periodically he would remove them to observe the state of digestion. Such experiments continued for a dozen years, leading to a new branch of science—the study of human digestion—and making celebrities of both Beaumont and St. Martin (whose tummy window stayed open for the rest of his life).

The earliest horse was about the size of a fox terrier.

A CLOSER LOOK

Hans Lippershey was a 17th-century maker of eyeglasses. One morning, having just completed a pair of lenses, he stood in his shop doorway and inspected his work for imperfections. As a final test he held both lenses up to the light and checked for minute flaws. What he saw next caused Lippershey to stagger back in amazement. Shaking his head in disbelief, he put the lenses up to his eyes once more. Again it happened—the church tower in the distance leapt out at him!

Hans had stumbled upon a way to make distant objects appear as if they were right in front of you. Lippershey had looked through two lenses at the same time—one concave (curved inward), the other convex (curved outward). Seeing a quick buck, he mounted the two lenses on a board and charged his customers to take a closer look at the distant church tower. After some experimentation he mounted the lenses inside a hollow tube, dubbing the nifty device his *kijkglas* ("look glass").

We know it as the telescope.

* * * * *

"People think of the inventor as a screwball, but no one ever asks the inventor what he thinks of other people."

—*Charles F. Kettering*

"There is a correlation between the creative and the screwball. So we must suffer the screwball gladly."

—*Kingman Brewster*

"Accident is the name of the greatest of all inventors."

—*Mark Twain*

Galileo made the first thermometer in around 1600.

MNEMONICS YOU MIGHT MNEED

You mnever mknow.

You think scientists are smart? That's what they'd like you to think. Well, guess what? All this time, they've been using mnemonics. Which, we have to admit, isn't exactly cheating. You probably came across some in school They're pretty excellent devices for remembering lists and necessary (or even unnecessary) facts. They work because new knowledge is more effectively stored in long-term memory if you can associate it with something familiar. Mnemonics focus on association and sometimes the more bizarre or funny your associations, the easier they are to call up when you need to remember something.

FOR EXAMPLE: ASTRONOMY

For remembering the order of the planets according to their distance from the Sun, a lot of people use what are called sentence mnemonics: Taking the first letter of each planet—Mercury, Venus, Earth, Mars, Jupiter, Saturn, Uranus, Neptune, Pluto—and making a sentence out of them. Like: My Very Excited Mother Just Sold Uncle Ned Pies. Get it? Here's more (including a slightly mnaughty one):

- My Very Educated Mother Just Sent Us Nine Pickles.
- Mother Very Eagerly Made Jelly Sandwiches Under No Protest.
- My Very Earnest Mother Just Served Us Nine Pizzas.
- My Very Educated Mother Just Showed Us Nine Planets.
- Many Very Eager Men Just Sat Under Nine Pines.
- Many Voters Earn Money Just Showing Up Near Polls.
- My Very Eager Mother Just Served Us Nothing.
- Mary's Violet Eyes Make John Stay Up Nights Praying.
- Men Very Easily Make Jugs Serve Useful Nocturnal Purposes.

Did you find the mnaughty one? Good for you. And you know, if you don't like any of our examples, you can make up some of your own (but keep it clean!).

Some insects have up to 4,000 muscles compared to about 600 muscles in a human body.

HOW TO SURVIVE AN AVALANCHE

*Look! It's snowing! Soft, powdery snow seems like
such an innocent substance. But when those snowdrifts
are piled high, watch out!*

Avalanches don't just happen in the Alps—around 2,000
are reported to the U.S. Forest Service Avalanche Center
in an average winter. Worldwide, avalanches kill an average of 135 luckless people a year. The swift-moving slides (up to
50 mph [80 kph]) don't stop at burying skiers. They can isolate
towns, block roads and passes, sweep cars from roads, and even
knock down buildings. Just a few recent examples:

- In February 2000, the Alaskan ski resort town of Girdwood was
  isolated for almost a week. Officials had to resort to dynamite to
  blast the roads clear.
- In January 2000, an avalanche in Norway pushed a bus into the
  sea, killing five.
- An avalanche slid into a Quebec Inuit village on New Year's
  Day 1999, collapsing a school gym and killing nine.

Avalanches can happen anywhere, except maybe Florida and
Africa. Read this handy guide so you know what to do just in case.

WALK SOFTLY AND CARRY A BIG SHOVEL
Of course, all this advice goes for you skiers out there, too (though
you probably won't be toting the shovel), but it's mostly for people
who inexplicably want to walk around in the freezing cold. So, if
you're going to be traveling in avalanche-prone areas, be sure to
use caution:

- Travel on ridge tops above avalanche paths, in dense timber,
  and on slopes of 25 degrees or less that aren't topped by
  steeper slopes.
- Cross slopes at the very top when possible.
- Climb or descend the edge of a slope rather than the center.
- Alter your route or go back when you detect unstable snow.

Snakes don't have ears; they "hear" by feeling vibrations from the ground.

- When crossing dangerous areas, split up your group and stay in constant visual or voice contact.
- Never walk up to the edge of a drop-off without first checking it carefully—it's common sense, but thousands have died this way.

You should also carry avalanche rescue gear at all times, including:

- A beacon, a.k.a. an avalanche transceiver
- A shovel
- Collapsible or ski-pole probe
- A day pack with enough equipment to spend the night

WHAT ARE FRIENDS FOR?

In the first place, you should have a partner with you; virtually all avalanche victims are dug out by someone else. With any luck you or your partner will be spared to rescue the other or to go for help. But if you're caught in a snowslide:

- First, try to escape to the side or grab a tree or rock.
- If you're knocked down and sliding with the snow, dump your pack and/or your poles and skis if you've got 'em, all of which weigh you down.
- "Swim" with the avalanche to try to stay on top and avoid trees.

If the worst happens, and you're buried by the snow:

- Rule number one: Try to keep calm (easier said than done, but you'll expire a lot faster if you panic and breathe in snow).
- Dig a breathing space around your face—as large as possible (your breath's heat will form an ice wall around you).
- If you've been knocked down and tumbled around, you may not know which way is up and which direction to dig. Ball up some snow and drop it in your breathing space. A couple of drops will reveal the way as gravity pulls the small ball downward.
- Dig slowly and calmly directly upward, taking care that bits of snow do not plug up your mouth, nose, and eyes.
- Call for help as often and as loudly as you can.

DON'T BE A STATISTIC

That covers the basics. Fewer than half of the avalanche victims who are completely buried survive. Nobody who has been buried deeper than 7 feet (6.4 m) has lived to tell of it.

Cats can jump as high as the length of their tail times five.

POOL SHARKS

How Olympic swimmers are beating the clock with a little help from high-tech science and low-tech fish

Freestyle competitive swimming seems like the simplest of sports, but at the world-class level, the clock is king, and shaving seconds (or hundredths of a second) off the prevailing record has become a science.

BEAT THE CLOCK

Swimmers like Australia's Ian "Thorpedo" Thorpe have to master a lot of components to bring in those gold medals. Among them:

- Reaction speed—ability to be quick off the mark at the start

- Acceleration—ability to reach maximum speed in the shortest possible time

- Maximum speed—peak swimming speed

- Speed-endurance—speed that swimmers can sustain for long-distance races.

SWIMMING IS SUCH A DRAG

To further complicate the situation, physics dictates that despite his super abilities, Thorpedo has to overcome the problem of drag when he tries to go faster. Drag is caused by the friction and pressure created by the water, which resists an object's movement (even when that object is as powerful a swimmer as Thorpe).

There's frontal drag when Thorpe swims and has to move water out of his way, and skin drag when water flows across the surface of his body (creating a turbulent wake that increases drag). Here's an example of the power of drag. Swimmers shave off surface hair because smooth skin creates less skin drag than hairy skin. This helps them gain about an extra second per 100 meters.

For 200 million years humans have been accustomed to moving through air. Water is nearly 800 times denser than air and 55 times more viscous (resistant to flow) than air. The world's best swimmers have to struggle to go faster than four miles an hour!

SIZE MATTERS

Genetics plays a big part in making great swimmers. A swimmer

The smallest spider, the Samoan moss spider, is smaller than a pin's head.

with the right stuff has a tall, lean body. Most elite male swimmers are over six feet (like Olympic gold medal winner Alex Popov at 6'7"). Long bodies give swimmers a longer reach for a powerful stroke, and being lean helps a swimmer cut through the water in as streamlined a fashion as possible.

YA GOTTA HAVE HEART

Superswimmers also have "big hearts." Studies show that the best swimmers have large heart muscles. Some long-distance swimmers have cardiovascular systems that deliver twice as much oxygen to muscle cells as the average young person who's reasonably fit.

TECHNIQUE MATTERS

It takes more than a "genetically correct" and well-conditioned body to bring home gold. Elite swimmers use constantly evolving technology. Videos, computer analysis, stroke digitalization, and physiological testing equipment are as much a part of world-class competitive swimming as the splash of water and the smell of chlorine.

HIGH-TECH IS ALL WET

If you don't believe that great swimmers and their patrons invest in serious science, you've probably never heard of a flume, which is a kind of water treadmill that coaches and swim scientists use to zero in on the strengths and weaknesses of competitive swimmers. Put a great swimmer like the U.S.'s Brooke Bennett in a flume and you can tape her winning form with stationary videocams above and below the water level. Stroke digitalization uses computers to identify points on the joints of her shoulder, elbow, wrist, and hand; it tracks these points through a stroke cycle so that even the slightest need for adjustment becomes obvious. And all the while, testing equipment is measuring Bennett's heart rate, oxygen levels, energy levels, and so on. Talk about fine-tuning.

FROM FLUMES TO FLIPPER

Athletes are also turning to scientists for research on the biome-chanics of some of the world's other great competitive swim-mers—dolphins and sharks. Even air-breathing mammals like dolphins can leave our best swimmers rocking in their wake. The best human swimmers expend tremendous energy to reach four mph (6.4 kph), but a dolphin can cruise by at 20 mph (30 kph)

Spiders appeared on Earth about 170 million years before the first dinosaurs.

without breaking a sweat, so to speak. Dolphins try to avoid the surface where "wave drag" slows them down. When they're migrating, dolphins swim underwater and lift themselves up out of the water when they need to breathe. Some competitive swimmers are making use of dolphin wisdom: They'll glide faster in a turn if they go deeper.

SWIMMING WITH SHARKS

Here's what you get when technology meets biomimicry. Sharks have denticles on their skin (scales that are actually tiny teeth all facing toward the tail) that direct the flow of water over a shark's body, creating a film that reduces drag. A British shark expert helped Speedo design a bodysuit for swimmers called the Fastskin. Made of a ridged material that mimics sharkskin, the suit is said to reduce drag by three percent. Does the Fastskin work? Ask Michael Klim and Grant Hackett, who won Olympic gold wearing Fastskin bodysuits at the 2000 Sydney games.

SWIM LIKE A FISH

Some fast-swimming fish have fins that can be tucked away in special grooves to make them more streamlined when they need to move fast. Now some swimmers are wearing (and swearing by) special, slithery bodysuits that compress their muscles and make their bodies more streamlined.

And just in case you were thinking of taking up the sport, the experts will tell you that what you wear will not replace training and preparation. Technology aside, it's the engine in the car that determines how fast it'll go.

* * * * *

THE FISH OLYMPICS

The 100 meter Olympic swimming freestyle record is about 48 seconds, a snail's pace to many of the ocean's regular inhabitants. The fastest fish in the ocean—a sailfish—can move as fast as 67 mph (100 kph), so it could complete the 100-meter human race in about 3.5 seconds.

LITTLE THINGS MEAN A LOT

Those little things that we take for granted were once some inventor's bouncing baby brainchild.

Ballpoint Pen: Invented by a Hungarian who manufactured them in a factory in England, which was eventually taken over by a French company called Bic. (So should we have been pronouncing it "beek" all this time? As in "fleek your beek"?)

Band-Aid: Invented by the husband of an accident-prone woman who was constantly cutting and burning herself in the kitchen.

Baseball Caps: Most players wore straw hats until the late 1860s, when they started wearing visored caps that were based on the Union and Confederate soldiers' uniforms.

Can Opener: Canned food was invented for the British Navy in 1815. The can opener wasn't invented until 50 years later. (While waiting, they used a chisel and a hammer.)

Cellophane: Move over, waxed paper. The inventor was trying to make a stainproof tablecloth and came up with the first clear food wrap instead.

Electric Blankets: Not based as you might think on the electric heating pad, but on the electrically heated flying suits that U.S. Air Force pilots wore during World War II.

Flyswatter: The first was a square piece of wire screen attached to a yardstick. The inventor wanted to call it a fly "bat," but "swatter" fans prevailed.

Jockey Shorts: A Midwestern underwear manufacturer copied the design of men's bathing suits that were popular in France at the time (the 1930s).

Levis: Their creator, Levi Strauss, decided to dye them indigo blue so most stains would disappear into the fabric.

Matches: The first match was a stick that the inventor (who was trying to invent a new kind of explosive) had used to stir his

---

Most snowflakes are 1/8 to 1/4 of an inch in width and height.

ingredients. When he tried to remove the dried glob on the end of the stick, it ignited.

Miniature Golf: Invented by an unusual man who loved his family as much as he loved playing golf. This way he could get his golfing fix and be with the wife and kiddies, too.

Motorcycle: The first motorcycle had three wheels, like a tricycle with a motor.

Neon Lights: H. G. Wells wrote about them in *When the Sleeper Awakes;* they weren't invented until 11 years after the book was published.

Paper Bag: The machine that makes paper bags as we know them today—with a flat bottom—was invented by a woman who worked as a bundler at a paper bag company where the flat-bottomed bags were made by hand.

Paper Cup: Because the inventor had in mind a disposable water cup that wouldn't carry germs, he called his invention "health cups." Luckily, his office happened to be in the same building as the Dixie Doll Company—voila!—Dixie Cups.

Paper Towels: When a defective roll of toilet paper—too heavy and very wrinkled—arrived at the Scott company's mill, somebody had the bright idea to sell it as paper towels.

Peanut Butter: Ground peanuts and peanut oil, it was the brainchild of a doctor whose patient was dying of "protein malnutrition" and, because of a stomach disorder, couldn't eat meat. Peanut butter never made it as a medicinal remedy, but boy, did it catch on as an easy way to get kids to eat protein.

Rear-View Mirror: The first was introduced at the Indy 500 in 1911. Up till then there were two people in each car: the driver and the mechanic, who also acted as lookout. That year, the inventor drove his rear-view-mirrored car across the finish line to finish first.

Roller Skates: The inventor wanted to make a grand entrance at a party, playing his violin while wearing his new "wheeled feet," but he crashed into a full-length mirror and broke his violin, the mirror, and his new skates.

One ragweed plant can release as many as one billion grains of pollen.

Running Shoes: A miler at the University of Oregon heated some rubber in a waffle iron to get the kind of traction he wanted on the soles of his running shoes. He started a shoe business and named the shoes Nike, after the Greek goddess of victory.

Scotch Tape: 3M invented it especially for Detroit automakers to use for painting their two-tone models. The automakers thought 3M had skimped on the tape, so they called it "scotch" tape ("scotch" being synonymous with "cheap" at the time). The name stuck, even if the tape didn't.

Shopping Carts: The idea didn't catch on right away—shoppers were used to carrying their own baskets around a store—so the inventor (who was also the market owner) hired some phonies to push the carts around and pretend they were shopping. That did the trick.

Stethoscope: A doctor who was too shy to put his ear to the chest of a pretty patient with a heart condition invented the stethoscope. To his surprise, he could hear her heart much more clearly.

Typewriter: The first typewriter had no shift key and only printed in capital letters. The apparent nonsensical scrambling of the letters on the keyboard was deliberate: to prevent the rods that printed the letters from jamming.

Vending Machine: Would you believe that vending machines have been around since the 17th century? The first one, in England, dispensed one pipeful of tobacco for a penny.

Wire Coat Hanger: When a worker at the Timberlake Wire and Novelty Company arrived at work and found all the coat hooks taken, he twisted some wire into what looked pretty much like the ones we use now, and proceeded to hang up his coat.

Wristwatches: They were originally designed for women; men who wore them were considered sissies. It took more than a hundred years—the end of World War I—for them to be acceptable as men's wear.

Yo-yo: The word "yo-yo" means "come-come" in Tagalog. It was used as a hunting weapon in the Philippines.

ASTRONAUTS DO IT SITTING DOWN

Astronauts can spend months on a space shuttle. Have you ever wondered, like we have, exactly what the "amenities" consist of?

They call it a WCS, not for "Water Closet Something-or-other," but for "Waste Containment System," and it makes the bathroom on a 747 look luxurious.

SPACE-AGE DECOR

It's actually a little bigger than a bathroom on an airplane, but instead of cornball wallpaper and rounded plastic edges, a WCS is all sharp edges, metallic, and studded with bolts, gauges, clamps, and strange-looking machines. And handholds and footrests. The overall effect is torture-chamber modern. The most inviting and familiar sight is a white toilet seat that sits on a metallic platform.

NUMBER ONE

First, let's look at the urinal arrangement. Each astronaut (and astronette) has a personal funnel that is attached to a hose for urinating. Fans suck air and urine through the funnel and hose into a waste water tank.

NUMBER TWO

For actual sitting on the john—and don't forget we're in zero gravity—the astronauts have to unscrew the lid first and position themselves on the toilet seat, attaching themselves to leg restraints and thigh bars. Like the number one arrangement, the toilet waste matter is sucked into the commode by vacuumlike fans.

FURTHER AMENITIES

The bathroom also contains dry and wet wipes to wash hands and faces. Curtains close off the area for privacy, so it's also used for changing clothes and taking what can't be very luxurious sponge baths.

THE BUG IN THE SYSTEM

The current "extended duration" or EDO WCS was designed for longer shuttle flights, and despite all those nuts and bolts, has leakage problems. Funny. You can send whole gangs of people into space, but designing a nonleaking toilet—now that's a challenge!

The average beard grows five inches (140 mm) per year.

"YOU THINK I'M MAD, DON'T YOU?"

They're not mad! It's the world that's mad!!
Bwa hah hah hah hah!!!

Look at it from the mad scientist's point of view. All he wants to do is reanimate the dead, or invent a transporter, or maybe just drink a mind-altering potion in the privacy of his own home. But the rest of the world seems to think that's wrong! What do *they* know?!? *They* didn't spend years digging up cadavers, mixing toxic chemicals, or exploring the eighth dimension! *They* probably don't have any advanced degrees! Foolish mortals! See? From the scientist's point of view, it makes perfect sense. Here are ten films to prove they're not mad—just misunderstood.

The Adventures of Buckaroo Bonzai
Across the 8th Dimension!
Yes, the exclamation point is part of the title. The mad scientist is Dr. Emilio Lizardo (John Lithgow), who went looking for trouble in the eighth dimension and found it when some goopy-looking alien took over his skull. Now he needs to get back to where he once belonged, and the only thing stopping him is Buckaroo Bonzai: scientist, rock 'n' roll star, and cultural icon. A true cult favorite among the brainy and socially maladapted. (They want to be Buckaroo Banzai, but they smell like Dr. Lizardo.) While it is a little obscure for some, it starts making twisted sense after the fifth or sixth viewing. Stick with it.

Coma
Here's a flick to make you nervous the next time you go in for a tummy tuck. Genevieve Bujold plays a doctor who is investigating her friend's death during minor surgery. One thing leads to another, and the next thing she knows, she's wandering through a big room filled with people hanging from tubes, their organs just waiting to be harvested! Apparently people forgot you could just check the "donor" box on your driver's license application. Michael Douglas plays her love interest and Richard Widmark is the doctor who keeps slipping the patients a little too much gas. So remember, next time you're in, ask for a local.

April 21, 1970, was the first celebration of Earth Day.

Dr. Jekyll and Mr. Hyde

Long before Anthony Hopkins got an Oscar for playing a doctor gone bad in *Silence of the Lambs*, Fredric March copped one in 1932 for this baby. You know how it works: Mild-mannered doctor by day goes drinking and then becomes an evil criminal jerk by night. Yes, it sounds no different than what happens at any convention—but in *this* case Dr. Jekyll isn't tossing back frilly drinks with umbrellas in them. This one's been remade a few times (including as a stoner comedy in the early 1980s, for which karmic punishment will certainly apply), but the Fredric March version is still the best.

Dr. Strangelove, or How I Learned to Stop Worrying and Love the Bomb

Even if the entire film weren't already a brilliant black comedy about the end of the world by way of nuclear holocaust (and it *is*), this would still be worth seeing for the great Peter Seller's portrayal of Dr. Strangelove, an expatriate Nazi scientist (very loosely modeled on Werner von Braun). Strangelove is intensely weird, from the top of his toupéed head to the fingertips of his out-of-control (and self-homicidal) right hand. If actual nuclear scientists were anything like him, we'd all be glowing piles of ash.

The Fly

Jeff Goldblum zaps himself in a transporter of his own making and makes it through to the other side, no problem. Well, *one* problem: The fly that went along for the ride is now in his DNA. Pretty soon he's superstrong and walking on the ceiling, which is cool, but he also loses fingers and teeth and has to vomit on his food to digest it, which is, um, icky. *The Fly* could simply have been a gross-out horrorfest (and it certainly is that—no pregnant woman should *ever* watch the birth scene), but director David Cronenberg makes it surprisingly touching in places. A remake of a 1950s B movie, this one is superior in every way.

Frankenstein

You have two choices: The classic 1931 version starring Colin Clive as Dr. Frankenstein and Boris Karloff as the grunting, rivet-necked monster, or the not-so-classic 1994 version with Kenneth Branagh as the good doctor and Robert De Niro as the monster (which certainly puts a whole new spin on the classic De Niro line, "You lookin' at *me*?"). The 1931 version is indelibly printed onto our cultural memory—the collective image of the Frankenstein monster is Boris Karloff's—but on the other hand, the 1994 version is much more faithful to the original 19th century novel by Mary Shelley. And it's in color! And don't forget *Young Frankenstein*, Mel Brooks's dazzling send-up of *Frankenstein* and classic horror films—a classic in its own right.

Hollow Man
Kevin Bacon turns invisible, and no, this is not an assessment of his movie career. In *Hollow Man* he plays an unethical scientist who uses his own untested process to become invisible. Then, as he must in a movie like this, he goes completely insane and starts sneaking into hot girls' apartments and killing off colleagues. Watch this for the special effects; the story is a bit, er, transparent.

The Island of Dr. Moreau
There are several versions of this tale of a mad scientist combining humans and animals, the most recent starring Marlon Brando as the doctor in question, channeling his *Apocalypse Now* Colonel Kurtz performance. You might prefer the 1977 version with Burt Lancaster—less flab, more acting. The author of the original novel, H. G. Wells, was doing his patented thing of using science fiction to make a social point—this time about the fine line between human and animal nature, but as with the Hollywood versions of *The Time Machine*, good luck finding much of a social point here, especially in the Brando version.

The Nutty Professor
Dr. Jekyll done for comedy. The original *Nutty Professor* had Jerry Lewis turning from maladapted loser/science professor into suave ladies' man, Buddy Love; the Eddie Murphy remake has him as maladapted *and* obese, but still turning into Mr. Love. They both have to bottle Buddy back up: He's suave, but he's also kind of a creep. It's a toss-up which version is better. The Lewis version is beloved by the French, but the Murphy version, filled with potty jokes, is more in line with contemporary tastes.

Re-Animator
In the mood for a really over-the-top splatterfest? *Re-Animator* has got the goods, a nasty—and nastily funny—flick in the *Frankenstein* mode (based on a story by creepmaster H. P. Lovecraft). In a nutshell: Testy medical student Herbert West (Jeffrey Combs) finds a formula to reanimate dead tissue, so he *does*. Hilarious and gory hijinks ensue. Not everyone's cup of tea, to be sure.

WHIZ KIDS

*You never know what useful thing a kid is going to invent
for a science fair, and the best of them win at the national level.
ere's a rundown of some of the inventions that turned up as
winners in recent national science fairs.*

Who: Ryan Patterson of Central High School,
Grand Junction, Colorado
Title of Project: Sign Language Translator
Contest: National Individual Winner, Siemens Westinghouse Science & Technology Competition, and First Place, Intel Science Talent Search (wow!)
The Particulars: Winning one prestigious national science competition wasn't enough for Ryan. His sign language translator looks like a golf glove with a small screen attached. A small computer translates sign language gestures into words on the screen. With this device, a hearing-impaired person does not need to rely on an interpreter. Ryan holds a patent for the device.

Who: Shira Billet and Dora Sosnowik of the Stella K. Abraham High School for Girls, Hewlett Bay Park, New York
Title of Project: Viscometer for Ultra Thin Films
Contest: National Team Winners, Siemens Westinghouse Science & Technology Competition
The Particulars: These smart girls invented a device that measures the viscosity of thin films of lubricants. What exactly is viscosity? We wondered that, too. It's how well a fluid resists flowing freely. (Ketchup is a good example of a high viscosity fluid.) The girls can expect their device to have uses in the many fields of industry where thin films of lubricants are used, from artificial joints to computer disk drives.

Who: Hanna and Heather Craig of East High, Anchorage, Alaska
Title of Project: Ice-Crawler, the Rescue Robot for Snow, Ice, and Glaciers
Contest: $50,000 Scholarship Team Winners, Siemens Westinghouse Science & Technology Competition
The Particulars: These young women invented a robot that they hope will be used to rescue people trapped in remote and wintry

environments. It uses two motors and moves on silicon-reinforced rubber tracks that help it to crawl over snow and ice. They worked on the project for two years before winning all that money.

Who: Branson Sparks, Alexandria Country Day School, Alexandria, Louisiana
Title of Project: Dismissed!
Contest: First Place, 2001 Discovery Channel Young Scientist Challenge
The Particulars: In a contest for younger students, Branson wrote a computer program to coordinate his school's dismissal process. The program, which uses computer sound files to call students' names over the public address system, streamlined the dismissal process, resulting in fewer traffic backups outside his school. It worked so well that the school still uses the system. Branson, the little devil, holds the copyright.

MY KID COULD DO THAT!

If you think your offspring could be the next Edison, encourage him or her to start early. Some of the winners worked on their projects for years. Chances are, your kid's school is already affiliated with a national science fair. If not, we've provided handy web links where you can seek more information. Many of the websites also show what the previous winners did to win.

Contest: Intel International Science and Engineering Fair
Website: http://www.sciserv.org/isef/index.asp
Grade Levels: 9th through 12th
Prizes: Scholarships, tuition grants, scientific equipment, and scientific trips.
This fair operates at the local, regional, state, and national levels. To enter, your kid needs to start at the school level and work his way up. All 50 states and 40 countries participate. The location of the international fair varies from year to year.

Contest: Intel Science Talent Search
Website: http://www.sciserv.org/sts/
Grade Levels: High-school seniors only
Prizes: Scholarships
This is more of a contest than a fair, but past winners have gone

---

The skin of a polar bear is black and its hair is clear—not white.

on to win no less than the Nobel Prize, as well as numerous other science awards. To enter, submit an entry by mail before the deadline. Forty finalists receive an all-expenses-paid trip to attend the Science Talent Institute in Washington, D.C., where the final winners are chosen.

Contest: Siemens Westinghouse Science & Technology Competition
Website: http://www.siemens-foundation.org/
Grade Levels: For Individual Contest, 12th only; for Team Contest, 9th through 12th
Prizes: Scholarships
This contest also works by submitting an entry, but finalists first have to compete in one of six regional competitions. Regional winners are invited to compete in the National Competition in Washington, D.C.

Contest: Discovery Channel Young Scientist Challenge
Website: http://school.discovery.com/sciencefaircentral/dysc/
Grade Levels: 5th through 8th
Prizes: Scholarships and scientific trips
Similar to the Intel International Science and Engineering Fair, this has contests at local, regional, state, and national levels. So far, most states participate. The final contest is in Washington.

Contest: International Science Olympiads
Website: The Olympiads have multiple websites.
    Mathematics: http://imo.math.ca/ (general info)
    Physics: http://www.jyu.fi/tdk/kastdk/olympiads/
    Chemistry: http://www.icho.sk/
    Biology: http://www.kbinirsnb.be/ibo/ibo.htm
    Informatics: http://olympiads.win.tue.nl/ioi/index.html
    Astronomy: http://issp.ac.ru/univer/astro/ioas_e.html
Grade Levels: High school.
Prizes: gold, silver, or bronze medals
Competitors are given problems to solve and tasks to perform, then their results are judged. Winners are awarded medals, just like in the Olympics. Each nation chooses five or six contestants or team members, depending on the competition. The international competition has a different home every year.

In Greek, *astro* meant "star" and *naut* meant "sailor."

DR. DREW

The virtually unknown African American doctor whose pioneering work in blood preservation has saved countless lives in every corner of the world.

He was an all-American halfback and captain of his Amherst College team, but because his older sister died of tuberculosis when she was only 15, Charles Richard Drew chose to devote his life to medicine rather than sports.

A BLOODHOUND IS BORN
Drew was born in 1904 in Washington, D.C. At age 24, he entered McGill University Medical School in Montreal, Canada, where he soon became interested in blood research. Later, at Columbia University Presbyterian Hospital (now Columbia Presbyterian Medical Center), he narrowed his field of research—to blood transfusions and the storing of blood.

EUREKA!
In 1940, Dr. Drew documented a new technique for storing blood. He'd discovered that by separating the liquid red blood cells from the near-solid plasma and freezing the two separately, blood could be preserved and reconstituted at a later date—even a much later date. Blood banks had been around for decades by then, but Drew's work made it possible to preserve and store blood for the long-term. Just the thing that was needed in the war effort.

BLOOD FOR BRITAIN
That same year he was asked to be the medical supervisor of "Blood for Britain." He took thousands of pints of dried plasma to England, where he organized a system of volunteer blood donors, centralized the collection of donated blood, and conceived of using a "blood mobile" to deliver the blood to where it was most needed.

When the project was taken over by the American Red Cross, Drew was named director of the Red Cross Blood Bank in New York. At the same time, he was assistant director of blood procurement for the National Research Council for the U.S. Army and

The architect of the attack on Pearl Harbor, Admiral Yamamoto, was a graduate of Harvard.

Navy. That was when and where—after all those years—the race issue reared its ugly head.

DR. DREW MAKES A WITHDRAWAL

During WWII, the army, the navy, and even the Red Cross had separate blood banks for blacks and whites, which was not only costly and time-consuming but, to Dr. Drew, absolutely ridiculous. He denounced the policy as unscientific, but the military stood firm. So Drew returned to Howard University Medical School, where he'd taught pathology in the 1930s.

Dr. Drew died tragically in an automobile accident in 1950. Rumors that he could have been saved but was denied a blood transfusion at the nearest hospital because he was black were untrue.

HONORABLE MENTIONS

In 1977, the American Red Cross headquarters in Washington, D.C., was renamed the Charles R. Drew Blood Center. In 1981, the U.S. Postal Service issued a stamp in his honor. Today every blood bank in the world is a living memorial to the genius and dedication of Dr. Charles Richard Drew.

* * *

HOW MANY JOHNS?

We've long been curious about the name "Johns Hopkins," as in Johns Hopkins famous hospital and school. Was there more than one John? Or were the hospital and school founded by someone whose last name was Johns and whose partner was someone named Hopkins?

Turns out the answer is one man named Johns Hopkins, a Quaker merchant from Maryland who, with profits from his investment in the B&O (that is, Baltimore and Ohio) Railroad, willed $7 million to found the university and hospital that still bear his name.

Hopkins died at 78 of pneumonia, some say because he was too cheap (he was a notorious skinflint) to buy a heavy overcoat, but the more likely story is that the winter of 1873 was exceptionally cold, and Hopkins insisted on walking to his office without a coat or overshoes (he was notoriously stubborn, too) on a day when the temperature plunged to 20 degrees below.

GODS OF SILICON

The modern computer was built one step at a time, as one inventor built on the work of another. Meet four of the giants on whose shoulders later innovators stand.

JACK ST. CLAIR KILBY: MICROCHIP MAN

In July 1958, Jack Kilby had been at his job just a few months at Texas Instruments. The entire plant shut down for a company-wide two-week vacation. Kilby hadn't earned a vacation yet, so virtually alone in the lab, he worked feverishly to come up with something to justify his employment.

Let's See...

At the time, the current that ran through electronic devices was conducted by transistors, the circuits of which required workers to hand-solder wires to hundreds, sometimes thousands, of miniscule transistors, resistors, capacitors, and other microscopic gizmos, which—as you can imagine—was labor-intensive, expensive, and prone to errors.

Micro-Management

With this in mind (and two weeks of quiet time), Kilby managed to etch the entire circuit—transistor, wires, capacitors, resistors, and all—into one single sliver of germanium crystal. These "integrated circuits" made room-sized computers obsolete. And they were unbelievably cheap to make; cheap enough to create a proliferation of electronic devices, including radios, microwaves, cell phones, VCRs, and TVs. Not only that, but Kilby and another TI scientist invented the handheld calculator—the first mass-market usage for the microchip we know and love today.

You Win Some, You Lose Some

Kilby snagged a Nobel Prize in Physics in 2000 for his work. When CNN asked him if he had any regrets about what his work hath wrought, he answered, "Just one...electronic greeting cards that deliver annoying messages." Kilby is still a consultant for TI.

RAY TOMLINSON: E-MAIL GURU

Ray Tomlinson was just goofing off at work one day when he created the way a lot of us communicate these days. After graduating from

MIT in 1965, he went to work at Bolt Beranek and Newman, the company that had contracted with the U.S. government to build ARPANET—the experimental military communications system that would later become the Internet.

Where He Was @
In 1971, Tomlinson was trying to figure out a way to send messages to other engineers on the project. He knew of a message-sending program that could send messages between users of the same ARPANET machine, but he also knew of another program that could send files from one remote computer to another—so why not messages? He tinkered some more and figured out how to use them both to get what he wanted. And he chose a symbol for message address lines to denote mail sent through ARPANET to remote machines: today's ubiquitous @.

He didn't consider his new message-sending convention to be a big deal; in fact, as *Forbes* reported in 1998, a BBN coworker said that when Tomlinson showed him his work, he said "Don't tell anyone! This isn't what we're supposed to be working on."

Traffic Jamming
But electronic mail caught on like wildfire. It wasn't the programming that was the breakthrough, it was the idea. Suddenly two users could send terse, information-filled messages to each another without the need for social niceties or for both to be available to chat at the same time. The number of e-mail messages sent grew by leaps and bounds on ARPANET. By 1973, a study found that 75 percent of all traffic on ARPANET was e-mail. Today we send millions of e-mails every day—it's changed the way we do business, talk to one another, and even the way we think.

Just Another Day at the Office
But Ray Tomlinson didn't get rich quick—in fact, he didn't get rich at all. If he'd decided to patent his idea and charge even a fraction of a cent for each e-mail sent, he'd be a billionaire by now. Instead he continues to work at BBN, content with his place in history as a man whose work will probably outlive his name.

JIM CLARK: LET'S GET GRAPHIC
Clark left school at 16, joined the navy, and ended up getting a doctorate in computer science. He was teaching at Stanford in

1978 when he came up with his life-changing idea. At the time, computers required thousands of lines of slow-reading code to produce 3-D graphics. Clark had a better idea—he built a chip specially modified to work with graphics rather than code. The resulting "Geometry Engine" was a revelation for engineers and architects that generated instantaneous computer designs instead of painstakingly hand-drawn blueprints.

Clark and a few colleagues founded Silicon Graphics, Inc. in 1982, a company that grew to a billion-dollar technology behemoth that put 3-D technology into the hands of desktop computer users.

Chairman of the Bored

By 1994 he was bored at SGI and looking for something new. With Marc Andreessen, the brilliant University of Illinois student who'd developed the Mosaic Web browser, he founded Netscape Communications Corp. and started building his next billion-dollar company. When Netscape went public (early, against conventional business wisdom, before they'd even shown a profit), its shares rose from $6 to $24 on the first day of trading. Three months later the stock traded at $70. Jim Clark was a billionaire, and so were a lot of other people.

Clear Sailing

Clark put part of his earnings into a healthcare information and technology company, WebMD, where he continues to be a director. He's also invested in building and sailing giant high-tech-enabled "smart boats," sailboats in which every component from mast to jib is automated and controlled by Silicon Graphics computers. Hey, it beats slaving away over a keyboard.

TIM BERNERS-LEE: WEB WEAVER

The World Wide Web might not have happened if Tim Berners-Lee had kept better office files.

Enquiring Minds

In 1980, the man who would create the ubiquitous "www" that sits in that topmost bar on your computer screen was into a six-month job as a software developer at CERN, the European Laboratory for Particle Physics in Geneva, Switzerland.

He'd left some of his notes at home in England. Wouldn't it

be great, he thought, if there was a piece of software that kept track of all the details in all his documents "that brains are supposed to be so good at remembering but that sometimes (his) wouldn't"? There wasn't such a program—so he wrote it himself and called it "Enquire." Of course, it only worked on his own personal files.

Just a Click Away
But Berners-Lee could see that Enquire had possibilities beyond that. He envisioned a system of open documents, all written in a common language and all linked together...which turned out to be those underlined words or phrases that we click on to take us to a different page or site.

Weaving His Web
He wrote a quick-and-dirty coding system called HTML (for hypertext markup language); came up with an addressing system that gave each file on his "web" a unique address, which he called a URL (uniform resource locator); and wrote a program that allowed documents with a URL to be accessed by computers across the Internet: HTTP (for hypertext transfer protocol). Finally, Berners-Lee took the step that would bring the whole world to what he would name the World Wide Web—the browser.

Thanks, I'm Just Browsing
The browser was the key to the Web. Up to this point, geeky computer types could send and receive information packets across the Internet, but doing so required a lot of technical knowledge the average person just didn't possess. Berners-Lee's browser made it as simple as clicking on a bit of colored, underlined text. And click the masses did—the load on the first Web server at info.cern.ch multiplied by 10 every year from 1991 to 1994. By 1996, the number of Web and the Internet users had hit 40 million. At one point the rate of users was doubling every 53 days.

Untangling the Web
Berners-Lee himself hasn't profited at all from his creations. He manages the nonprofit W3 Consortium (which oversees development of web technology standards) from a plain, tiny office at MIT. The protocols he created are a household name—but Berners-Lee is content to keep working behind the scenes.

Artist Paul Gauguin worked on the Panama Canal in 1887.

A DOTTY IDEA

Elbert Botts's brainchild wasn't just a bump in the road.

You may have run over Elbert Dysart Botts's invention today. Never heard of him? Well, he's the innovative guy who developed Botts Dots, the raised reflective markers seen on roads and freeways throughout America.

MEET DR. BOTTS

Botts earned his doctorate in chemistry from the University of Wisconsin and taught for 16 years at San Jose State University. When WWII broke out, he went to work for the government as a chemist. Then he landed a job as a chemist in research and development at CalTrans (the Californian Department of Transportation), where he was assigned the task of creating reflective paint for freeways that could be seen in heavy rain.

YIKES, SPIKES!

That's when Botts dreamed up the idea of raised markers, which he called Reflective Pavement Markers, or RPMs (known by the nickname "Botts Dots"). Unfortunately, the ceramic markers cracked apart after being rolled over, exposing the spikes that held them to the road surface, which—as you might have guessed—was bad news for tires. But one of Botts's former students came up with a solution. He developed a durable, fast-drying epoxy that replaced the spikes.

FOLLOWING THE DOTTED LINE

Elbert Botts retired from CalTrans in 1960 and died two years later at age 69. Even though he never got to see his invention installed on warm-weather roads all over the country (he died three years before the first Botts Dots were installed in Northern California in 1963), we hope he knows that from now on, every time we hear that "thump-thump-thump" under our car wheels, we'll be thanking him for keeping us awake and out of everybody else's lane.

Nearly 50 percent of the newspapers in the world are published in the U.S. and Canada.

A SONY OF HIS OWNY

After WWII, Japanese companies flooded the American market with cheap, poorly made products. The words "Made in Japan" translated to "schlock." But Akio Morita changed that.

The Morita family had been brewing sake and soy sauce for 14 generations when Akio was born in 1921. As the oldest son, he was expected to take over the business, but Akio was more interested in tinkering with electronics.

His first business, Tokyo Telecommunications Engineering Corporation, was housed in a bombed-out department store in the ruins of postwar Tokyo. He had a partner who focused on engineering and product design, while he handled marketing, personnel, and financing—the business end.

Their first product was an automatic rice cooker, which might have been a hit if the postwar Japanese economy hadn't been devastated by the war. No one could afford to buy it. That's when Morita realized he had to look elsewhere for his markets—to the West.

MAKING A TAPE
First on the agenda was a tape recorder. But Morita and his partner couldn't find a source for magnetic tape, so they made their own by grinding up magnets and sticking the powder to strips of paper so that they could test their prototypes. They perfected Japan's first magnetic tape recorder in 1950, and after some aggressive marketing by Morita, it was a modest success.

OPTICAL ILLUSION
In trying to design a pocket-size radio for the American market, Morita found that the smallest radio he could make was still a little too large. So he had his salesmen wear shirts with bigger pockets, so the radio could slip in and out during demonstrations. The radios they sold became the first commercially successful transistor radios.

MAYBE THE BEST IDEA HE EVER HAD
Morita decided to scrap the mouth-filling "Tokyo Telecommunications Engineering Corporation" for a name that would be easy to

pronounce and easy to remember. In 1958, he changed the company's name to Sony, from the Latin word *sonus*, which means sound, and *sonny*, which he thought was a "friendly" term that also sounded like the sun.

In 1961, Sony became the first Japanese corporation to have its stock listed on the New York Stock Exchange. Later it became the first Japanese company to build a manufacturing facility in the U.S.

SO, N.Y.

Morita moved his family to New York City in 1963 because he wanted to learn all he could about Americans and their culture, so that Sony could design products tailored to the American market. A lot of people in the industry thought a tape player without a record function would never catch on, but Morita knew he could make the device much smaller and more portable without it. He added some headphones and in 1979 the Walkman was born.

MR. NICE GUY

Akio Morita's excellent communication skills and great charm allowed him to easily bridge the cultural gap between Japan and the West—he seemed to captivate everyone he came into contact with. True, he was a workaholic, but he also liked sports and remained very active throughout his life, even taking up water-skiing, scuba diving, and wind surfing in his 60s.

SONY PICTURES, ETC.

Sony developed the first successful battery-powered portable TV, the Trinitron picture tube (which set a new standard of quality for color TV), and the first color home video recorder (the now-defunct Betamax). Not to mention these media standards: the three-inch floppy drive, 8 mm videotape, and, in a joint effort with Phillips, the audio CD. Pretty good track record for a kid who might have ended up pushing soy sauce.

In fact, Morita died of pneumonia in 1999 at age 78. At the time of his death, he was the most famous Japanese citizen in the world and Sony was the number one consumer brand in the U.S.

Lionel Rothschild, House of Commons, was the first Jewish member of Parliament in 1858.

BANKER FOR THE LITTLE GUY

A. P. Giannini was the first to challenge the unwritten rule that banks should only lend money to people who don't need it.

Amadeo Pietro Giannini learned the value of a dollar the hard way. He was only seven years old when he saw his father killed in a fight with another man over exactly that amount—one lousy dollar. The elder Giannini had been a farmer; both he and A. P.'s mother were Italian immigrants. After his father's death, his mother married Lorenzo Scatena, who was in the produce business. A. P. quit school at 14 to help his stepfather, who was so impressed by his stepson that he made him a partner in the business.

EARLY RETIREMENT
A. P. helped build the business—and his reputation—by being fair and honest. He did so well that he was able to retire at 31 by selling his half of the business to his employees. But his retirement didn't last long; a group of San Francisco businessmen asked him to serve on the board of a small savings and loan that catered to the Italian- American community, and Giannini accepted.

Back in those days, banks only loaned money to large businesses and other assorted rich folks. When A. P. couldn't convince the other members of the board to extend credit to hard-working poor people, he decided to start his own bank. He lined up some investors and started what he called "The Bank of Italy" in a converted saloon. He even kept one of the bartenders on as an assistant teller.

The Bank of Italy was the first to offer home mortgages, auto loans, and installment credit. A. P. built his business by reaching out to the immigrant poor, even going door-to-door to explain his services to folks who didn't know anything at all about banks.

THAT'S THINKING AHEAD
In the aftermath of the 1906 San Francisco earthquake, the fire that swept the city was getting a little too close to his bank, so he

borrowed a wagon, collected all his gold, currency, and records, and brought it all to his home. A few days later, while the other banks in town were still closed, A. P. set up shop amid the rubble with a plank stretched across a couple of beer barrels serving as his desk. The loans he extended—in many cases based on little more than a handshake—helped rebuild the city.

THE ROAD—AND THE POND—TO SUCCESS
Giannini always worked harder and longer than his competitors. Once, when he was riding his horse out of town to visit a farmer to close a deal, he saw a competitor behind him who he knew was on his way to the same farmer's house. Giannini took a shortcut, raced ahead, dismounted his horse, swam across a small pond, and ran the rest of the way to the farmhouse to get his contract signed before the other man arrived.

BRANCHING OUT
Because so many of his customers had to travel long distances to do business with him, he decided to open a branch of his bank in San Jose in 1909. Then he started buying up other banks and opening new ones all over California and from there, in other major American cities.

In 1928, he purchased the Bank of America, an old and very respected institution in New York City, and consolidated all of his banks under that name. He continued to open branches all over the U.S., making Bank of America the first nationwide bank; by 1945, it was the largest in the country.

TWICE AS NICE
Giannini was a liberal in a conservative business, but he wasn't just being a nice guy. All of his innovations like loans to ordinary people and installment payments, were sound business decisions that revolutionized the banking business and generated substantial profits for his shareholders. He also helped large and small businesses that were down on their luck or out of favor. His financial backing of the California wine and movie industries was instrumental in their growth. He created a motion-picture loan division and helped Charlie Chaplin, Douglas Fairbanks, D. W. Griffith, and

Bette Nesmith, mother of Monkee Mike Nesmith, invented Liquid Paper in the 1950s.

Mary Pickford start United Artists. Giannini loaned Disney $2 million when he went over budget on *Snow White*. A. P. also is remembered for many visionary projects, including the financing of the building of the Golden Gate Bridge.

He was more than generous with his employees—literally. The profit sharing and stock ownership plans he instituted for them would guarantee their loyalty and his own success. But it wasn't money he was after; it was the good that it could do.

A MAN OF MODEST MEANS

The man who tried to retire at 31 was still at the helm when he died in 1949, at the age of 79. His estate was valued at a modest $500,000, because although he could have amassed a huge fortune in his lifetime, he was never interested in accumulating wealth and often didn't take a salary. He used most of the money he made to start foundations that funded scholarships, and supported medical and agricultural research.

Time magazine named Giannini one of the most important 100 persons of the 20th century.

* * *

"It's no use to decide what's going to happen unless you have the courage of your convictions. Many a brilliant idea has been lost because the man who dreamed it lacked the spunk or the spine to put it across" —A. P. Giannini

* * *

SILLY RUMORS

In his autobiography, TV producer Aaron Spelling (*Charlie's Angels, Starsky and Hutch, Beverly Hills 90210*) set the record straight about the mansion in Los Angeles, California, he shares with wife, Candy. Yes, it does have 12 bedrooms. And a bowling alley, a screening room, a sports bar, a video game/pool room, a swimming pool, and a wine cellar. But contrary to gossip, the house does not have a skating rink. How do these rumors get started?

Chez Spelling also has two rooms set aside for wrapping presents (because "Candy loves to give presents").

THE OTHER BABE

She was a whiz at sports—and she'd be the first to tell you.
Brash and supremely confident, her aim was "to be
the greatest athlete that ever lived."

B abe Didrikson Zaharias said that she got the nickname
"Babe" early in her teens from boys who were amazed at her
long-distance homers. But as she grew older, observers
noticed more Ty Cobb in her, a darkness and a rage that made
losing intolerable. It was an unnamed hostility that seemed to fuel
her competitive fire.

TEXAS TOMBOY
Mildred Didrikson was born in Port Arthur, Texas, in 1911. She
was a natural athlete. In high school she played virtually every
sport except football. But that didn't win her any popularity contests.
Her prima donna attitude, which included boasting and constant
attention seeking, alienated most of her classmates. Did she care?
Doubtful. She had better things to do.

HOOPS, AND WE DON'T MEAN EARRINGS
Basketball was her first stepping stone. At school she played for
the All City and All State teams, after which an insurance company hired her as a typist (85 wpm) so she could keep her amateur
standing and play on their basketball team.

A TEAM UNTO HERSELF
In 1932, she entered the Amateur Athletic Union women's
national track and field competition as an individual contestant.
She caused a sensation at the opening parade when she marched
as the entire team representing the Employers Casualty Insurance
Company of Dallas. She won six events, broke four women's world
records, and, with 30 overall points, scored eight points more than
the University of Illinois, the second place winner.

SHE WUZ ROBBED!
Her performance qualified her for the 1932 Olympics, which
began just two weeks later in Los Angeles, California. Olympic

rules limited her to three events. She took two gold medals—for the javelin and hurdles—and a silver in the high jump. She cleared the same height as the top finisher in the high jump, but her jump was considered a foul because she went over the bar headfirst—the judges called it "diving." (Babe's "diving" style was legalized soon after that.) Foul or not, the world couldn't help but notice her. Babe was an overnight sensation.

BABE TURNS PRO

She lost her amateur standing after a picture of her appeared in an automobile ad. Her folks needed money, so Babe turned professional. She didn't hesitate to capitalize on her own abilities or to turn a profit from her name. She spent the next two years promoting herself: a brief stint in vaudeville playing the harmonica (while running on a treadmill); pitching in some Major League spring-training games; and touring, first with a billiards exhibition, then a men and women's basketball team called Babe Didrikson's All-Americans, and finally as the only nonbearded member of an otherwise all-male, bearded baseball road team called the House of David.

THE GREATEST, BUT…

There was very little that she couldn't do. In addition to basketball, baseball, billiards, and track, she played tennis, golf, and handball, and she skated, cycled, swam, and bowled. When someone asked her if there was anything she didn't play, she wisecracked, "Yeah, dolls."

Anyone as talented as Babe Didrikson was bound to attract a lot of press. Famed sportswriter Grantland Rice called her "the greatest athlete of all…for all time." Other writers condemned her for not being feminine. She lived in the olden days when female athletes were thought of as unseemly, or even freakish. But not for a moment was our Babe a feminist. She didn't care about women's liberation—all she wanted was to play sports.

THE SECRET TO GOOD GOLF

When asked how she could regularly drive a golf ball some 250 yards though she didn't weigh more than 145 pounds, she said, "You've got to loosen your girdle and let it rip."

Babe got serious about golf in 1933 and won the Texas Women's Championship in 1935. After which, the U.S. Golf

Association ruled that "for the best interest of the game," Babe was not an amateur because she had competed professionally in other sports.

At the 1938 Los Angeles Open, she was paired with George Zaharias, a "bad guy" wrestler who was making a fortune as "the Weeping Greek from Cripple Creek." They married 11 months later, and George took over as her manager and advisor.

The Golf Association reinstated her as an amateur in 1945; in 1946, she won an amazing 13 consecutive tournaments. The next year, she was the first American to win the British Amateur. For three straight years (1945–47) the Associated Press named her the Female Athlete of the Year. She turned pro in the summer of 1947, after winning 17 of 18 tournaments. In 1948 Babe won her first U.S. Women's Open, the World Championship, and the All-American Open.

With George and Hall-of-Famers Patty Berg and Fred Corcoran, she founded the Ladies Professional Golf Association in 1949. She continued her impressive performance on the LPGA tour for the next several years.

THE 19TH HOLE

Shortly after winning the inaugural Babe Zaharias Open in Beaumont, Texas, in April 1953, Babe learned she had cancer of the colon. Surgeons removed the tumor, but discovered the cancer had spread into her lymph nodes. Her cancer was inoperable. The next year she won her third U.S. Women's Open—by 12 strokes, mind you—on the way to five titles and her sixth AP Female Athlete of the Year award.

But the pain in her lower spine, caused by the cancer, became unbearable and she stopped golfing. On September 27, 1956, she died in Galveston, at the age of 45.

She's remembered to this day as the athlete whose pursuit of greatness changed women's sports forever.

* * *

"The formula for success is simple: practice and concentration, then more practice and more concentration."

—Babe Didrikson Zaharias

Henry Ford was fascinated with soybeans and used them for automotive paint and parts.

YA GOTTA HAVE HEART

Americans often confuse her with Filipina shoe-fetishist Imelda Marcos. Wrong! While Imelda was collecting those shoes, Corazon Aquino was battling Imelda's husband, Ferdinand, for presidency of the Philippines.

Born in 1933 into a family that had made its fortune in sugar and rice, Corazon (which means "heart") Aquino grew up in the midst of wealth and power. Her father was a congressman and her grandfather was a senator, but she never thought she'd be called upon to be a politician herself. She was educated at fancy private schools in Philadelphia and New York, held degrees in French and math, and thought about studying law. However, when she married politician Benigno "Ninoy" Aquino, Jr., in 1954, she settled for being a wife and mother.

THE PARTY ISN'T OVER TILL I SAY SO
She basked for a while in the glory that was Ninoy. He was a political wunderkind. He'd already been the youngest mayor of his town (at 22) and the youngest governor of his province (at 29). He was shaping up as a powerful threat to President Ferdinand Marcos, who was nearing the end of his second term, which was constitutionally mandated as the maximum anyone could serve.

That should have cleared the field for Ninoy to step in. But in one swift move in 1972, Marcos declared martial law, installed himself as permanent president, and jailed most of his political enemies, including Ninoy. Eight years later, Ninoy was released. Marcos allowed him to visit the U.S. for heart surgery but warned him that if he returned to the Philippines he would face a death sentence.

AVERAGE AMERICAN HOUSEWIFE
Ninoy and Cory settled in a Boston suburb, but they kept a sharp eye on the First Couple of the Philippines. As Ninoy recuperated he grew more restless every day, and for good reason. In a country where seven out of ten Filipinos were certifiably poor, Ferdinand and Imelda were looting the National Treasury to the tune of $5 billion. Not even a death sentence could keep Ninoy from going back.

SWIFT INJUSTICE
In 1983, leaving Cory at home in Boston, he boarded a plane bound for the Philippines. When his plane landed, soldiers hustled him away at gunpoint and shot him right there on the tarmac. Marcos had killed off the only man who could threaten his position.

CORY FOR PRESIDENT!
It took Ninoy's supporters a few years to talk Cory into running for president in Ninoy's place. When she finally agreed, Marcos said he wasn't worried—he even called for an immediate election. Yet he couldn't have been as confident as he seemed because on the February 1986 election day, his thugs went around ripping up ballots, paying for votes, and intimidating voters at gunpoint.

TANKS VS. NUNS
It set the country aflame. Thousands of people flooded the streets in protest. The election was condemned by Filipino Catholic bishops and by the U.S. Senate. Two of Marcos's high officials rebelled, declaring Aquino the true winner. The tanks that Marcos had sent to disperse the crowds ground to a halt in front of a group of rosary-clutching nuns kneeling in their path. His loyalists were defecting in droves. All the world was watching.

Just one day after Marcos had himself falsely inaugurated, he had to flee to Hawaii, exiled forever. Reports vary on the number of pairs of shoes that his wife had to leave behind, but according to the former First Lady herself, the precise number was 1,060.

CORY AS PRESIDENT
Hailed as the savior of her country, Cory had a lot to live up to—too much, in fact. She faced heavy odds. Guerrilla war continued to threaten the Philippines, as did massive poverty. Cory served two terms (and survived seven coup attempts). She left office in 1992, succeeded by General Fidel Ramos, a military man who had thrown his support behind her presidency in 1986—and who had saved the Aquino government from the aforesaid attempted coups.

Cory hadn't been a perfect president, but she'd tried to govern her people fairly. She lives in the Philippines today, a powerful and admired symbol of righteous rule.

KING OF KETCHUP

Richard Nixon smothered cottage cheese with it; Japanese eat it on rice; and one ice-cream manufacturer tried to make it a flavor. Here's a story you'll relish, about the man whose name became synonymous with the condiment so popular that it's found in nearly every fridge in America.

Hundreds of years ago, the Chinese used the brine from pickled fish as a dipping sauce. They called it "ke-tsiap." From there it made its way to Malaysia, where the name was modified to "kechap." In the 1680s, Dutch and British explorers brought the concoction back to Europe, where the upper classes spiced it up with goodies like pickled mushrooms, anchovies, kidney beans, and walnuts. Eventually, the Brits bottled it and called it "catsup." By the late 1700s, the recipe found its way to New England, where tomatoes were added to the mix. Mid-19th-century entrepreneurs exploited the American taste for sweet food and started selling catsup made with tomatoes, vinegar, sugar, cinnamon, cayenne, and salt. But it wasn't until the 1870s that H. J. Heinz came up with the recipe that our taste buds would recognize today.

A BORN SALESMAN
Henry John Heinz was born in Pittsburgh, Pennsylvania, on October 11, 1844. His father, another Henry, had come to the U.S. from Bavaria only four years earlier. At the age of 12, H. J. began selling his mother's homemade horseradish sauce door to door.

EXHIBIT A...THE TOMATO
At the time, the typical American diet was a pretty dreary affair, consisting mostly of bread, potatoes, root veggies like carrots, turnips, rutabagas, parsnips, and beets, and meat—usually dried, smoked, or salted. Pickles were still something that, by and large, were available only in wintertime. Tomatoes were considered an exotic Mexican fruit.

HORSERADISH AS FAR AS THE EYE CAN SEE
By 1869, Heinz had a burgeoning condiment business and a partner, Clarence Noble. They bottled their horseradish sauce (and pickles,

---

sauerkraut, vinegar, and so on) under the name Heinz and Noble, and they delivered their goodies by horse-drawn wagons to grocers in and around Pittsburgh. They had 100 acres of garden along the Allegheny River—including 30 acres of horseradish—along with 24 horses, a dozen wagons, and a vinegar factory in St. Louis. In 1875, Heinz bought 600 acres in Illinois in pursuit of new sources of cucumbers. (A similar search drives the plot of the next *Star Trek* movie, we've heard.)

KETCHING UP
A banking panic that same year forced the business into bankruptcy, but H. J., with his brother and cousin, bounced back. In the depression brought on by the banking collapse, 1876 proved to be a hard first year, but one in which a new product was introduced— Heinz sweet tomato ketchup. Next came red and green pepper sauces, then cider vinegar, apple butter, chili sauce, mincemeat (a finely chopped mixture of raisins, apples, and spices, with or without meat), mustard, tomato soup, olives, pickled onions, pickled cauliflower, baked beans, and the first sweet pickles (and sweet pickle relish) to ever hit the market.

HOME SWEET FACTORY
Not only that. In an era when long hours, poor working conditions, and low pay were the norm for urban workers in America, Heinz put into practice what was then a radical notion—that workers should be treated well on the job. Conditions at his factories were often better than the workers had at home.

TRAVELING SALESMAN
Then, long before globalization became a buzzword, Heinz sailed with his family to England, including in his luggage a bag packed with "seven varieties of our finest and newest goods." Ten years later the first overseas office opened near the Tower of London. Heinz's products eventually became so successful in the U.K. that most British shoppers thought Heinz was a British company.

THE PRINCE OF PICKLES
By 1896, Heinz was a household name and H. J. himself had become a millionaire. How did he do it? Three years earlier, at the

A coffee pot with a sieve to strain away the grounds was not invented until 1806.

Chicago World's Fair, everyone who attended the Heinz exhibit—more than 1 million vacationers from around the world—left the fair with a free pickle pin. Although a green plaster-of-Paris pin may sound a little, well, cheesy, it proved to be one of the most effective promotional items in the history of retailing.

HIS LUCKY NUMBER?

The ideas kept coming. Heinz's next idea proved to be another marketing coup, one of the greatest in the history of retailing, in fact. Here's how the story goes: The company was still in need of an easily recognizable slogan. So, while riding on a New York City elevated subway car one day, Heinz spotted a sign above a local store that said "21 Styles of Shoes." He decided that his own products weren't styles, but varieties. And although he had more than 57 foods in production at the time, the numbers five and seven held a special significance for him and his wife Sallie, so he adopted the slogan "57 Varieties."

MAYBE NOT

While the story about the train is true, the part about the numbers five and seven holding some sort of special significance for Henry Heinz and his wife could best be described as a pile of horse…in this case, let's say horseradish. The story may have been an attempt on the part of the folks running the Heinz Corporation to keep the Henry Heinz mystique alive. Maybe there's a more likely explanation.

It's hard to say exactly what may have been going through the mind of the pickle peddler from Pittsburgh when he came up with it. According to some accounts, he simply liked the way the number 57 looked in print. In all likelihood, when Heinz had his epiphany on the train in 1896, he simply miscounted his products. (He actually had at least 62 at the time.) When he returned to his office, he probably already had the slogan "57 Varieties" embedded in his brain and nothing—not even an accurate product count—was going to change his vision.

In any case, it's clear that the "57" in Heinz 57 really stands for incredibly savvy marketing. He took what was for all intents and purposes an arbitrary number and attached it to his brand name. It cost him absolutely nothing. Over the last century, millions if not billions of people have probably asked themselves or others, "I wonder what the 57 stands for in Heinz 57?" You can't buy that kind of publicity.

THERE'S A PICKLE LOVER BORN EVERY MINUTE

Now that Heinz was an instantly recognizable national brand, H. J. was ready to take things to the next level. Literally. With all the subtlety of a P. T. Barnum (or Donald Trump, to update the image a bit), Heinz erected a 40-foot-high flashing electric pickle—New York City's first electric sign (1900)—in the heart of Midtown Manhattan. And a 90-foot pickle at the end of a 900-foot pier in Atlantic City.

In the same year that the Big Apple pickle went up, there were 100 manufacturers of ketchup, but even now Heinz ketchup is the standard by which other ketchups are rated. The man who made it happen died of pneumonia in 1919 at the age of 75, but his name (and his ketchup) live on.

* * *

LET THEM EAT CHEESECAKE

When you hear the name Sara Lee, do you think of some femme in an apron slaving away over a hot oven, turning out cakes by the hundreds and thousands? Forget it.

The real Sarah Lee never went near the kitchens that made her famous. In 1935, Charles Lubin and his brother-in-law bought a chain of small neighborhood bakeries. In 1949 they parted ways, Charles retaining the company. His first solo product was a cream cheesecake named for his eight-year-old daughter, Sara Lee Lubin. The business was wildly successful, as we know. And little Sarah Lee (Lubin) Schupf grew up to become one of America's best-known and most generous women philanthropists.

PARK IT!

Every car on the list below has been waiting for someone like you to come along. Can you drive all 40 autos into their assigned parking spaces in the grid so that they all fit, crossword-style?

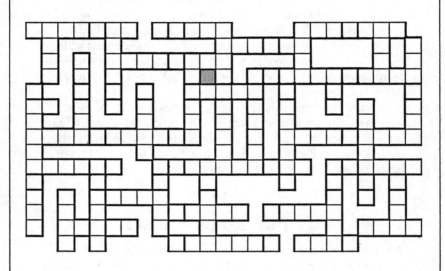

2-letter word	Isuzu	Lancia	**9-letter word**
MG	Lotus	Suzuki	Excalibur
	Simca	Toyota	
3-letter word	Steyr		**10-letter words**
Reo	Stutz	**7-letter words**	Ambassador
	Tatra	Citroën	Oldsmobile
4-letter words	Volvo	Daimler	Studebaker
Audi		Hyundai	
Benz	**6-letter words**	Lagonda	**11-letter words**
Jeep	Auburn	Sunbeam	Aston Martin
Nash	Austin	Triumph	Lamborghini
Saab	Desoto		
Yugo	DuPont	**8-letter words**	
	Hudson	Borgward	
5-letter words	Hummer	Mercedes	
Eagle	Kaiser		

ANSWER, PAGE 371

GROSS STUFF

*Your body makes all kinds of disgusting goo. Our
favorite pick: the stuff that comes out of your nose.*

BOOGERS
They're green, they're gooey, and they're gross.
Everybody has them. But what exactly is a
booger? Basically this little slimeball is the result of your
nose protecting your body. Picture this: you take a deep
breath and a piece of dust whooshes into your nostrils.
That dust particle instantly meets little tiny nose hairs—
called *cilia*—which are there to stop the dust from going
any farther.

But it doesn't always work, and sometimes the dust
gets past the nose hairs. If it does, it will bump into the
mucous membrane, which has a surface something like a
sticky fly strip or piece of masking tape. This membrane
makes a gooey liquid called *mucus* that catches and
destroys any dust or bacteria trying to invade your body.
How? It surrounds the dust or bacteria, and *voila!*
You've got a booger. The exact color is determined by
what kind of particles came into your nose.

Once the mucus is used up, your body whips up
another batch. Your body can make as much as a
quart of mucus a
day. That's equal
to four glasses of
milk!

> You can pick your friends...
> And you can pick your nose...
> But you can't pick your friend's nose.

More than half of the bones in your body are in your hands and feet.

BUT IT SAYS ON THE LABEL...

Think that you can tell what's in the products you buy by reading the labels? Think again. Here 're four examples that show how companies stretch the truth to increase sales.

FRESH IS FROZEN

The Label Says: "This Turkey Never Frozen"

You Assume: It's fresh turkey.

Actually: According to government rules, to be called "fresh," a turkey has to be stored at above 26°F—the freezing point for poultry. But the label still doesn't have to say "frozen" unless it was stored at 0°F (or below). So a company can legally say it was never frozen...even if it was stored at 1°F.

YOUR LAWN OR YOUR LIFE?

The Label Says: "Pesticide Ingredients," then lists them

You Assume: All the ingredients—particularly the toxic ones—are on the list.

Actually: According to a recent study, "over 600 toxic chemicals included in pesticides aren't disclosed on the brand labels." Why not? "Under federal regulations, these chemicals don't have to be listed if they are *inert* ingredients—chemicals that assist in killing bugs or weeds, but aren't the active agent of destruction." Why aren't they listed? Pesticide companies say they need to protect trade secrets.

DO IT AGAIN
The Label Says: "Recycled Paper"
You Assume: It's been used by a consumer—as newspaper, office paper, cardboard, etc.—then sent to a recycling center, and turned back into paper.
Actually: The only time you can be sure that's true is if the label says "Post-Consumer." Otherwise, it could be something else. Paper manufacturers dump paper from the mill floor back into the paper pulp...and the government allows them to call this paper "recycled."

DEM BONES
The Label Says: "Chicken Nuggets"
You Assume: It's chicken meat.
Actually: According to the National Consumer League, when convenience foods such as chicken frankfurters, chicken nuggets, and turkey bologna are processed, there's no telling what's in them. "Mechanically deboned poultry may contain bone fragments, marrow, kidneys, skin, and lungs as by-products of the process. These by-products are not listed as ingredients, though, so consumers don't know that they are eating this material....Labeling requirements allow the poultry industry to hide behind a vague description of product as 'chicken meat.'"

A WORLD OF SCHOOL LUNCHES

Ever wonder what kids are eating at school in other countries?

JAPAN. Most schools don't have cafeterias, so kids eat in their classrooms. Schools serve a variety of meats, fishes, vegetables, and sea plants. A typical meal consists of stew (or curry), boiled vegetables, a sandwich, and salad, with milk and ice cream.

MEXICO. The school day ends at 2 p.m., so kids usually wait until they get home to eat. But for kids who are really hungry, vendors wait outside with spicy snacks: watermelon and hot sauce, cucumber spears doused in chili powder, and popcorn with salsa.

FRANCE. By law, kids are not allowed to bring a lunch to school. But they do get a two-hour break to eat a gourmet meal in the *cafétéria* ("cafeteria"). Sample lunch: They start with a beet and endive salad, followed by hen with rice in white sauce, Camembert cheese, and for dessert, chocolate mousse.

GERMANY. Most schools don't have kitchens, so they have the meals delivered. Students eat in the *Speisesaal* ("dining room"). A typical lunch consists of chicken schnitzel (a breaded cutlet) with sauce, mixed vegetables, and salted boiled potatoes.

ASK THE EXPERTS

Everyone's got a question or two they'd like answered. Here are a few questions, with answers from some top trivia experts.

STUCK ON YOU

Q: *Why do tongues stick to cold metal?*

A: "It's not only our tongue—it's any warm, wet body part. 'It becomes "flash frozen" to the cold object,' notes geochemist John Kelley of the University of Alaska. 'Because metal is such a good conductor, the heat of your body is immediately transferred, and all surface moisture becomes crystallized.' The classic treatment is to pour warm water on the compromised appendage. This will melt the ice crystals, but will do little to restore your sense of pride." (From *Why Moths Hate Thomas Edison*, edited by Hampton Sides)

DOES ZIT REALLY MATTER?

Q: *Will I really get zits if I eat chocolate, fried foods, etc?*

A: "No. The good news from the dermatologists is that that's just an old wives' tale. In a study performed at Yale University, teens consumed large amounts of chocolate. Even those who were prone to acne didn't show a significant difference. In fact, doctors say that there are no foods that cause pimples—unless you're allergic to a specific food, in which case the allergy shows up as a rash. Since adults can eat chocolate and fried foods without breaking out, this is obvious common sense." (From *Old Wives' Tales*, by Sue Castle)

THE ROOT OF THE PROBLEM

Q: *Why is root beer called "beer" when it isn't beer at all?*

A: "It's pretty much consumer fraud. In the early 1870s, Charles Hires was served a root and herb tea at a country inn, and liked it so much he decided to market it as a soft drink. As an anti-alcohol prohibitionist, Hires hoped that drinkers would abandon liquor in favor of his root tea. But just to be safe, he decided to call it a 'Root Beer.'

"The ploy worked well. In fact, too well. The success of root 'beer' brought down the wrath of the Women's Christian Temperance Union, which called for a boycott of the soft drink. From 1895 to 1898, a war against root beer was waged in the newspapers, nearly destroying the Hires Co. Finally, an independent lab analyzed samples of the soft drink and concluded that root beer contained 'less alcohol than a loaf of bread.' The WCTU apologized, and sales of Hires Root Beer rebounded." (From *Just Curious Jeeves*, by Jack Mingo and Erin Barrett)

*   *   *

REAL-LIFE SIGNS IN ENGLISH
FOUND IN FOREIGN COUNTRIES

On a Viennese restaurant menu: "Fried milk, children sandwiches, roast cattle and boiled sheep."

In a Swiss inn: "Special today—no ice cream."

The Native Americans of New Mexico have been eating popcorn for more than 5,000 years.

TONGUE TWISTERS

Ready for a workout? Try to say each of these three times fast…and pay no attention to the person banging on the bathroom door, asking what's going on in there.

"What ails Alex?" asks Alice.

Ada made a gator hate her, so the gator ate her.

Six sly shavers sheared six shy sheep.

The big bloke bled in the big blue bed.

The bottom of the butter bucket is the buttered bucket bottom.

A well-read redhead.

Wire-rimmed wheels.

Edgar at eight ate eight eggs a day.

Can a flying fish flee far from a free fish fry?

An itchy rich witch.

Pass the pink peas please.

The fickle finger of fate flips fat frogs flat.

Fleas fly from fries.

Some shun summer sunshine.

Mr. Spink thinks the sphinx stinks.

THE KID WHO PEED OUT THE FIRE

We'd like to nominate this amazing kid for an award to honor his uncanny ability to think on his feet. Here are some fireworks you've (probably) never seen.

It all began in Philadelphia on July 4, 1777, when people started to celebrate by shooting rifles, lighting candles, waving banners...and Independence Day was born.

But no 4th of July can match the celebration of 1854 in Bristol, Rhode Island. That year, several houses were accidentally set on fire by firecrackers and by the wadding (a small piece of cloth used to pack the gunpowder) from fired guns. But a kid saved the day. Here's the actual account from the local newspaper, *The Bristol Phoenix*,

> "A portion of the wadding of one of the guns lodged upon the roof of the Baptist church and set it on fire....A lad named Morris, about twelve years of age ascended by the lightning rod and attempted to extinguish the flames by scraping dust upon them with his feet, but finding it of no avail, he began to spit upon them, still flames increased until he had the presence of mind to unbutton his pants and play his own engine so effectually that he entirely extinguished the fire."

According to the *Phoenix*, a large crowd saluted the lad with loud "huzzahs." That's the spirit!

I WANT MY MTV!

Sure, the world existed before Music Television...
but it was far less interesting.

THE EARLY DAYS

• In 1981 TV exec Robert Pittman had an idea for a new cable station: Get record companies to provide free programming (videos) and have hip VJs introduce them and share "insider" gossip about the stars.

• Sounds like an obvious way to appeal to kids' love of television and music. Yet, when MTV was launched on August 1, 1981, no one imagined it would become so big.

• The first video ever aired was "Video Killed the Radio Star" by the Buggles, which is ironic because that's exactly what happened. The music industry used to be dependent on radio airplay. Today, if you want to make it big in the music business, you have to get your music video on MTV.

GROWING PAINS

• Its first two years were slow. Then, in 1983, New York and Los Angeles began to offer MTV on their cable systems. By 1986 it was seen in 28 million homes.

• Stars like Michael Jackson, Madonna, and U2 saw the potential of MTV and created elaborate videos to showcase their songs. It worked: both MTV and the performers became mega-popular.

There are 32 leather panels and 642 stitches on a regulation soccer ball.

- By the late 1980s, MTV had become… well, boring and predictable. How did they spice up the format? They added shows like *MTV News, Yo! MTV Raps, Remote Control, TRL, Beavis and Butt-Head,* and *Unplugged.*

WE ARE THE WORLD

- MTV Europe was launched in 1987, followed by MTV Asia in 1991 and MTV Latino in 1993.

- MTV became a political force during the 1992 presidential election. Its "Rock the Vote" campaign encouraged young people to register to vote. Presidential candidates were invited to discuss issues on the air with first-time voters. Among the candidates taking advantage of "Rock the Vote" was Bill Clinton, whose appeal to young people helped him get elected.

- Twenty years after MTV aired the first video, they introduced a new show, featuring the daily life of aging rock star Ozzy Osbourne and his family. *The Osbournes* quickly became the most-watched show in MTV's history.

- Today, it's estimated that a billion people in 164 countries watch MTV in 18 different languages.

MTV FACTS

- Michael Jackson was the first black artist to have a video aired on the music channel.

- In 1992 MTV started the reality TV craze with *The Real World.*

- Got their start on MTV: Pauly Shore, Carson Daly, Jon Stewart, Carmen Electra.

BASEBALL SUPERSTITIONS

When a major-league baseball player is in a slump, he usually spends some extra time practicing. For some, though, that's not enough. Here are a few of the superstitions players follow for luck.

• **Wade Boggs,** one of the game's all-time best hitters, ate chicken before every game.

• Dodger manager **Tommy Lasorda** always ate linguine before a game—with red clam sauce if the team was facing a right-handed pitcher, white clam sauce if it was a lefty.

• Pitcher **Luis Tiant** wore a special loincloth around his waist under his uniform to "ward off evil."

• During **Leo Durocher**'s 40-year career as a player and manager, he'd keep winning streaks alive by not changing his clothes—underwear included—until his team lost.

• **Babe Ruth** *always* touched second base on his way to the dugout at the end of each inning. **Willie Mays** always *kicked* second base as he left the field.

• Red Sox shortstop **Nomar Garciaparra** steps on each dugout step with both feet when he enters the field.

• Yankees shortstop **Phil Rizzuto** put a wad of gum on the button of his cap and only removed it when the team lost.

HOW TO BECOME A MILLIONAIRE IN 30 DAYS

Do you have to work to make money? Not according to our friend Jess Braillier, who showed us this get-rich-quick scheme.

EASY STREET

Want to make an easy $10 million and change? Hey, who doesn't? But how? Be an NBA star? Be a movie star? Create an Internet start-up? Well, you could try those ways...or you could try this perfectly legal scam.

First, find someone with lots of money (A wealthy relative is a logical target). Offer to do some daily chore for them, like picking up after the dog or taking out the garbage. But don't act too excited, or you'll risk raising their suspicions.

WHAT TO DO

Now tell Uncle Billfold or Aunt Moneybags that for this daily chore, you'll charge just 1¢ the first day. And that each day after that, you'll charge just twice as much as the day before. Your average sucker will figure, "Let's see, that's one cent the first day, two cents the next day, and, uh, only four cents the next day—hey, sure, it's a deal."

Congratulations! You've just done it. In 30 days, you'll be a multimillionaire. Check it out!

Day 1, you earn $0.01	**Day 20,** you earn $5,242.88
Day 2, you earn $0.02	**Day 21,** you earn $10,485.76
Day 3, you earn $0.04	**Day 22,** you earn $20,971.52
Day 4, you earn $0.08	**Day 23,** you earn $41,943.04
Day 5, you earn $0.16	**Day 24,** you earn $83,886.08
Day 6, you earn $0.32	**Day 25,** you earn $167,772.16
Day 7, you earn $0.64	**Day 26,** you earn $335,544.32
Day 8, you earn $1.28	**Day 27,** you earn $671,088.64
Day 9, you earn $2.56	**Day 28,** you earn........$1,342,177.28
Day 10, you earn $5.12	**Day 29,** you earn........$2,684,354.56
Day 11, you earn $10.24	**Day 30,** you earn........$5,368,709.12
Day 12, you earn $20.48	
Day 13, you earn $40.96	
Day 14, you earn $81.92	
Day 15, you earn $163.84	
Day 16, you earn $327.68	
Day 17, you earn $655.36	
Day 18, you earn $1,310.72	
Day 19, you earn $2,621.44	

Grand total for all 30 days: $10,737,418.23!
(*Don't spend it all in one place.*)

Snails have teeth.

CARNIVAL TRICKS

*Do the booths at carnivals and traveling circuses seem rigged
to you? Well, many of them are. Here are some booths
to look out for—and some tips on how to beat them.*

T he Booth: "Ring a Bottle"
The Object: Throw a ring over the neck of a
soft-drink bottle from about five feet away.
How It's Rigged: The game isn't rigged, but it
doesn't have to be—it's almost impossible to win.

• In 1978 researchers tossed 7,000 rings at a
grouping of 100 bottles. They recorded 12
wins—an average of one shot in every 583
throws. What's more, all of the 12 winning
tosses were *bounced* on; not a single aimed
shot had gone over the bottles. In fact, the
light, plastic rings wouldn't stay on the bottles even if dropped from a height of three
inches directly over the neck of the bottle.
How to Win: The only way to win is to throw two
rings over a bottle neck at the same time...but carnival
operators usually won't let you throw more than one at
a time.

The Booth: "The Milk Can"
The Object: Toss a softball into a 10-gallon milk can.
How It's Rigged: Most carnival cans aren't ordinary
dairy cans. For the midway game, an extra piece of

---

steel is attached to the rim of the can, reducing the size of the opening from $6\frac{1}{2}$ inches down to $4\frac{3}{8}$ inches.

How to Win:

• Give the ball a backspin and try to hit the back edge of the can.

• Another way: Toss the ball as high as you can, so that it drops straight into the hole. This isn't always easy: operators often hang prizes from the rafters of the booth to make high tosses difficult.

The Booth: "The Bushel Basket"

The Object: Toss softballs into a bushel basket from a distance of about six feet.

How It's Rigged: The bottom of the basket is connected to the baseboard in such a way that it has a lot of spring to it, so the ball will usually bounce out.

• Some carnies use a heavier ball when demonstrating the game or to give to players for a practice shot. Then, when play begins, they switch to a lighter ball that's harder to keep in the basket.

How to Win:

• Ask to use the same ball the carny used.

• The best throw is to aim high, and aim for the lip or the sides of the basket. The worst place to put the ball is directly on the bottom of the basket.

Q: What's one thing that snakes can do, but insects can't? A: Sneeze

THE STORY OF LITTLE LEAGUE

Today the Little League is an American tradition,
but it only came about because someone kept
a promise he made... to himself.

ACCIDENT OF FATE
It started one afternoon in 1938. A man named Carl Stotz went out into his Williamsport, Pennsylvania, yard to play catch with his two nephews. They wanted to play baseball, but the yard was too small. So they just had a game of catch.

On one throw, a nephew tossed the ball so far that Stotz had to run into the neighbor's yard. He recalled years later, "As I stretched to catch the ball, I stepped into the cutoff stems of a lilac bush that were sticking up several inches above the ground. A sharp stub tore through my sock and scraped my ankle. The pain was intense."

GOOD OL' DAYS

As Stotz sat nursing his ankle, he suddenly remembered that he had played on the same kind of rough ground when he was a kid... and he remembered a promise he'd made to himself when he was a young boy.

Back then, equipment was scarce—he and his friends hit balls with sticks because they didn't have bats. They

World's largest fish: the whale shark can grow 50 feet long and weigh several tons.

used baseballs until the skins came off, and then patched them up with tape and used them until there wasn't anything left to tape back together. Some of his friends had even played barefoot because they didn't have any shoes.

"I remembered thinking to myself, 'When I grow up, I'm gonna have a baseball team for boys, complete with uniforms and equipment. They'll play on a real field like the big guys, with cheering crowds at every game.'"

Right then and there, Stotz decided to keep his boyhood promise.

DOWNSIZING THE GAME

He spent the next few months organizing teams and rounding up sponsors to pay for the equipment. At the same time, he set about "shrinking" the game of baseball so 9- to 12-year-old kids could really play.

Stotz found child-sized bats and equipment for his teams, and at every team practice he experimented until he found the ideal size for a field. About the only thing Stotz didn't change was the size of the baseball itself. He wanted kids to be able to practice with any baseball they already had on hand.

"Remember, this was 1938, and the Great Depression was still with many families," he wrote in his autobiography. "I was afraid the expense of buying special balls would be too much for some families and might keep boys from becoming Little Leaguers."

Ha Ha! Q: Why did the chicken cross the playground? A: To get to the other slide.

BATTER UP

Stotz finally set the date of the first game: June 6, 1939. But what was the new league going to be called? He'd considered calling it Junior League Baseball or the Little Boys' League, but he couldn't decide. So he let the sports editor of the local Williamsport newspaper choose...and he picked Little League.

Little League grew slowly over the next several years, but by the end of 1950, there were more than 700 local leagues all over the United States. There was even one in British Columbia, Canada—the first outside the U.S.

By 2000, there were more than 7,300 leagues in 102 countries. And in case you're wondering, that's 2,845,425 kids, all playing the game that Carl Stotz started with a dream—Little League baseball.

LITTLE LEAGUE FACTS

• Originally, Little League was for boys only. In 1974 the rules were changed to allow girls to play, too.

• The first team to win the Little League World Series was the Maynard Midgets from Williamsport, Pa., in 1947.

• In the big leagues, the distance from home plate to first base is 90 feet. In Little League, it's 60 feet.

• The Little League Pledge: "I trust in God. / I love my country and will respect its laws. / I will play fair and strive to win. / But win or lose I will always do my best."

• The game of tee ball was invented in 1960 in Bagdad, Florida, by Dayton Hobbs.

Makes sense: One term for a group of giraffes is a *tower*.

DUMB CROOKS

*From the BRI's crime blotter, here's
proof that crime doesn't pay.*

WRONG PLACE, WRONG TIME

A not-too-observant man tried to rob a bank on the ground floor of a busy building in New York. If he had checked it out carefully before he decided to rob that particular bank, he might have known the FBI had offices there.

But he didn't. What's more, he picked the worst possible day to rob the place—payday! Why? Several armed FBI agents were waiting in line to deposit their paychecks. So when the foolish robber told the teller to put the money in the bag, he instantly heard the clicking of 15 guns behind him...and was quickly arrested.

TURN THE OTHER CHEEK

In a packed courtroom in Athens, Texas, Judge Jim Parsons sentenced 40-year-old Ray Mason to eight years in prison. But just before the police moved in to haul him off to jail, Mason yelled, "Hey, judge, look at this!" Then he pulled down his pants and mooned the judge—and everyone else in the courtroom. Judge Parsons was not amused. He charged Mason with contempt of court and gave him an extra six months in the can.

COOKING WITH UNCLE JOHN

What do you say we make a big bowl of snot? What ingredients are used to make fake snot? Pretty much the same ones that make real snot: protein, sugar, and water. Now, let's get cooking!

BOOGIE MAN

FAKE SNOT

Ingredients:
- three packages of unflavored gelatin (the protein)
- light corn syrup (the sugar)
- about ½ cup water

Recipe: You'll need an adult to help you with this recipe. First, heat the water in a pan until it boils. Remove it from the heat and sprinkle in the packages of gelatin. Let this mixture soften a few minutes and then stir it with a fork. Add enough corn syrup to make 1 cup of thin, goopy glop. Stir the glop with the fork. While you're stirring it, lift the fork to pull out long strands of snot. As the "snot" begins to cool, it will thicken. Add more water, if you need to, a spoonful at a time, to keep it nice and slimy.

Say it out loud: "It looks like boogers but it's not."

EXTRA BONUS: FAKE BOOGERS!

You can make fake boogers, too. Real boogers are formed when mucus coats a tiny dust particle in your nose and then dries out and hardens.

That's how you make fake boogers, too. Just take the fake snot, toss in about a pinch of dust and... *eureka!* You've got fake boogers! Now go wipe one on a wall. You could even put one in your friend's sandwich...

* * *

HE'S GONNA BLOW!

When you have a cold, you just reach for a box of tissue to help you with your snotty noses. But before there were disposable tissues, people carried handkerchiefs, or "snot rags"—a practice that started more than 2,000 years ago in Rome.

Of course, people didn't always use hankies. Many people just wiped their noses on their sleeves. But in the 1500s King Francis I of France thought it was gross and decided to put a stop to the filthy habit. He ordered buttons sewn on all men's coat sleeves to make them use their handkerchiefs instead of their sleeves. In the 1700s, Admiral Nelson had buttons sewn on the sleeves of all all British naval uniforms for the same reason, as did Napoleon for the French military in the 1800s.

And that's why men's coats have buttons on their sleeves today.

DUMB CROOKS

And still more proof that crime doesn't pay.

C OULDN'T BUY A CLUE
A man walked into a gas station with a knife and demanded that the attendant give him all the money in the cash register. The attendant replied that he had to buy something before she could open the register. The confused robber told her that he had no money, so he couldn't buy anything. The clever attendant told him that she was very sorry, but there was nothing she could do—she had to follow the rules. And the would-be crook left...empty-handed.

LOVESICK LOSER

While robbing a bank, the thief fell head-over-heels in love with the teller he was robbing. He got away, but he was so smitten that he actually called her, *at the bank*...to ask for a date! She talked to him—but not to make a date. She kept him on the line long enough for the police to trace the call.

HELLO, MY NAME IS...

In Long Beach, California, several employees of a large aerospace company got the bright idea to rob a bank on their lunch hour. They had it all planned out—except for one thing: They forgot to remove their I.D. tags while they were robbing the bank.

ROYAL SLOBS

Before there were bathrooms, toilets, and indoor plumbing,
where did people go? Just about anywhere they felt like
going. And that included kings and queens, who
had some pretty disgusting habits.

King James I of England (reigned 1603–25) loved hunting so much that he wouldn't leave the saddle, even to go to the bathroom. The king just went in his pants and had his servants clean him up after he got home.

King Henry IV of France tried to do something about repulsive toilet habits. In 1606 he passed a law forbidding anyone to pee or poop in the corners of his palace in Paris. His son, **The Dauphin (Louis XIII),** issued a similar warning—no one was allowed to pee or poop on the floors or under stairways, either. But no one obeyed, including the prince. The very day that he made his announcement, he was caught peeing against the wall of his bedroom.

King Charles II of England fled to Oxford in 1665 to escape the plague. The people of Oxford thought the king was a royal slob. English historian Anthony Wood wrote about the king and his entourage in his diary: "Although they were neat in their apparel, they were nasty and beastly, leaving their excrement in every corner; in chimneys, studies, coalhouses, and cellars."

Two thousand years ago, Europeans washed by coating themselves with mud, then scraping it off.

King Louis XIV of France (1638–1715) thought that everything he did was royally important—including going to the bathroom. One of his favorite things to do was greet guests while seated "on the throne." Some people didn't mind doing business with the king while he was doing *his* business. They even paid to see his bare bottom, seated on the royal pot. Other people were disgusted by it, especially ambassadors from foreign lands. But that didn't stop Louis. He even announced his engagement while sitting on the pot.

*   *   *

MORE BATHROOM LORE

• In 1490 Leonardo da Vinci designed an entire sanitary city with enough toilets for everyone. Spiral staircases led to all the bathrooms. Why spiral? So there were no corners for people to pee in.

• In the 18th century, a Dr. Benjamin discovered a well in his back garden that had terrible-tasting water. Health spas were popular at the time, and the townspeople figured that anything that tasted bad had minerals in it and must be good for you. They drank the well dry only to discover it was connected to the doctor's septic tank.

• The first baron of Grimthorpe, Edmund Beckett Denison (who designed the famous clock called Big Ben in London) built a bathroom that locked a person in until they flushed the toilet.

Thirty-one percent of U.S. households have a dog. Twenty-seven percent have a cat.

DECODING HARRY POTTER, PART I

Where does J. K. Rowling get her ideas for the characters and details in the Harry Potter *books? Some of them bear an amazing resemblance to characters in Greek and Roman mythology.*

T**he lightning bolt.** Harry's famous scar is the symbol of Zeus, god of the sky and supreme god of the ancient Greeks.

Hermione. Hermione is the mythological daughter of King Menelaus of Sparta, Greece, and Helen of Troy—both mortals, just as Hermione's parents are Muggles.

Minerva McGonagall, one of the teachers at Hogwarts. Minerva is the Roman goddess of wisdom and of war and peace. She prefers reason to violence, except when pushed, just like Professor McGonagall.

Argus Filch. The caretaker of Hogwarts seems to know (almost) everything that goes on around the school. He is very much like the mythical Greek watchman, Argus the All-Seeing, who has 100 eyes that never close.

Fluffy, the giant three-headed guard dog. The entrance to Hades, the mythological Greek underworld, is guarded by the monster *Cerberus*. Like Fluffy, *Cerberus* is a giant three-headed dog. Also like Fluffy, he is lulled to sleep by sweet music.

ANIMALS TO THE RESCUE

Amazing tales of heroic beasts.

HIP HIP HOORAY
What mammals are responsible for the most human deaths on the continent of Africa? Believe it or not, hippos. But they're not all killers. Some of them are downright kindhearted—like the hippo a *Life* magazine photographer saw in Kruger National Park, South Africa.

A baby impala (a type of antelope) had gone to the river for a drink when a crocodile grabbed it. As the croc started to drag the impala under the water, a nearby hippo saw what was happening and charged. The crocodile was so frightened that he let go of the impala.

Suddenly free, the impala tried to run, but it was so injured that it collapsed on the edge of the river. The hippo pushed its lower jaw under the dying animal and gently lifted it to its feet, but the tiny impala collapsed again. The hippo put its lips to the little impala's wounds trying to stop the bleeding, but it did no good. As a final effort, the hippo tried to resuscitate the animal by opening its jaws and taking the impala's head into his own cavernous mouth, trying to breathe life into it, but it was too late. The hippo stayed with the little impala until it died.

WATCH THE BIRDIE!

When a sparrow crashed into a chimpanzee cage at the zoo in Basel, Switzerland, one of the chimps immediately scooped it up in its hand. A zookeeper who was watching expected to see the chimp eat the bird. But instead of eating it, the chimp just held the bird tenderly and studied it.

Other chimpanzees became curious and came over to see the bird. It was carefully passed from one chimp to another. Each chimpanzee examined the little creature, holding it gently in its hand, taking obvious care not to hurt it. Finally, one of the chimps brought the frightened bird to the front of the cage and carefully handed it to the very surprised zookeeper...who released it.

ELEPHANT BABYSITTERS

One afternoon, an African woman placed her baby in the shade of a tree while she worked. Soon after, an elephant herd strolled by and saw the baby. The elephants seemed to worry that the baby would be disturbed by flies, which can be a problem in that part of Africa. The mother watched, amazed, as several of the elephants pulled big leaves from the trees and covered the sleeping babe with them. The elephants were so gentle and quiet that they didn't even wake the baby. When the baby was covered, the elephants continued on their way.

SPARK IN THE DARK

Here's a science experiment you can do for little more than a buck.

hat You Need:
- Pack of Wint-O-Green Lifesavers
- Very dark room or closet

What You Do:

1. Go into the room (take a friend or a mirror).

2. Bite into the Lifesaver. Whoa! It sparks.

You just discovered triboluminescence! What? *Triboluminescence* is light produced by striking or rubbing two special substances together. The electrons in the atoms of each substance are like little sponges absorbing the energy from the friction. When the friction stops, they release the energy...and it becomes light.

Do you have to use a Wint-O-Green Lifesaver? No. It will work with some other substances, but Wint-O-Greens work best. Why? They contain wintergreen oil, (methyl salicylate), which is actually fluorescent.

Pop blows its top! Want to create a soda volcano? Here's another experiment. Open a brand-new two-liter bottle of soda pop and drop in three or four Wint-O-Green Lifesavers. *Don't replace the cap.* When the carbon dioxide (CO_2) in the soda meets the Lifesavers, it will make big bubbles that will shoot out of the soda bottle. *Warning!* Do this trick in the kitchen sink or shower!

DECODING HARRY POTTER, PART II

Wizard-in-training Harry Potter learns a lot of magic spells at Hogwarts School. They may sound strange and mysterious, but the words actually come from Latin, the language of the ancient Romans.

The Spell: Accio! (the summoning charm)
Latin Translation: "To summon."

The Spell: Cruciatus! (One of the "unforgivable curses," it causes excruciating pain in the victim.)
Latin translation: "To torture."

The Spell: Diffindo! (a charm used to break something open)
Latin Translation: "To split or open."

The Spell: Expelliarmus! (the disarming spell)
Latin Translation: *Expello* means "to drive out." It is combined with *arma*, which means "weapon."

The Spell: Finite incantatem! (the spell that stops the effects of all currently operating spells)
Latin Translation: *Fino* means "end," and *incantare* means "to enchant."

The Spell: Imperio! (Another "unforgivable curse," it causes the victim to be completely under the wand-waver's command.)
Latin Translation: *Impero* means "to order, or command."

The Spell: Lumos! (the chant that causes a small beam of light to shine from the end of a wand)
Latin Translation: *Lumen* means "light."

All-time bestselling children's storybook: *The Poky Little Puppy,* by Janette Sebring Lowrey.

SIM MAN

If Uncle John were to create a simulated house, there'd be a bathroom in every room—even in the closets. And, of course, every bathroom would have a bookshelf.

DIGITAL REALITY

What's the bestselling computer game of all time? Is it a wild car-chase game? An auto theft game? A bullet-ridden blood-and-guts game? Guess again—it's *The Sims*, where players build a home, create a family, and design a neighborhood.

Players control the digital people and get them to do exciting things like take out the garbage, go to work, or make new friends. They marry other *Sim* people and even have *Sim* babies. The goal: To **simulate** life and build a healthy, sane world.

MEET MR. WRIGHT

And who came up with this brilliant idea? A guy named Will Wright. Wright has been creating simulations ever since he was a kid. He started out playing with model ships and airplanes and then got into computers so he could build robots.

The first computer game Wright designed was a helicopter action game called *Raid on Bungeling Bay*. That was in 1984. He discovered he had more fun building the levels for *Bungeling Bay* than flying the helicopters. That gave him the idea for *SimCity*, his first *Sim* game.

SIM UNIVERSE

He spent two years trying to sell the idea for *SimCity— The City Simulator*, without success. So Wright and a partner, Jeff Braun, formed their own company, *Maxis*, and built *SimCity* in 1989. It was so successful that Wright followed up with *SimEarth*, *SimAnt*, and *Sim-Copter*. *The Sims* appeared in 2000 and with all of its expansion packs has sold 18 million copies to date.

Now, with *Sims Online*, practically everyone can play it—and can play together. Your digital family can interact with other digital families online. Wright says, "There's a lot more of *SimCity* in this game than *Sims*. Instead of playing in a small neighborhood of about 10 houses, you're playing in a large city of around 30,000 and building an entire city—kind of a collaboration with everyone. You can form businesses or a household with other players."

HOW A GAME DESIGNER RELAXES

What does Will Wright do with his time? Besides working on more Sims creations, he surfs the fan sites every day and downloads cool things that Sim-maniacs have created. "It's really ironic," he says. "Now it's the fans out there who are entertaining us, the developers, with their creations."

Wright feels that playing games is not just for kids, it's for everyone. He rides around his office on an electric scooter, still builds robots and, along with his daughter, Cassidy, is a frequent competitor in TV's *BattleBots* tournaments.

FOOD FIGHTS

*Sounds like leftovers in the school cafeteria, but they're
stories of food that was used as weapons in real wars.*

SAY CHEESE

The army of Uruguay once fought a sea battle using a new kind of cannonball: cheese. It happened in the 1840s when a dictator from Argentina tried to take over the country. He ordered his ships to blockade the port city of Montevideo, the capital. The people of Uruguay fought back from their ships in the harbor—until they ran out of ammunition. Then someone got a bright idea: raid the galleys of the ships and load their cannons with very old, hard Edam cheeses. They fired the cheese at the enemy...and won!

SPUD MISSILES

In World War II, the naval destroyer U.S.S. *O'Bannon* sank a Japanese submarine using...potatoes. It happened in the Pacific Ocean. First, the Americans shot off the sub's conning tower, stopping it from diving, but the sub was so close that they couldn't fire their big guns at it. Then, for some reason, the Japanese sailors came out on deck and the *O'Bannon* crew pelted them with potatoes. Thinking the potatoes were hand grenades, the Japanese threw their guns overboard, then panicked and submerged the sub. It sank. A plaque honoring the event was donated by Maine potato growers.

Camel's milk will not curdle.

COMING SOON

Inventions you might see in the next 10 minutes or the next 10 years.

D ISPOSABLE CELL PHONE
Designed by a British inventor, it's a wafer-thin computer chip stuck on a piece of paper the size of a credit card. The phone, called P.S. Call Me, comes with a miniature earpiece and is good for only one call...then you throw it away.

DR. TOILET
Imagine a toilet that analyzes your pee and poop and then sends an e-mail to your doctor if it detects anything wrong. It also tells you if you need to add fiber to your diet. Not only that: it plays music, too!

NUTRITION PATCH
Don't like your veggies? Then don't eat them, absorb them! The military is working on a stick-on patch designed for extreme circumstances that will send vitamins and nutrients through the skin.

ELECTRONIC NEWSPAPER
Picture this: Your morning paper arrives on *e-paper*—a flexible "paper" that continually updates itself throughout the day. You download the news and read it, then roll it up and go. Or use it to download a book. Hooray, no more heavy backpacks!

A cat has 32 muscles in each ear.

PUZZLES ANSWER KEY

DOG DOO! GOOD GOD!

1. Dennis **sinned.**
2. Was it a rat **I saw?**
3. 'Tis in a Desoto **sedan I sit.**
4. Red rum, sir, **is murder.**
5. Damnit, **I'm mad!**
6. Do geese **see God?**
7. A slut nixes **sex in Tulsa.**
8. Lapses? Order **red roses, pal.**
9. "Desserts," **I stressed.**
10. If I had a **hi-fi...**
11. Ed, I saw Harpo Marx **ram Oprah W aside.**
12. Yawn. Madonna fan? **No damn way.**
13. Lisa Bonet ate **no basil.**
14. Do nine men interpret? **"Nine men," I nod.**
15. Are we not drawn onward, we few, **drawn onward to new era?**

PALINDROMIC PEOPLE

1. Roy
2. Enid
3. Stella
4. Max
5. Naomi
6. Norma

A LITTLE LIST

The 3 Most Dangerous Foods to Eat in a Car

1. Coffee
2. Tacos
3. Chili

SNAP, CRACKLE, FLOP

The made-up cereals are Mysterios, Grape Ape, and Post Jelly Donuts.

MR. & MS. QUIZ

1. **Women** are more likely to be naturally blond. One of every 14 women in America is a natural blonde; only one out of every 16 men is.

2. **Men** are more likely to laugh more. The average American male laughs 69 times a day; the average woman, 55.

3. **Women** are more likely to sleep more.

4. **Men** are more likely to snore (big surprise there).

5. **Women** are more likely to be born at night.

6. **Women** are more likely to purchase men's clothing in U.S. stores—about two-thirds of all men's clothing is bought by women.

7. **Men** are more likely to run stoplights.

8. **Women** are more likely to switch lanes without signaling.

9. **Men** are more likely to be left-handed. There are roughly 50% more left-handed males than females.

10. **Women** are more likely to get migraines.

11. **Men** are more likely to get an ulcer.

12. **Men** are more likely to get hiccups.

13. **Men** are *six times* more likely to get struck by lightning.

14. **Men** are more likely to leave their hotel rooms cleaner.

15. **Women** are more likely to lock themselves out of their hotel rooms.

16. **Women** are more likely to take longer showers—13 minutes on average, compared with the average man's 11.4 minutes.

17. **Women** blink nearly twice as much as men.

18. **Men**—we should say, boys—are four times more likely to stutter than girls are.

19. **Women** are almost twice as likely to buy gifts for Mother's Day.

20. **Men** are twice as likely to fall out of bed while in the hospital.

21. **Women** are more likely to talk to their cars.

22. **Men** are twice as likely to hold the TV remote.

23. **Men** are also twice as likely to lose the TV remote.

24. **Women** generally have a keener sense of smell.

THE KING'S THINGS

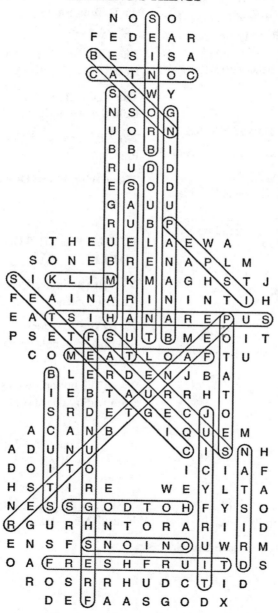

EYE OF THE BEHOLDER

d. Marilyn didn't remove her upper molars to emphasize her cheekbones—that was Marlene Dietrich's beauty secret.

FILL IN THE LIMERICKS

1. suicide, automobiles, died
2. seeds, grass, weeds
3. died, fermented, inside
4. dribbling, highway (or freeway or roadway), sibling
5. paw, wife, father-in-law
6. light, way, night
7. sin, could, again
8. wager, part, Major
9. stew, about, too
10. Natchez, clothes, scratchez(s)

COMING UP SHORT

The 9 Planets: Uranus

The 8 Members of TV's Brady Family: Peter

The 5 Great Lakes: Ontario

The 5 Original Members of the Rolling Stones: Charlie Watts

The 4 H's in the 4-H Club: Heart

The 13 Original U.S. Colonies: Georgia

The Life Savers' "5 Flavors": Pineapple

The 4 Teletubbies: Dipsy

WOULD WE LIE TO YOU—THREE?

1 – a (It's an indication of high alcohol content.)

2 – b (The manufacturer only had pink food coloring on hand.)

3 – c (The buttons keep you from wiping your nose on your sleeve.)

4 – a (Walking beneath a ladder violates the "Holy Trinity" symbol.)

5 – c (You dig really deep beneath the water.)

TRUE CONFESSIONS

HOW FAMOUS CAN YOU GET?

IT SLICES! IT DICES!

1 – g (GLH#9 Hair-in-a-can:
"You can use it on your dog!")

2 – e (Inside the Eggshell
Scrambler: "You'll use it a lot
and every time you do, you'll
save washing a bowl and fork!")

3 – a (The Miracle Mop: "It
lets you wring out the head
without putting your hands into
the dirty water!")

4 – c (The Pocket Fisherman:
"Attaches to your belt, or fits in
the glove compartment of your
car!")

5 – d (The Ronco Bottle and Jar
Cutter: "A hobby for Dad, craft
for the kids, a great gift for Mom!")

6 – b (The Ronco Rhinestone
and Stud Setter: "It changes
everyday clothing into exciting
fashions!")

7 – f (The Veg-O-Matic: "No
one likes dicing onions...the
only tears you'll shed will be
tears of joy!")

TAKING DEBATE

e. It was the bathroom tissue
issue. As reported in an article
called "Uncle John's Stall of
Fame" in *Uncle John's All-
Purpose Extra Strength Bathroom Reader*, Ms. Landers'
own opinion was that the paper
should come over the top. Why?
"Fine quality toilet paper has
designs that are right side up,"
she explained.

PLAY D'OH

1. I'm not normally a religious
man, but if you're up there, save
me, Superman!

2. Son, you tried your best and
you failed miserably. The lesson
is, never try.

3. If you really want something in this life you have to
work for it. Now quiet! They're
about to announce the lottery
numbers.

PARK IT!

```
H Y U N D A I   V O L V O           S U N B E A M
  U           U           L A N C I A         A       U   D
  G     D   B O R G W A R D             A     A         D   A
  O     E   U         U       S   L A M B O R G H I N I
A       S   R     T   S I M C A     E       E           M
M   G   O   N     A   T   O   G     R       O     T     L
B       T         T   I   B   O     C               R   E
A S T O N M A R T I N     I   N     E X C A L I B U R
S                 T       L   D     D                 U
S U Z U K I     S T U D E B A K E R     H U M M E R
A       A       T     U         S       U     P   A
D   N   I S U Z U     P         D       D     H   G
O   A   S       T O Y O T A     L O T U S         L
R   S T E Y R   Z     N                 O   J E E P
    H   R         C I T R O E N     B E N Z
```

If you're not familiar with all the makes and models on our list, here's some info on the more obscure among them:

Auburn: An American car company started in Auburn, Indiana by the Eckhart Carriage Company in the early 1900s.

Borgward: Founded by German engineer Carl Borgward (1890–1963), and famous among aficionados for the Lloyd, the Hansa, and the Isabella.

Steyr: An Austrian company founded in 1920 that's today known as Steyr-Puch.

Tatra: A Czechoslovakian company that produced its first car in the late 1800s.

THE TIME IT TAKES

Here are the answers in order:

1 second for a hummingbird's wings to beat 70 times

58 seconds for the elevator in Toronto's CN Tower to reach the top (1,518 feet)

4 hours for the *Titanic* to sink after it struck the iceberg

7 days for a newborn baby to wet or soil 80 diapers

30 days for a human hair to grow half an inch

12 weeks for a U.S. Marine to go through boot camp

1 year for Los Angeles to move two inches closer to San Francisco (due to the shifting of tectonic plates)

25 years equals the time the average American spends asleep in a lifetime

95 years for Easter to recur on the same date

500,000 years for plutonium-239 to become harmless

LOST IN TRANSLATION

Dr. No

THE 7 "OFFICIAL" ATTRIBUTES OF THE PILLSBURY DOUGHBOY

1. His skin must look like dough: "off-white, smooth, but not glossy"

2. Slightly luminous, but no sheen

3. No knees, elbows, wrists, fingers, ears, or ankles

4. Rear views do not include "buns"

5. Walks with a "swagger"

6. tomach is proportional to the rest of his body

7. He is not portly

BASEBALL NAMES

The fakes are the San Francisco Giants (named in 1886 when their proud manager addressed them as "my big fellows, my giants" after a particularly stunning victory), the Cleveland Indians (when Luis Francis Sockalexis, the first American Indian to play pro baseball and a popular Cleveland player, died in 1913, the team was named in his honor), and the San Diego Padres (whose name was chosen in a name-our-team contest).

HELLO? DOLLY?

The quote: Dolly Parton once *lost* a Dolly Parton look-alike contest.

The clue answers:

A. COLOR
B. PLATOON
C. DONATELLO
D. STORE
E. NICKEL
F. TODAY
G. YOLKS
H. PLANT

I FOUND IT ON EBAY

Date with Brady: $6.19

Frog purse: $5.50

Butt picture: $1

Civil War dirt: $2.75

Wedding dress: $15.50

Francis D. Cornworth's
     virginity: $10 million

Ali's X-ray: $255.01

Set of eyeballs: $613

Elian's raft: $280 (minimum
     bid was not met)

Cadaver bag: $15

MIX-UP AT THE HONKY-TONK

1. "He's Been DRUNK Since His Wife's Gone PUNK"

2. "I Don't Know Whether to KILL Myself or Go BOWLING"

3. "If FINGERPRINTS Showed Up on SKIN, Wonder Whose I'd Find on You"

4. "I'll MARRY You Tomorrow but Let's HONEYMOON Tonite"

5. "I've Been FLUSHED from the BATHROOM of Your Heart"

6. "I've Got the HUNGRIES for Your Love and I'm Waiting in Your WELFARE Line"

7. "Mama Get the HAMMER (There's a FLY on Papa's Head)"

8. "TOUCH Me with More Than Your HANDS"

9. "She Made TOOTHPICKS Out of the TIMBER of My Heart"

10. "When We Get Back to the FARM (That's When We Really Go to TOWN)"

THE LAST PAGE

FELLOW BATHROOM READERS:
The fight for good bathroom reading should never be taken loosely—we must do our duty and sit firmly for what we believe in, even while the rest of the world is taking pot shots at us.

We'll be brief: now that we've proven we're not simply a flush-in-the-pan, we invite you to take the plunge: Sit Down and Be Counted! Become a member of the Bathroom Readers' Institute. Send a self-addressed, stamped, business-sized envelope to: BRI, PO Box 1117, Ashland, Oregon 97520. You'll receive your free membership card, receive discounts when ordering directly through the BRI, and earn a permanent spot on the BRI honor roll!

If you like reading our books...
VISIT THE BRI'S WEBSITE!
www.bathroomreader.com

- Visit "The Throne Room"—a great place to read!
- Receive our irregular newsletters via email
- Submit your own articles and ideas
- Order additional *Bathroom Readers*
- Become a BRI member
Go with the Flow...

Well, we're out of space, and when you've gotta go, you've gotta go. Tanks for all your support. Hope to hear from you soon.

Meanwhile, remember:

Keep on flushin'!